To Joyce

Don L Meredith

Jean Saunders

sincerely

Jack R Lewis

Mar 8, 2009

Photo by Holland Studio of Photography, Germantown, Tennessee

Annie May Alston Lewis
November 26, 1917—March 9, 2006

"All these people were still living by faith when they died."
(Hebrews 11:13; NIV)

Still Living by
Faith

STILL LIVING BY FAITH

A Collection of Lectures

Annie May Alston Lewis

Compiled and Edited by
Jean Lewis Saunders and
Don L. Meredith

RESOURCE PUBLICATIONS
2205 S. Benton
Searcy, AR 72143

ISBN-13: 978-0-9818128-3-0
ISBN-10: 0-9818128-3-X

The background photo on the cover is the Oliver and Norma Rogers Research Center at the Harding Graduate School of Religion in Memphis, Tennessee. The Research Center, built in 2006, is an addition to the L. M. Graves Memorial Library where Annie May Alston Lewis was the head librarian from 1962 through 1983. The east tower outside the Research Center, called the Lewis Tower, was dedicated to Jack P. Lewis, Annie May Lewis, and Clyde Lewis. Photo by Jeff Montgomery, Harding University Public Relations Office.

Cover photo of Annie May Alston Lewis was taken by Mike James, Harding University Public Relations Office.

CONTENTS

PREFACE

The idea for this book began with the wish to honor Annie May on her 85th birthday, which was on November 26, 2002. The project turned out to require more time and attention than that deadline would allow. During the years that followed, her health began to deteriorate more quickly. Following her death on March 9, 2006, it was our conviction that Annie May's Sunday school lessons and other talks had inspired and edified hundreds of people and needed to be collected and shared.

The lessons cover a span of about 40 years. They were assembled from notes of talks presented to her Sunday school classes, ladies' Bible classes, and lectureship audiences. The talks are filled with her rich "asides" which reflect on her own time, era, and heart. They show her love of friends and family, of work and students, of psalms and hymns, all of which were very much a part of the fabric of her life and devotion.

We do not know when most of the lessons were presented, so they are not in any order of presentation. They were literally plucked from an old metal filing cabinet and put together to see what might be made of them. Some are more polished than others because of their original settings.

Some lessons were presented several times for different audiences. We offer no apology for the repetition of examples, points, and Scriptures. Annie May was a teacher, and teachers repeat. As she used to say, when God puts something in more than once, he wants you to take notice of it.

Annie May's notes were provided by her husband, Dr. Jack P. Lewis. Most had been typed on her old Royal manual typewriter. Notes were in the margins in her notoriously illegible handwriting—sometimes just a word or two which would remind her of something but which had little meaning to later readers. These lesson notes were deciphered and transcribed by her niece Jean Saunders. They were read, sorted, and edited by Betty Copeland, Susan Rubio, Bonnie Barnes, and Don Meredith. All Scripture references were checked and the version noted. All Scripture references are RSV unless otherwise noted.

Because they began as notes for oral presentations, they contained no documentation. But as many as possible of the sources she mentioned have been located by Don Meredith and Jean Saunders, added as footnotes in the text, and listed in the Bibliography at the end of the book. Sources which could not be located are so indicated.

This book has been a labor of love by many. We as a group loved her and did what we could, some much and some little, to bring this book into being. Thanks go to Uncle Jack for providing the challenge; to Don for his hours of diligently searching for sources, for not wanting to give up; to Betty and Susan for reading, correcting, reading again, and remembering how Annie May would have said it; to Daddy for finding which book those hymns were in; to Bonnie, Betty, and Carisse for helping me write this Preface; and to Carisse for direction, for encouragement, and for calling me to admit that I loved the challenge.

The lessons are organized according to the theme of the last formal presentation Annie May gave to a ladies' Bible class at White Station Church of Christ in Memphis, Tennessee—"Living with Debilitating Illness." She describes her life and her activities. I have divided the book into the same three sections—"The Way It Was," "The Way It Is," and "The Way It Is Going to Be"—and then assigned lessons to that section which were about the kinds of things she was doing at that time in her life.

One of her statements speaks volumes about the thrust of her teaching and study and relationships with people: "It is the long look at eternity that clarifies the ultimate issues of stewardship." Her life was one long look at and toward eternity.

I chose Hebrews 11:13, one of her favorites, to inspire the title of the book: *Still Living by Faith*. It is reflected in all of the lessons in references to stewardship, faithfulness, staying the course, being single minded, having a pilgrim mentality, and selfless service. Until the day she died, she was still asking about the ladies she had taught in her Outreach class—"Was Mary there today?" She was still living by faith when she died. And she is still living by the faith of those whom she taught.

Jean Lewis Saunders
Memphis, TN

BIOGRAPHICAL SKETCH

Professionally, Annie May Alston Lewis was a librarian and teacher. She attended David Lipscomb College for two years and graduated from Harding College in 1939 with a degree in English. She taught in public schools for a few years and completed a B.S. degree in library science from George Peabody College in 1943.

Dr. George Benson asked her to come to Harding to teach English in 1944. She preferred a position in the library; but because there was no opening, she accepted the invitation to teach English. In 1947 she became head librarian and worked tirelessly (many times 10 hours a day) to improve the quality of the library. A few years later when Harding received its accreditation, the library received the highest praise from the visitation team. During these years in the summers, she worked on and completed an M.A. degree from the University of Chicago in 1952.

Annie May's father died in 1952, and she took a leave of absence from Harding to be with her mother. When the librarian who had taken her place left, Dr. Benson again invited her back to Harding as the librarian, and she served in that capacity from 1956 to 1962.

In 1962 after several invitations from W. B. West, Jr., Annie May agreed to come to Memphis to become the librarian at the Harding University Graduate School of Religion. She had accepted a unique position. She became the first theological librarian in the churches of Christ and was entrusted with the responsibility of building from scratch a quality collection to support a theological graduate program. She attacked this project with the same hard work and determination that characterized her tenure at Searcy. She put in long hours to build the library.

She was the first member of the churches of Christ to become a member of the American Theological Library Association, the national organization for theological librarians. She attended the annual meetings and developed relationships with librarians from other theological schools. These contacts were immensely helpful to her in learning what to add to the collection and how to get these materials. At her request several donated books and periodicals to the library.

To become familiar with the subject area, Annie May enrolled in the M.A. program at Harding Graduate School and took courses while working full time as librarian. She completed the program in 1967, becoming one of the early women in the churches of Christ to have a graduate theological degree. In the late 1960s, she developed a course at the Graduate School to help students improve their writing and research skills and to familiarize them with the basic research tools in theology. Because of her work, Harding Graduate School is still one of the few seminaries that offer such a required course.

When Annie May came to Memphis, the Harding Graduate School library contained only about 5,000 volumes and subscribed to only 82 periodicals. When she retired in 1983, it had almost 69,000 volumes and received 582 periodicals. She not only left a good theological collection but a great legacy for succeeding librarians, who would be respected members of and vital participants in the academic community. During her career she also mentored several who became librarians.

Annie May was active in library professional organizations and served in leadership roles in each. During her years in Arkansas she served as president of the Arkansas Library Association. She was a charter member of the Tennessee Theological Library Association, a charter member of the Christian College Librarians, and a member of the Memphis Area Library Council from its earliest days. She was honored several times for her work. She was listed in *Who's Who in America, Who's Who of American Women*, and *Outstanding Educators of America*. She received the 20th Century Christian Literature Award in 1975. In 1968 she became the first woman to be honored as a distinguished alumna by Harding College, and in 1979 she and Dr. Lewis were joint recipients of Harding University's Distinguished Service Award. She was the only person twice honored as alumna of the year by Harding Graduate School, in 1993 and again posthumously in April 2006. In the latter case, the award was to be given to the alumnus who best exemplified the school's 2006 theme of "holiness." The alumni and administration felt no one better exemplified that theme.

Most people who knew and admired Annie May did not know her as a librarian but as a Christian woman who exemplified the holiness that led to her last earthly award. She was born into a godly family in Henning, Tennessee, on November 26, 1917. Through word and example, her loving parents and siblings instilled in her the importance of family and, more important, the significance of being a part of God's family. Two brothers died before she was born, but she grew up with her brother, Jack, and sister, Margaret. These also preceded her in death, Jack in 1968 and Margaret in 1974. When her mother was no longer able to live alone, she moved into Annie May's one-bedroom apartment, and Annie May lovingly cared for her for eight years until her death in April 1973. She dearly loved Betty Alston, her sister-in-law, and her nephews and nieces, Jackie, Susan, Meg, and Roy, all of whom cherish her memory.

The small Henning congregation nurtured Annie May, and she was privileged to hear such gifted preachers as Dr. L. C. Sears, Dr. Jack P. Lewis, James A. Harding, and L. K. Harding teach God's Word. At the age of 12, she was baptized by L. K. Harding.

During her student days at Harding, she was influenced by the sacrificial service of the teachers and their wives and their faith in God's providential care. There she witnessed a simple lifestyle that she embraced all her life. It was also here that she became convinced that "everyone ought to hear about Jesus at least once." It was this conviction that motivated her to be involved in the training and encouragement of preachers and missionaries.

On November 23, 1978, just three days before her sixty-first birthday, Annie May married Dr. Jack P. Lewis, long-time friend and fellow professor at the Harding Graduate School of Religion.

They shared a love for the church, a love for the Bible, a love for teaching, a commitment to a simple lifestyle, and a spirit of generosity for God's work. Both taught Bible classes at the Church of Christ at White Station for many years and both served on its missions committee. She encouraged Dr. Lewis in his research and writing, proofread what he wrote, and frequently traveled with him when he lectured. She particularly enjoyed the annual Society of Biblical Literature meetings where she could visit with former Harding Graduate School students.

Annie May encouraged anyone she felt needed it, whether college president, dean, fellow Christian, preacher, missionary, or student. For many years she mailed a regular newsletter to missionaries and sent notes, phoned, or spoke a word of encouragement to hundreds. Her hospitality knew no limits; it included good food and fellowship offered to every conceivable category of people, especially missionaries and foreign students from Harding Graduate School. As one lady observed, "Annie May had a great capacity to love," and that love knew no social, ethnic, racial, or educational bounds. After her retirement she used her additional time to visit nursing homes and to become involved in the Each One Teach One literacy program.

Annie May taught a ladies' Bible class at the Church of Christ at White Station for over 30 years. For a few years, she taught on Tuesday morning, Sunday morning, and Wednesday night. When the congregation began a bus program to bring in children for Sunday Bible school, she began a class for the mothers of the children who came. All of these ladies were eventually baptized, and a few still attend regularly. This class soon became a favorite of other ladies, and she continued to teach as long as her health permitted. Through her teaching and mentoring, she blessed their lives and developed a multitude of daughters of faith.

Stewardship and frugality were consistent traits in Annie May's life. She never hesitated to ask for funds for the library or for other worthy causes, but she never asked for anything for herself. She lived very simply and never sought the finer things of life but sent her money to people and institutions she felt needed it. Her idea of a fancy meal out was a hamburger and maybe some pistachio almond ice cream.

Prayer was a significant and regular part of Annie May's daily devotional life, and she believed strongly in its efficacy. She prayed faithfully for a host of people daily and enlisted others to pray for those she was especially concerned about.

Annie May loved the Bible and felt it should be the center of any Sunday school class. A lady who sat with her at the nursing home overheard her say, "Books, books everywhere, but there's really only one book." She was a devoted Bible student and instilled in others a love for it and a desire to study it. In her last three months in the hospital, she frequently asked the ladies who sat with her to read from the Bible, particularly the Psalms, many of which she had committed to memory. Her knowledge of and love for the Bible are very apparent in the lessons in this book.

On March 9, 2006, Annie May went to receive the award she longed for and wrote of in the last selection in this collection. Truly she embodied the statement she once made in an interview, "Where there's a need, try to fill it because you belong to the Lord."

Don L. Meredith, Head Librarian
Harding University Graduate School of Religion
Memphis, TN

ACKNOWLEDGMENTS

The following people spent countless hours typing and scanning from old manuscripts, proofreading, editing, organizing, verifying Scripture references, advising—and the list of skills required to compile this collection of Annie May's lessons goes on and on. Special thanks go to:

Bonnie Ulrey Barnes

Carisse Mickey Berryhill

Betty Bird Copeland

Ellis L. Haguewood

Denise B. Hunt

H. Clyde Lewis

Jack P. Lewis

Don L. Meredith

Evelyn R. Meredith

Susan B. Rubio

Jean Lewis Saunders

INTRODUCTION

"The reason for Bible study is to get to know God—to see him more clearly and to love him more dearly. Our lives are manifestations of what we think about God."

Annie May Alston Lewis

Annie May Alston
Harding College *Petit Jean* Yearbook
1946

1
Living with Debilitating Illness

The Way It Was

With apologies to Jimmy Stewart, I have had a wonderful life. I had the best parents who, though they did not have the blessings of a Christian education, wanted it for their children and sacrificed so that we might have it.

I attended David Lipscomb College for two years and had the blessings of classes under Brother and Sister E. H. Ijams. Lipscomb was a junior college back then, so my last two years were spent at Harding. Those years were pure joy. I have often said that I am thankful that when I went to Harding the school was small with about 400 students, and we were all poor—students and teachers. The teachers defined service for us. Wives took in washing and ironing, kept boarders, and sold milk and eggs. I was visiting in the home of Mrs. B. F. Rhodes, whose husband was the History Department. The student who was living with the Rhodes came in and asked her what to prepare for lunch. Mrs. Rhodes answered, "Potatoes and beans." And the student just stood there expecting something else. Mrs. Rhodes continued, "That is all that there is. There is not anything more." When I graduated, I hated to leave, and I cried and cried.

I taught in public schools several years, but I was delighted when the opportunity came for me to go back to Harding. Dr. Benson called and said that there was a vacancy in the English Department. I told him that I had just finished my first library degree, and that I would like to work in the library. He replied, "The vacancy is in English." I told him that I would come. So I taught English for three years, and then I moved to the library. I served as librarian for 13 years. I meanwhile took another library degree from the University of Chicago, which better prepared me for my next job. I was not eager to leave Harding in Searcy. At the insistence of Dr. West, however, I came to the Graduate School in 1962; and to this day, I think it was the best job in the world. I retired in 1983 after 21 years. I was glad to turn the keys over to Don Meredith. He has proven to be as good as I knew he would be. His wife, Evelyn, was on the staff; and she was so efficient! Then Billie Thomason always made me look better than I was. She was impartial and worked 13 years for me and 13 for Don. She is a perfect example of Proverbs 17:22: "A cheerful heart is a good medicine."

But while I was at the Graduate School, I also endured some very sad times. In 1968, my brother died suddenly, leaving his wife and four children. Then in 1973 my mother died of congestive heart failure. One of the Lord's greatest blessings in my whole life was to have her live with me the last eight years of her life. She was the perfect example of patience and kindness and always had a smile for me when I came in. She often had a letter on my pillow. My sister, who taught in Florida, spent the summer months with us and also the long Christmas vacations. She had cancer and was often in the hospital here. After my mother's death, White Station had a surprise party for me, which proved to be a trip to Germany to visit three weeks with my close friend Irene Johnson, who spent 30 years as a missionary in Germany. She literally grew a church from her teaching of children. Years later when she returned to Germany, she saw her children active as leaders and teachers. That joyful experience in Germany was short-lived, however, since my sister died the following spring. But through these bad times, I had so much support through the White Station congregation and the Graduate School, and especially from the students who lived in the apartments. Many of you will remember Waymon and Charla Hinson. Charla worked in the library, and we shared many meals together.

Then in 1975 Jack's wife died, and it was a sad time for him and his sons. Jack and I had been friends from Searcy days, and I had read his papers. He always said that if he had a comma in,

I said, "Take it out"; and if he did not have one, I said, "Put it in." I suppose the sadness both of us had experienced became the basis of our wonderful friendship, and in 1978 we were married at my sister-in-law's home in Searcy. Again God was so good to give me Jack. He had preached in my hometown, and my family had the highest regard for him.

In 1982–83, the year I retired, Jack had a fellowship to the Albright Institute for Archaeological Research in Jerusalem, and we spent the academic year there. That was a wonderful learning experience. I did volunteer work in the library and met scholars I had known only through footnotes. I received a basket of oranges in a contest for having been the person who spent the most time sitting in the garden in the sun during the winter. We worshiped with the Arabic congregation, and that was wonderful. There were several blind people in the congregation. Jack preached in the morning, and at night we attended and heard a sermon in Arabic while we read our English Bibles. We drank gallons of tea, ate bushels of oranges, and were invited into many homes where we ate delicious Arabic food. My friend Ileene Huffard knows how to prepare those dishes. We did not always share a common language with our hosts, but the hospitality was warm. Tea in an Arabic home, even the poorest one, included an apple, an orange, a banana, cake, and a small square of chocolate. It was impolite to leave before the chocolate. One day we had tea with the maid of the Albright Institute. She lived in the old city, and her home really was like a cave; but she had all the food that anyone else would have had.

Jack studied at the École Biblique, which is the French school of archaeology, from Monday through Friday. He was studying the Book of Obadiah, which has one chapter, and he is still working on it. But on Saturday we got on the buses and went sightseeing. One Saturday when it was cold in Jerusalem, we went to Jericho, which is 17 miles away and 1,200 feet below sea level. We found ourselves in a very warm climate. One of my favorite sites was Emmaus because I love the resurrection story about Emmaus.

While in Jerusalem I had pneumonia twice, but I had good doctors there. We got to the doctor's office, which had a small waiting room and an examination room, and found him to be receptionist, nurse, and doctor all in one. I asked Jack to look at the certificates on the wall, and he discovered that the doctor's degree was from Columbia in New York. We had to go to a laboratory in another place to have a specimen tested and later had to go back to pick up the laboratory report. The second doctor, whom we visited later, had a degree from England and had his own laboratory.

In my retirement I could do the two things I wanted to do: I worked in the literacy program and visited in the nursing home, both of which I did as long as I was physically able. Through these years I had the blessing of teaching the Bible on Sunday morning, Tuesday morning, and Wednesday night. One of the most enjoyable moments was when I had Susan Rubio, Betty Copeland, Peggy Haguewood, and Jean Saunders, who were in the Tuesday morning class, ask if we could have another Bible study on Thursday nights at my apartment. I was delighted to teach these young mothers who were eager for more Bible study. The only class I asked if I could teach was the bus mothers' class. At one time we had up to 35 in the class.

Jack was conducting tours, and after our marriage we traveled to places I had only dreamed about: China, Taiwan, Japan, Australia, and New Zealand, from which polar explorations departed. We visited Tahiti, Europe, and Israel; and then on our own, we traveled to Scotland and followed Robert Burns all the way across the country. The next year we went to the Grand Tetons, Yellowstone, and Glacier National Park. So you can see that I have had a wonderful life and memories to last a lifetime. We have hundreds of slides if we can find them.

O how kindly hast Thou led me,
Heav'nly Father, day by day;
Found my dwelling, clothed and fed me,
Furnished friends to cheer my way!
Didst Thou bless me, didst Thou chasten,
With Thy smile or with Thy rod,
'Twas that still my step might hasten
Homeward, heav'nward, to my God.

O how slowly have I often
Followed where Thy hand would draw!
How Thy kindness failed to soften!
How Thy chast'ning failed to awe!
Make me for Thy rest more ready,
As Thy path is longer trod;
Keep me in Thy friendship steady,
Till Thou call me home, my God.[1]

The Way It Is

In about 1995, I was preparing lunch for guests and turned around to put chicken salad in the refrigerator. To my total surprise, I fell and broke a hip. But after a partial replacement, that summer I was able to go to the Holy Land with a group of members of the White Station church. A couple of years later, I went with the group to Turkey to see the sites of the seven churches, which I often referred to as one pile of rocks after another. I have no appreciation for archaeology and only endure slides that others seem naturally to enjoy. I told Sy Gitin, director of the Institute of Archaeology in Jerusalem, that I really did not care for archaeology. He returned to me, "Don't worry! My wife leaves when I start talking about archaeology." This trip also took us to the Greek islands and the spectacular views to be seen there. It was wonderful to see the Isle of Patmos where the apostle John was a prisoner.

Then in fairly quick succession came a broken wrist, another broken hip requiring a partial replacement, and then April of last year a broken upper arm requiring a plate. Another hard fall in July gave a back injury. In addition to these difficulties, I have a lack of energy because of chronic bronchitis.

My independence of getting in the car and driving where I wanted to go came to an end. I miss traveling with Jack, preparing and teaching Bible classes, and visiting relatives. This summer I am hoping to attend the Alston reunion in northwestern Arkansas at the last of July. I miss having students over for meals.

---

[1]Thomas Grinfield, "O How Kindly Hast Thou Led Me," *Great Songs*.

At times I have been disappointed in myself, but never in God.

But the blessings far outweigh the difficulties. First, I am thankful for Jesus; he comes at the top of my list of helpers. And then I am thankful for Jack, who deserves a purple heart. When someone asks me what I want Jack to be remembered for, I say that it is his books and articles. But Susan Rubio said, "No. I will remember him for how he takes care of my Annie May." He gives me my morning shower and dresses me. Jack tucks me in bed at night.

I never did care much about dress, but I did notice my shoes on the wrong foot one day. Phillip Morrison tells the story that someone asked him if Annie May had improved Jack's dress. He answered, "No! Now she dresses like he does." I never did like to shop, and Jack says when I do try to shop, I say, "Blouse, come out to meet me." He gives me great encouragement by telling me that I am getting stronger. We walk around the fellowship hall corridor multiple times almost every day. I might not do the walking were it not for Jack, who insists that I must do it.

Whatever is done in the kitchen, Jack is the doer of it. We have not gone hungry. White Station cooks have gone way beyond the call of duty. I have had prayers and cards from around the world, especially from students who are in the mission field. I have encouragement from Jim Hambrick and others at therapy. There is an African-American man at therapy; when I said I was 83, he said over and over, "I do not believe it. I will tell my church about you." Then the children at Harding Academy encourage me. One of Susan Douglas' students in the first grade, when she saw that I was leaning on Jack's arm instead of using the walker, said, "I can see that she is walking better." There has been encouragement from all the staff here at White Station.

I have encouragement from strangers. Year before last we did not get to go to Jack's professional meeting in Boston because I was in the hospital recovering from pneumonia. Last year's meeting was in Nashville, and I was determined to try to go. We stopped at a restroom on the way, and a woman I did not know said, "Mrs. Lewis, may I help you?" She turned out to be Mrs. John Lipsey, a member at Highland but a stranger to me. I was wheeled around the convention hall in a wheelchair and enjoyed it all.

For 22 years Jack and I have hosted a worship service for those attending this convention who would like to come. We had the service in our hotel room until we overflowed it and were finally able to rent a room in the hotel. This year we had 120 who came for worship. We had singing, prayers, Bible reading, and communion, and I think I will not see anything like it this side of heaven. Many who come are our former students. The invitation is an open one, and people from all branches of the Restoration Movement come for worship.

I will admit there are some sad times for me. Jack came in one day from work, and I was crying. I was determined that he was not going to come in and find me crying anymore. I have not quite kept that resolution, but I have made an effort to. I try not to compare myself with others. I try not to say, "I wish I could." We have a story in our extended family of a golden wedding anniversary celebration. The daughter-in-law came in about the time for the affair to begin and asked what she could do to help. Her mother-in-law replied, "You can be pleasant." I do try to be pleasant, especially at home.

The Bible is my textbook. Once I was in the hospital and did not feel like reading. Betty Copeland came and said, "I know you do not feel like talking. I am just going to read the Bible," and she read page after page. On the trip to Scotland, we had the privilege of seeing Sir Walter Scott's vast library. On his deathbed he told his son-in-law to get the book for him. When asked which book, he answered, "There is but one book."

I have underlined verses that mean a lot to me, and I will give you a few of those. I would encourage you to underline verses that do the same for you.

Second Samuel 12:22, 23: After David's sin with Bathsheba, Nathan appears to him and tells him the famous parable of the ewe lamb. David said, "I have sinned against the LORD" (v. 13), and all sin is against the Lord. The Lord forgave him but told him that his child would die. After the child's death, David washed, ate food, and worshiped the Lord. When the servants did not understand David's actions, he said to them, "I shall go to him, but he will not return to me" (v. 23). This verse brought the most comfort to me of any biblical passage after my mother's death.

I live with the Psalms. As soon as I finish 150, I go back to the first one.

Psalm 27:1: "The LORD is my light and my salvation; whom shall I fear? The LORD is the stronghold of my life; of whom shall I be afraid?"

Psalm 27:13: "I believe that I shall see the goodness of the LORD in the land of the living!"

Psalm 27:14: "Wait for the LORD; be strong, and let your heart take courage; yea, wait for the LORD!" This was Andy T. Ritchie's favorite psalm, and Andy was blind in his last years.

Psalm 37:25: "I have been young, and now am old; yet I have not seen the righteous forsaken or his children begging bread." This was a favorite passage of brother James A. Harding, for whom Harding is named and who also baptized my father. He preached this verse and lived it out. Much has been written on his faith and his total dependence on God. He was greatly influenced by George Müller of England. Müller had the conviction that God would supply every need if he sought God's kingdom first. Müller had built five orphans' homes and cared for ten thousand orphans. He never asked for a gift, but he handled two hundred thousand dollars a year for his orphanages. Once when they were down to the last crust with nothing for breakfast, a wealthy contributor called and asked how they were doing. Müller could have told him that they had nothing for breakfast; but Müller replied, "They are doing as well as the Lord wants them to," and the visitor went away. When he left, Müller dropped to his knees and prayed; in a few minutes the man returned. He said, "I have five hundred pounds [which would be equivalent to about twenty-five hundred dollars] which I have decided to give to some cause, and I have decided that I could not give it to a better cause than your orphanage."[2] In Harding's last years, he suffered from Alzheimer's; but he was well provided for by his daughter and her husband, who was a doctor.

---

[2]Source unknown. George Fredrick Müller (1805–1898) was a Christian evangelist and coordinator of orphanages in Bristol, England. http://en.wikipedia.org/wiki/George_M%C3%BCller (accessed March 23, 2009).

Psalm 57:2: "I cry to God Most High, to God who fulfils his purpose for me"; repeated in Psalm 138:8a: "The LORD will fulfill his purpose for me."

Psalm 103:14: "For he knows our frame; he remembers that we are dust."

Psalm 118:24: "This is the day which the LORD has made; let us rejoice and be glad in it." I try to say that every morning.

Psalm 119, especially verse 71: "It is good for me that I was afflicted, that I might learn thy statutes."

Habakkuk 3:17–19: "Though the fig tree do not blossom, nor fruit be on the vines, the produce of the olive fail and the fields yield no food, the flock be cut off from the fold and there be no herd in the stalls, yet I will rejoice in the LORD, I will joy in the God of my salvation. GOD, the Lord, is my strength; he makes my feet like hinds' feet, he makes me tread upon my high places."

Isaiah 40:28–31: "Have you not known? Have you not heard? The LORD is the everlasting God, the Creator of the ends of the earth. He does not faint or grow weary, his understanding is unsearchable. He gives power to the faint, and to him who has no might he increases strength. Even youths shall faint and be weary, and young men shall fall exhausted; but they who wait for the LORD shall renew their strength, they shall mount up with wings like eagles, they shall run and not be weary, they shall walk and not faint."

Nehemiah 8:10: Nehemiah, who directed the rebuilding of the wall after the destruction of Jerusalem, said to the workmen, "Go your way, eat the fat and drink sweet wine and send portions to him for whom nothing is prepared; for this day is holy to our Lord; and do not be grieved, for the joy of the LORD is your strength." After Brother Gordon Teel at the college church in Searcy had preached a series of sermons designed to provoke us to doing more than we were doing, I said to him, "I wish you would preach a sermon on joy," and he preached on this text.

Lamentations 3:22–24: "The steadfast love of the LORD never ceases, his mercies never come to an end; they are new every morning; great is thy faithfulness. 'The LORD is my portion,' says my soul, 'therefore I will hope in him.'"

The last book I taught was the Book of Jeremiah; in fact, Betty Copeland finished the book for me. The thirty-second chapter is one of the greatest chapters on faith building in the Old Testament. Jeremiah's cousin wanted Jeremiah to buy a field from him, but it was in the time of the siege of Jerusalem by Babylon and it seemed futile; nevertheless, Jeremiah bought it. The Lord told him that fields and houses would again be bought in this land, and after 70 years the people did return. But twice in that chapter of Jeremiah, the Lord says, "I am the LORD . . . is anything too hard for me?" (32:27; see v. 17).

There are two New Testament passages that you already know well:

Romans 8:28: "We know that in everything God works for good with those who love him, who are called according to his purpose."

James 1:2, 3: "Count it all joy, my brethren, when you meet various trials, for you know that the testing of your faith produces steadfastness."

The sands have been washed in the footprints
Of the Stranger on Galilee's shore,
And the voice that subdued the rough billows
Is heard in Judea no more;
But the path of that lone Galilean
With joy I will follow today;
And the toils of the road will seem nothing
When I get to the end of the way;
And the toils of the road will seem nothing
When I get to the end of the way.

There are so many hills to climb upward,
I often am longing for rest;
But He who appoints me my pathway
Knows just what is needful and best.
I know in His word He has promised
That my strength it shall be as my day;
And the toils of the road will seem nothing
When I get to the end of the way;

And the toils of the road will seem nothing
When I get to the end of the way.[3]

The Way It Is Going to Be

Browning was right: "The best is yet to be."[4]

One of the most comforting passages of the Bible is Revelation 21:4: "He will wipe away every tear from their eyes, and death shall be no more, neither shall there be mourning nor crying nor pain any more." I remember that Jack taught a class many years ago on Revelation. And he said about this verse that God did not leave wiping away the tears to anyone else. He would do it himself.

An elderly man was asked whom he wanted to see first in heaven. He said, "Jesus, because he makes it possible to see all the others." My daddy said, "I do not mind dying. I hate to leave my family." And I think that is the way most of us feel. I look forward to seeing my two brothers—Roy, six years old, and Luther, ten years old—who died before I was born. I am looking forward to seeing the members of the honor roll of faithful people in Hebrews 11. The NIV says, "All these people were still living by faith when they died" (v. 13). In the New Testament, I think it would be Paul that I would like to see first.

Sing the wondrous love of Jesus,
Sing His mercy and His grace;
In the mansions bright and blessed,
He'll prepare for us a place.

While we walk the pilgrim pathway,
Clouds will overspread the sky;
But when trav'ling days are over,
Not a shadow, not a sigh.

Onward to the prize before us!
Soon His beauty we'll behold;

---

[3]Charlie D. Tillman, "The Sands Have Been Washed," *Great Songs*.
[4]Browning, "Rabbi Ben Ezra," 89.

Soon the pearly gates will open—
We shall tread the streets of gold.

When we all get to heaven,
What a day of rejoicing that will be!
When we all see Jesus,
We'll sing and shout the victory.[5]

Just think:

. . . of stepping on shore
And finding it heaven
Of touching a hand and finding it God's
Of breathing new air and finding it celestial
Of waking up in glory and finding it home.[6]

[Presented at White Station Church of Christ, Memphis, Tennessee, Summer 2003.]

---

[5]E. E. Hewitt, "Sing the Wondrous Love," *Great Songs*.
[6]Singer and Wyrtzen, "Finally Home."

THE WAY IT WAS

"We need to remind ourselves periodically that the Great Commission did not have a termination date; it is still in force. Whether it's teaching your own child in the home, teaching informally your next-door neighbor across the kitchen table, participating in organized personal work programs, going on campaigns, serving as a missionary here or overseas—wherever—we must be telling the Good News to somebody who has not yet heard it."

Annie May Alston Lewis

Photo by Mike James, Harding University Public Relations Office

Annie May Alston Lewis
November 23, 1978

2

Devotion

When we have a worship service during which the song leader honors requests that members make, among the most frequently requested titles are "My God and I," "I Come to the Garden Alone," and "Just a Closer Walk with Thee." I would like to suggest, however, that songs such as these may give us a good feeling and we may even think about the words, but these expressions in song are only the tip of the iceberg when compared to a deep devotional life. I want to talk about ways and means to develop this life, which I believe will contribute greatly to spiritual maturity.

Do you want a closer walk with God? Jesus asked the man who had been paralyzed for 38 years (John 5:2–9) if he wanted to be healed. On the surface that seemed like a ridiculous question. But the paralytic began to shift blame to others; there was nobody to help him get in the pool. There are, after all, benefits to being an invalid: No one expects anything of you; you do not have to work; you do not have to face the active pressures others face. For the first time in 38 years, probably, the real issue was spelled out for this man. Did he or did he not want to change? When he said "yes," then the process of healing began. It is never too late to start growing again no matter how old we are.

A university professor, a devout Christian, asked his son who had come east to medical school and had returned home an unbeliever if he wanted to believe. He did not marshal out all of the proofs for the existence of God, but in his wisdom he asked the one crucial question: Do you want to believe?

Once we have a vision of God as Isaiah had—a God high and

lifted up—and see the God who is everywhere; who has all power; who knows everything; who is faithful to every promise; who defines mercy, grace, holiness, and love; once we see what he has done for us in Christ Jesus, who died for us while we were still sinners, that question becomes a rhetorical one. We wouldn't need someone to tell us the five steps to a devotional life any more than I would need you to tell me five ways I can love my husband more or five ways I can be more devoted to my parents. Devotion would come naturally.

Time

You say you don't have time for a devotional life. You say, "Just look at my calendar." How do you find time? Lawrence Clark Powell, the bookman of a past generation, was the librarian at the University of California. Someone asked him how he found time to read all of the books he read. His spontaneous response was, "I take it." He thought that absolutely no excuse for failure to read was acceptable if you were going to be a librarian.[1]

We know all too well that we find time for what we really want to do. If we say we haven't time for a devotional life, then we don't love God above all else in the world—heart, soul, mind, and strength.

Everybody I know is busy, even those people who are residents in nursing homes. Our lives are filled with things to do, people to meet, projects to finish, letters to write, calls to make, and appointments to keep. I did not keep a calendar until after I retired from 44 years as teacher and librarian. One day two friends and I were lamenting the fact that we never saw each other except at the funeral homes. The daughter of one very wisely said, "Put it on the calendar." We did, and we had lunch together. We should schedule our time with God with the same realism that we schedule our time with people.

We need, in the words of Paul, to redeem the time (Eph. 5:16; Col. 4:5; KJV) while walking or driving or in unanticipated delays—waiting in doctors' offices, waiting for a very long train

---

[1]Powell, *The Alchemy of Books*, 100.

to go by, waiting for a wreck on the interstate to be cleared. Have your New Testament always with you. I doubt that any of us lead a life as busy as Jesus did. In Mark 1:32-39 we read that the whole town came crowding around the door. He cured many who were suffering from diseases of one kind or another, and he also cast out many demons. In the morning, long before dawn, he got up and left the house and went off to a lonely place to pray there. His time in prayer enabled him to say, "Let us go on to the next towns, that I may preach there also" (v. 38). Jesus was concerned with only one thing—doing the will of his Father.

E. Glenn Hinson says that the problem of time is neither too much nor too little but in ourselves and in our attitudes toward time. It's a matter of stewardship of time. He says there are three ways in which we fail to make the most of our time: (1) By non-use—by wasting it. (2) By misuse—using time for the wrong purposes—not for actual evil but by having our priorities molded by the advertising media. He is not denying the need for recreation or leisure. (3) By overuse[2]—the problem which Wayne Oates calls "workaholism."[3]

Hinson gives us something to think about. He says that if we are honest with ourselves, we will find that the time dilemma is one of ego.[4] Activity is important to self-esteem. When we are asked how we are, we give a litany of activities. John Claypool deals with the same insight in his chapter "Who Is Your Audience?" in his book *The Light within You*. He says that each of us has a select audience before whom we play the drama of our lives. It may be only one person or a group of persons, but what others think exerts enormous influence over our daily actions.[5] For most of us, our audience tends to be our peer group—the people in church or club or neighborhood or profession. Jesus dealt with this in Matthew 6:1: "Beware of practicing your piety before men in order to be seen by them." On the other hand, God is the best possible audience. He loves us best, and he knows us

---

[2]Hinson, *A Serious Call*, 88–92.

[3]Oates, *Confessions of a Workaholic*.

[4]Hinson, *A Serious Call*, 90.

[5]Claypool, *The Light within You*, 43–50.

best. The secret of Jesus' life and joy and power lies right at this point: He knew God as his Father, and he played his whole life to God and to God alone. "Whatever your task, work heartily, as serving the Lord and not men" (Col. 3:23).

Michael Quoist, in his book *Prayers*, says that all men complain that they haven't enough time. They look at their lives from too human a point of view. There is always time to do what God wants us to do, but we must put ourselves completely into each moment that he offers us.[6]

Solitude

The one thing all writers on the subject of the devotional life agree on is that without solitude it is virtually impossible to live a spiritual life. There must be a time and place for God and him alone. In Jesus' Sermon on the Mount, he tells us to go into our private room and when we have shut the door, pray to our Father (Matt. 6:6). Thomas Merton says that we don't go into the desert to escape people but to learn how to find them; we do not leave them in order to have nothing more to do with them but to find out the way to do them the most good. However, he adds this is only a secondary end. The one end that includes all others is the love of God.[7] We need to do what the psalmist said: "Be still, and know that I am God" (Ps. 46:10).

Most congregations I know have yearly retreats for men and women, but that is not enough. The piano teacher will say you must practice every day; the Greek teacher will tell you to study vocabulary every day. So it is with our devotional life. We need to make time every day to be alone with God. We may start with 15 minutes and then we will, I believe, find out we want to spend more time—30 minutes or an hour.

Life Lived from the Center

All that we have said so far is preamble. Now we come to

---

[6]Quoist, *Prayers*, 96.
[7]Merton, *New Seeds*, 52–53.

the body of the lesson. The first commandment is to love God with all our heart, soul, mind, and strength (Mark 12:30). We sometimes think our attention should be divided between God and our neighbor. But Jesus asks for a single-minded commitment to God and to God alone. It is this unconditional and unreserved love for God that leads us to care for our neighbors. "It is in God that we find our neighbors and discover our responsibility to them."[8] From the day his parents found him in the temple, Jesus speaks about his Father as the source of all of his words and actions. All through his life, Jesus considers his relationship with the Father as the beginning, center, and end of his ministry. All he says and does, he says and does in the name of the Father. He comes from the Father and returns to the Father, and it is in his Father's house that he wants to prepare a place for us.

Mary Ellen Ashcroft tells this story:

> When I was expecting our second child, my husband was offered the opportunity to visit some churches in the United States. He was excited about bringing some ideas from these churches back into our parish in Cape Town. I was devastated. Six weeks without my husband! One day I had tea with an older woman in the church. "How are you?" she asked. I sighed, "I find it so awful when Ernie's not around. I feel only half here, and so I just kind of wander around."
>
> "It kinda makes you wonder who your first love is, doesn't it?" I was speechless. I felt angry. But I respected her as a woman and a friend. That night I thought about what she had said to me and asked God to forgive me for substituting my husband for God. Since then I miss Ernie when we are apart, but some of the desperation is gone.[9]

Religion is not something to be added to our other duties. Life with God is the center of life, and it remodels and inte-

---

[8]Nouwen, *The Living Reminder*, 31.
[9]Ashcroft, *Temptations Women Face*, 191.

grates all else. It gives singleness of eye. We need to internalize the "one thing" passages: "One thing have I asked of the LORD, that will I seek after; that I may dwell in the house of the LORD all the days of my life, to behold the beauty of the LORD, and to inquire in his temple" (Ps. 27:4). Jesus' statement to the rich young ruler, "One thing you still lack" (Luke 18:22). Jesus to Martha, "One thing is needful" (Luke 10:42). Paul's "one thing I do . . . I press on toward the goal for the prize of the upward call of God in Christ Jesus" (Phil. 3:13, 14). Thomas Kelly, in *A Testament of Devotion*, comments:

> We are not skilled in the inner life . . . . We are trying to be several selves at once, without all our selves being organized by a single, mastering Life within us. Each of us tends to be, not a single self, but a whole committee of selves. There is a civic self, the parental self, the financial self, the religious self, the society self, the professional self, the literary self. . . . We are not integrated. . . . We feel honestly the pull of many obligations and try to fulfill them all. . . . We've seen such lives, integrated, unworried by the tangles of close decisions, unhurried, cheery, fresh, positive. These are not people of dallying idleness . . . ; they are busy carrying their full load as well as we, but without any chafing of the shoulders with the burden, with quiet joy and springing step.[10]

They lead lives of peace and power and joy because their lives are lived from a "divine Center" where "No" as well as "Yes" can be said with confidence.

If you read very much in devotional literature, the name of John Woolman will appear. He was the eighteenth-century Quaker preacher who wrote and spoke much against slavery. He was a bookkeeper in a mercantile house but later learned the tailor's trade. He simplified his life on the basis of its relation to the divine Center. He never let the demands of his business grow beyond his real needs. When too many customers came, he sent

---

[10]Kelly, *A Testament of Devotion*, 114–16.

them elsewhere to more needy merchants and tailors. He had that singleness of eye.

Richard Foster, whose name is a household word in any study of the devotional life, treats as many as a dozen areas of life in his search for the disciplined life.[11] I have chosen three to center on because I believe they are of primary importance on any scale. They are Bible study, prayer, and meditation.

Bible Study

David Watson commented on the days before his operation for the cancer that ultimately took his life:

> As I spent time chewing over the endless assurances and promises to be found in the Bible, so my faith in the living God grew stronger and held me safe in his hands. God's word to us, especially his word spoken by his Spirit through the Bible, is the very ingredient that feeds our faith. If we feed our souls regularly on God's word, several times each day, we should become robust spiritually just as we feed on ordinary food several times each day and become robust physically. Nothing is more important than hearing and obeying the word of God.[12]

I am not sympathetic with those today who disparage knowing Bible facts, although I know that facts are not the be-all and end-all of Scripture study. Whether you can name all of David's brothers is not so important, but it is imperative that you know the story of David. Whether you can name all of the spies is not so important, but you should know about their lack of faith in the God who was able to deliver them. Your salvation does not depend on whether you can describe all of the furnishings in the tabernacle, but you should know its significance in Jewish worship. I think you should know about Bezalel, the builder of the tabernacle, about whom the Lord said in Exodus 31, "I have filled

---

[11]Foster, *The Celebration of Discipline.*
[12]Watson, *Fear No Evil*, 39.

him with the Spirit of God, with ability and intelligence, with knowledge and all craftsmanship, to devise artistic designs, to work in gold, silver, and bronze, in cutting stones for setting, and in carving wood, for work in every craft" (vv. 3–5). These are gifts as well as those in the New Testament in Romans 12, in 1 Corinthians 12, and in Ephesians 4.

The reason for Bible study that encompasses all others is to get to know God. We get to know God as we get to know people, by spending time with them so that we know what they would want us to say and to do. Clyde Lewis, Jack's brother, and his wife, Griffie, were married for 50 years. Griffie suffered a stroke, which left her with impaired speech and the loss of the use of one hand. Since that time Clyde has done everything for her; he bathes her, dresses her, cooks, cleans house, and anticipates her every need. When the words she wants to say won't come out the right way, she says, "Clyde," and he becomes her spokesman. But it's 50 years together in life and in love that make it all possible. Living with God in his Word is the way we get to know how he wants us to live and how we should respond to any situation.

Elie Wiesel says that God made man because God loves stories.[13] We need to know these stories so well that we tell them to our children and hear them say, "Tell it again."

I have a dream—that we will get beyond the three chapters a day and five on Sunday mentality so that we can, with the writer of Psalm 119 in meditating on the law of God, speak of seeking the Lord with our whole heart (vv. 2, 10, 34, 58, 69, and 145) and of delighting in the law (vv. 16, 24, 35, 47, 70, 77, 92, 143, and 174). The Psalms were the devotional literature for the early church. For many years I have asked my class on Sunday morning to read a psalm every day in addition to their *Power for Today*. If you read five psalms a day, you can read them all in a month and then start over. I have a friend who, after serious surgery in which she could not focus her vision for some days, said that as soon as she could, she picked up her Bible and read Psalm 1 through 150 at one sitting. Another friend said after her hus-

[13]Wiesel, *Gates of the Forest*.

band's grave illness, "I could not have made it through the last 15 days without the Psalms." The Methodist minister Fred Morris said that Psalm 23 "had carried him through the gruesome hours in the Brazilian torture chamber and had given him peace in his darkest hour."[14] Every emotion to which man is subject is present in the Psalms.

The Psalms provide the prayer and praise with which we express our response to the Gospel. The first Christians sang in thanksgiving psalms and hymns and spiritual songs (Col. 3:16), and since those days the Psalms have been the inspiration of the hymn writers of Christendom. We increase our appreciation for this body of literature when we sing or read the hymns based on the Psalms: "Savior, Grant Me Rest and Peace" from Psalm 4:8—"In peace I will both lie down and sleep; for thou alone, O LORD, makest me dwell in safety"; "O Lord, Our Lord" from Psalm 8:1—"How majestic is thy name in all the earth"; "Thou, My Everlasting Portion" from Psalm 16:5—"The LORD is my chosen portion and my cup; thou holdest my lot"; "The Statutes of the Lord" from Psalm 119:97—"Oh, how love I thy law"; and "He Took Me Out of the Pit" from Psalm 40:2—"He drew me up from the desolate pit, out of the miry bog, and set my feet upon a rock, making my steps secure."

In the Psalms the individual soul deals in its own right with God. It is "thou" and "I." To the psalmists God is more real, more personal, more the center of everything. They know better how to pray, to praise, and to meditate on God. John Calvin said the Psalms have opened to us "familiar access to God."[15]

I hope you have known the sheer joy of discovering for yourself—not from any sermon or Bible class—a biblical truth or a deeper understanding of a biblical passage, a relationship between verses and chapters. Then you can share that discovery with another who loves to study the Bible.

Books have been written on how to study the Bible. One of the best experiences I ever had in Bible study was the Book of Jeremiah taught by Don Sime at the Harding University Gradu-

---

[14]Nouwen, *The Living Reminder*, 70.
[15]Calvin, *Commentary*, 1:xxxviii.

ate School of Religion. We read the book several times and were told to outline it. As you may know, you really cannot outline that book; it doesn't lend itself to outlining. But in the attempt, we did learn a great deal about the book. You need to avail yourself of good dictionaries, encyclopedias, atlases, and commentaries.

The non-negotiable place of Bible study is nowhere better stated than by the apostle John when he says, "And this is eternal life, that they know thee the only true God, and Jesus Christ whom thou hast sent" (John 17:3).

Prayer

Among Americans there now seems to be an enormous interest in the subject of prayer. The current *Books in Print* lists nearly 2,000 titles on prayer, meditation, and techniques for spiritual growth. A major publisher of serious religious books says that books on prayer, after the Bible, are its biggest sellers. An article in the January 6, 1992, issue of *Newsweek* quoted the late Rabbi Abraham Heschel, who has been called the greatest modern theologian of the spiritual life: "To pray is to bring God back into the world . . . to expand his presence." For Heschel, talking *about* God is idle chatter unless one first learns to talk *to* God. According to a study at the National Opinion Research Center, three-fourths (78 percent) of Americans pray at least once a week; more than half (57 percent) pray at least once a day. Even among the 13 percent of Americans who are atheists or agnostics, nearly one in five still prays daily. Forty-two percent ask for material things when they pray. Meditative prayer increases with age. Forty-five percent of 18- to 24-year-olds pray meditatively; 70 percent of 65-year-olds do so.

Charles Gonzalez, rector of the Jesuit community at Georgetown University, Washington, D.C., said, "I pray and pray regularly because I must do it to live."[16] R. T. Clark, a schoolmate of mine at Harding, a pioneer in space medicine, said on one of our

---

[16]Source unknown. Charles G. Gonzalez is a lecturer of theology at Georgetown University in Washington, D.C. http://explore.georgetown.edu/people/cgg9/?PageTemplateID=153 (accessed March 23, 2009).

retreats, "I run to live"; and though his heart finally gave out, running prolonged his life. In the same way, we need to pray to live; prayer can prolong our lives. I think those of us who feel we must pray to live consider prayer as conversation with God in which we tell him in all naturalness everything that concerns us. F. J. Sheed said,

> Our wants concern us deeply. But no conversation with anyone can consist wholly of asking for things, and in our conversation with God we should progress from thinking about ourselves to thinking about him, from talking about ourselves to talking about him. Our prayer should move from telling him of our wants, to thanking him for his gifts, on through sorrow for what has gone wrong in our relation with him to adoration and love.[17]

When we go to God in prayer, we need to go not as a stranger but as someone whom God has known through long familiarity. Dean Willard Sperry of the Harvard Divinity School used to tell this story to his students. He said his mother told him to be in the home of each family in the church where he ministered at least twice a year so when there was sickness, death, or another need in that family, he would go to visit not as a stranger but as a friend.[18]

If you don't know the language of prayer, then read some of the great prayers in the Bible—those of Ezra, Nehemiah, Daniel, and, of course, those in the Psalms. Tell God that is your prayer. The more we pray to our heavenly Father, the more we will realize that we cannot live without that solitary communion with him. I sometimes think that the greatest punishment we could receive in the afterlife would be the loss of the opportunity to talk with God. My father died 40 years ago, and to this day I long to hear his voice and miss talking with him. I recently heard

---

[17]Source unknown. Frank J. Sheed (1897–1981) was a popular Catholic writer and apologist. http://en.wikipedia.org/wiki/Frank_Sheed (accessed March 23, 2009).

[18]Sperry, Class Lecture Notes of Jack P. Lewis, Homiletics.

Jim Bill McInteer say, "In these last years of my life, I want to stress prayer." He also tells us, "One of my private devotionals is a bit public. In my diary I call it my 'prayer walk.' Until I learned better, I had a radio stuck in my ear hearing news reports and music so as not to lose any time. No more! Frankly, I don't want to walk with you—I want those 30 minutes to walk alone and pray. No radio, just one-half hour to talk to the Lord and await his answers."

Meditation

Paul tells us in Philippians 4:8, "Whatever is true, whatever is honorable, whatever is just, whatever is pure, whatever is lovely, whatever is gracious, if there is any excellence, if there is anything worthy of praise, think about these things." It is very difficult these days to meditate on these things because we are bombarded by television, newspapers, and magazines with all the ugly side of life. The media fill our lives with thoughts that are untrue, dishonorable, unjust, impure, unlovely, and ungracious. Thomas Merton, one of the most prolific writers on the devotional life, said that he never looked at television.[19] A rigid discipline is required to fill our minds with all the good we can. If we do not make a firm effort to do this, then we will be exposed to the same outcome as the man out of whom the unclean spirit was cast.

Jean Leclercq, the Benedictine medieval scholar, writes,

> To meditate is to read a text and to learn it "by heart" in the fullest sense of this expression, that is, with one's whole being: with the body, since the mouth pronounced it, with the memory which fixes it, with the intelligence which understands its meaning, and with the will which desires to put it into practice.[20]

---

[19]Merton, *New Seeds*, 86.

[20]Leclercq, *The Love of Learning*, 21–22.

The psalmist in 119 speaks of meditating on the law in verses 15, 23, 27, 48, 78, 97, 99, and 148.

The Bible is the basic source for meditation providing content for thought. Henri Nouwen reminds us that good memories offer good guidance.[21] The prophets reminded people of God's care and compassion. Jesus reminded his contemporaries of their history—Elijah and Elisha, Jonah and Solomon. The historical Psalms such as Psalms 78, 105, and 106 are constant reminders of God's care in past history. The agony of the palmist in Psalm 77 is so intense that he questions God's justice and love. But then to encourage himself, he says he will call to mind the deeds of the Lord and remember God's wonders of old. "I will meditate on all thy work, and muse on thy mighty deeds" (v. 12).

When we become anxious because of uncertainties, we need to focus on Jesus' words, "Do not fear, only believe" (Mark 5:36). Once we have expressed our fears and accepted them, we can let them go. If we encounter a spate of disappointments and a dearth of satisfactions, we may be tempted to become discouraged and experience spiritual fatigue. Then listen to Jesus' invitation, "Come to me, all who labor and are heavy laden, and I will give you rest" (Matt. 11:28). If we are concerned about priorities, we need to meditate on the Parable of the Pearl of Great Price (Matt. 13:45, 46). If we need guidance in times of decision-making, we need to think about God's chosen people who arrived at their destination but, fearing an encounter with the inhabitants of the land, lost their nerve and wandered in the wilderness for 40 years. After the death of that generation, the next generation accepted the risk of entering the new land, leaving the pattern of aimless wandering.

William Hulme recalls an incident in his own life in which he found himself in sharp conflict with his teenage son. "What I said is final—that's it—period." The son reacted with passive and sullen resistance. As a father, Hulme attempted to fortify his rightness with all sorts of justifications. Then he remembered, "Love does not insist on its own way" (1 Cor. 13:5). He was not

---

[21]Nouwen, *The Living Reminder*, 59.

ready to tell his son of any change in his approach. His pride was in the way. Fortunately, the son was also rethinking his role in the conflict. Before the father got around to approaching the son, the son approached him with a compromise suggestion and was quite taken aback by his father's receptiveness. The recall of Scripture brought reconciliation between him and his son.[22]

We should meditate on heaven every day. Charlie Hodge says, "We should think about heaven thirty minutes daily."[23] We should read the words of the hymn,

> One sweetly solemn tho't
> Comes to me o'er and o'er:
> Today I'm nearer to my home
> Than e'er I've been before.[24]

That is truth for the young as well as for the aged.

Goal

The goal in the devotional life is to live our lives so that there is no compartmentalization, but all of life becomes one magnificent devotion to God. That time spent in Bible study, prayer, and meditation cannot be separated from our day-to-day living. In Mark 12:28ff. the teacher of the Law said that Jesus had given him the right answer when asked which was the most important commandment. Later in the chapter, Jesus issued a warning against the teachers of the Law who walked around in flowing robes and had important seats in the synagogue and at banquets but devoured widows' houses. Their religion and their lives didn't mesh.

Jesus is the only one who ever lived whose devotional life was in perfect tandem with every other aspect of his life. We would hope that by a deeper devotional life our characters will be shaped by God. Like the young man in Hawthorne's story of

---

[22]Hulme, *Let the Spirit In*, 68.

[23]Hodge, *My Daily Walk*, 157.

[24]Phoebe Cary, "One Sweetly Solemn Thought," *Great Songs*.

"The Great Stone Face" who admired the sculpture on the cliff until he resembled it,[25] we may, in some small way, become mirrors of God. The simple monk known as Brother Lawrence seems to have embraced this idea when he said, "The time of business does not with me differ from the time of prayer; and in the noise and clatter of my kitchen, while several persons are at the same time calling for different things, I possess God in as great tranquility as if I were upon my knees at the blessed sacrament."[26]

Phillip Morrison expresses the idea in "My Prayer":

> Dear Lord,
> You know how long I've struggled . . .
> with my personal devotional life . . .
> trying to find the time to make the time for study, meditation, prayer.
>
> Thank you for Randy Harris,
> who introduced me to the prayers of Michael Quoist;
>
> For Coach Don Meyer,
> who made me a fan
> of the One Year Bible;
>
> For my loving parents,
> who piqued my interest
> with Hurlbut's Bible stories;
>
> For Mary Margaret,
> whose quiet example and encouragement
> set such a high standard.
>
> Thank you for leading me to learn
> the incomparable value of
> a quiet time with your Word,
> a private place for prayer,

---

[25]Hawthorne, *Twice-Told Tales*, 21–42.
[26]Lawrence, *The Practice*, 9.

treasured moments to talk with you,
the serenity which washes over me
When I know you are near.

Thank you also for letting me learn
that devotional life can be
spontaneous as well as planned,
prayers can be a single sentence,
spiritual awareness can begin with
a raindrop, Niagara, anthill or Alp,
wherever your nearness is felt.

It's an awesome reality
that I'm only beginning to grasp:
All my life is lived in devotion
when all my heart, soul, and mind
are devoted to thee,
my Rock and my Redeemer.

Thank you, Lord, for those times I
carve out, set aside, reserve for thee.
And thank you, Lord, for those unexpected
serendipitous moments when my heart leaps
at the wonder of your presence.[27]

[Date and occasion of this speech are unknown.]

[27]Morrison, "My Prayer," 12.

3

THE CHRISTIAN AS A LEARNER

The word *disciple* is generally taken to mean a person whose chief concern is with learning; he is essentially a learner. As Christians we have not taken very seriously what the Bible has to say about learning and teaching. We have long taught that obedience to a biblical command is not dependent on the number of times that command is expressed; a one-time command is sufficient. Yet if we would check our concordances to see the numerous allusions to teaching and learning throughout the whole Bible, we might be astonished to see how lightly we have taken this body of teaching. Teaching and learning are not options which we may choose or reject. They are commands to be followed.

The Bible teaches us that there are many lessons to be learned and taught, but we will focus on learning and teaching God's Word. Emphasis is given to this command in all three divisions of the Old Testament—the Law, the Prophets, and the Writings—with a concentration of references in the Book of Deuteronomy and in the Book of Psalms. Deuteronomy is replete with the Lord's admonition to learn the laws, statutes, and ordinances of the Lord. The Psalms echo again and again the prominence of the Law, the Lord's way, truth, testimonies, and statutes in the lives of God's people. Psalm 119 with its 176 verses has repeated allusions to teaching and learning God's Law.

Looking at the references in the Old Testament regarding the learning and teaching of God's Law, we see that a number of characteristics surround this command. First is that of parental responsibility. "And these words which I command you this day shall be upon your heart; and you shall teach them diligently to your children, and shall talk of them when you sit in your house, and when you walk by the way, and when you lie down, and when you rise" (Deut. 6:6, 7).

Psalm 78:5–7 reveals the method by which God's law is to be kept alive in the heart of the people, and again it is by the father's teaching of the children:

> He established a testimony in Jacob, and appointed a law in Israel, which he commanded our fathers to teach to their children; that the next generation might know them, the children yet unborn, and arise and tell them to their children, so that they should set their hope in God, and not forget the works of God, but keep his commandments.

Never was there a point in time when such instruction could be relaxed, and if such did occur, the results were tragic. The stark reality of such a condition is vividly seen in Joshua 24:31 and repeated in Judges 2:7–10:

> And the people served the LORD all the days of Joshua, and all the days of the elders who outlived Joshua, who had seen all the great work which the LORD had done for Israel. And Joshua the son of Nun, the servant of the LORD, died at the age of one hundred and ten years. . . . And all that generation also were gathered to their fathers; and there arose another generation after them, who did not know the LORD or the work which he had done for Israel.

In early Jewish education, there was no substitute for the father. As teacher of his children, the father served as a living and dynamic communicator of divine truth. Jewish law laid it down that a father must explain the great festivals to his son:

> When your son asks you in time to come, "What is the meaning of the testimonies and the statutes and the ordinances which the LORD our God has commanded you?" then you shall say to your son, "We were Pharaoh's slaves

in Egypt; and the LORD brought us out of Egypt with a mighty hand" (Deut. 6:20-21).

Although the father seems to have borne the major responsibility of teaching God's laws to his children, the Book of Proverbs indicates that mothers shared in this teaching role. "Hear, my son, your father's instruction, and reject not your mother's teaching" (Prov. 1:8), and "My son, keep your father's commandment, and forsake not your mother's teaching" (Prov. 6:20). The first verse of the oft-quoted worthy woman passage (Prov. 31) may have been overlooked: "The words of Lemuel, king of Massa, which his mother taught him."

That the child's training was to begin early is indicated by the writer of Ecclesiastes: "Remember also your Creator in the days of your youth, before the evil days come, and the years draw nigh, when you will say, 'I have no pleasure in them'" (Eccles. 12:1). This same emphasis on early training is echoed in Josephus: "If anyone should question one of us concerning the laws, he would more easily repeat them all than his own name; since we learn them from our first consciousness, we have them, as it were, engraven on our souls."[1]

A marked characteristic of this teaching was the diligence with which it was to be done. The Deuteronomy 6:6, 7 passage instructs that you "shall talk of them [words which I command you] when you sit in your house, and when you walk by the way, and when you lie down, and when you rise." In his speech to Joshua, after the death of Moses, God instructs that "this book of the law shall not depart out of your mouth, but you shall meditate on it day and night" (Josh. 1:8a). Psalm 1 pronounces a blessing on the man who meditates on the law day and night (Ps. 1:2). Encompassing all aspects of their lives, teaching God's law was not relegated to a single specified hour during the week.

Accompanying instruction in God's law was the ingredient of discipline. Instruction and discipline are inseparably linked in the Old Testament. Discipline was to be regarded as a mark of God's love and concern in instructing those whom he loves. "He

---

[1]Josephus, *Against Apion*, 2:19.

who chastens the nations, does he not chastise? He who teaches men knowledge, the LORD, knows the thoughts of man, that they are but a breath. Blessed is the man whom thou dost chasten, O LORD, and whom thou dost teach out of thy law" (Ps. 94:10-12). God knew that it was not possible to teach without discipline.

The disciplined instruction in God's law was not a burden to be borne but a joy to be experienced. The reader of Psalm 119 must be impressed with the recurrent phrases "In the way of thy testimonies I delight" (v. 14), "I will delight in thy statutes" (v. 16), and "Lead me in the path of thy commandments, for I delight in it" (v. 35). In that psalm, the word *delight* is used ten times in reference to the Lord's commands, testimonies, and statutes.

The joy of the commandment is a theme which recurs in Jewish writings. To the pious Jew, the commandments were to be practiced with joy, since only those laws which Israel accepted with joy were considered to have been observed. The pious Jew sang of his joy in practicing that law and of the consolation it provided, which made him forget all trials and persecution.

Further, in the Old Testament, the study of God's Word is conceived of as a continuing and growing activity, so that Solomon, the wisest of men, could speak of a wise man increasing in learning (Prov. 1:5; 9:9).

That knowledge of God's will can never be divorced from doing God's will is evident throughout the Old Testament. Over and over again Israel was told, "You shall therefore love the LORD your God, and keep his charge, his statutes, his ordinances, and his commandments always" (Deut. 11:1). After knowing the command, then the keeping and doing of that command naturally follows in God's order.

The priority of study or doing was propounded in a conference of rabbis at Lydda: Is studying the greater thing, or doing? R. Tarfon gave his voice for doing, but R. Akiba for study, and the decision was unanimous in his favor on the ground that "study leads to doing."[2]

Ezra's order was the correct one: "For Ezra had set his heart to study the law of the LORD, and to do it, and to teach his stat-

[2]Kiddushin 40b.

utes and ordinances in Israel" (Ezra 7:10).

In keeping with the order set by Ezra, the two prerequisites to teaching others are studying and doing God's will. Any attempt to teach without having fulfilled the first two requirements is futile. Deuteronomy 4:10b is a representative passage on the responsibility of teaching—". . . so that they may learn to fear me all the days that they live upon the earth, and that they may teach their children so." The psalmist says God "commanded our fathers to teach their children; that the next generation might know them, the children yet unborn, and arise and tell them to their children" (Ps. 78:5b, 6). God's charge is that each generation teach the following generation.

The same emphasis on learning God's will, doing his will, and teaching others is brought over into the New Testament. In the Gospels Jesus is addressed 16 times as "rabbi" and 41 times as "teacher." He taught in the cities (Matt. 11:1), beside the sea (Mark 4:1), and in the synagogue (Mark 6:2). He taught the multitudes (Mark 2:13); he taught his disciples (Matt. 5:1, 2). He taught a single person as she sat at his feet (Luke 10:39).

There is little knowledge of how Jesus was educated. His education probably consisted of what he was taught by his mother and father supplemented by the teaching of the local synagogue school. We know that Timothy's first teachers were his grandmother and his mother.

In Paul's admonition to Timothy (2 Tim. 2:2), four generations of spiritual offspring are involved in teaching the Gospel—Paul, Timothy, faithful men, and others. Good teaching had produced a chain reaction.

The New Testament continues the Old Testament concept of continuing in the word and growing in that word. It is Jesus himself who identified his disciples as those who continue in his Word (John 8:31), Paul who prays for the Colossians that they may increase "in the knowledge of God" (Col. 1:10), and Peter whose final plea is that the Christians would grow in the "knowledge of our Lord and Savior Jesus Christ" (2 Pet. 3:18). The writer of the Letter to the Hebrews speaks of going on to maturity and proceeds to more advanced subjects (Heb. 6:1, 2).

Jesus set the perfect example of doing what he taught. Children must know that parents hold to a firm belief that the study of the Bible is more important than the study involved in a profession, and that a *summa cum laude* without a knowledge of the Bible is an empty honor. Children must know that parents consider the study of God's Word vital to their very existence. When we sing, "How shall the young secure their hearts?" the answer must be a reaffirmation of our faith in "Thy Word." Robert Dale in his lectures on Ephesians has shown us our first priority:

> . . . under God, the primary condition of a successful Christian education is that *the parents should care more for the loyalty of their children to Christ than for anything besides*, more for this than for their health, their intellectual vigour and brilliance, their material prosperity, their social position, their exemption from great sorrows and great misfortunes.[3]

God knew that it was not possible to learn without discipline. Teachers and parents alike need to re-learn this basic principle—without discipline there is no learning. And children must know that an intensive study of the Bible is a joy; it brings a delight unequalled by any other pursuit.

The study of God's will was not sufficient under either the Old or New Covenant; neither can it be so today. God sets every person down in a network of relationships where he must be some kind of link between the generations and, whether he knows it or not, leave his particular touch on the lives of those around him. The ultimate translation for Scripture is not a book but a life. For most of us, our deeds do not match our words, and the challenge that they be brought more nearly into harmony with each other is a constant one. We want to live as we pray. We want to live as we teach. We want to live as we sing. We want to live as we speak. We want to love in deed and in truth.

It was in God's wisdom that he gave us Hebrews 11. The Bible had given definitions of faith, but we couldn't fully know what faith is until we saw Abraham leave his home, not knowing where he was going, just because God told him to; until we saw

---

[3]Dale, *The Epistle to the Ephesians*, 395.

Abraham ready to offer Isaac; until we saw Moses leave Egypt and not be afraid; and until we saw Rahab protect the spies.

Our children must see that Word lived out in our lives if they are ever to be convinced that we truly believe. In his introduction to *Christian Nurture*, which was written more than 100 years ago, Luther Weigle summarizes Bushnell as follows: "It is the Christian life of the parent, his good sense and the completeness of his own devotion to the will of God as shown him in Christ, that matters most."[4]

And finally, it is imperative that this learning of God's will be passed on to others in this present age. The Great Commission is as current today as it was in the day that Jesus gave it to his disciples. The use of the present participle in Matthew 28:20 suggests that the learning program of the Christian never comes to an end. Somehow the realization of the debt we owe must cause us to teach wherever there is one who has not heard that Jesus died for him. Jesus is coming back, and all of our excuses for failing to teach others will seem so feeble when we stand before him who spent his life teaching others.

The comments that we are prone to make about times changing, young people changing, the different age in which we live, and the countless demands that are made upon us in no way alter the truth that without a knowledge of God's Word, we and our children will perish; but with this knowledge lived out in our lives and teaching its truth to others, we can have that life which is life indeed.

A few years before his death, Karl Barth addressed students at the University of Chicago. Afterward he was asked to name the greatest discovery men could make in the New Testament. Drawing from a lifetime of serious study and thought, the old man responded, "Jesus loves me—this I know—for the Bible tells me so."[5] It will take a lifetime of study to grasp this truth and an eternity to thank him for it.

The universality of this command is seen in Moses' statement near the end of his life:

---

[4]Weigle, "Introduction," xxxvi-xxxvii.

[5]Barth, *Fragments*, 124.

> And Moses commanded them [priests and elders of Israel], "At the end of every seven years, at the set time of the year of release, at the feast of booths, when all Israel comes to appear before the LORD your God at the place which he will choose, you shall read this law before all Israel in their hearing. Assemble the people, men, women, and little ones, and the sojourner within your towns, that they may hear and learn to fear the LORD your God, and be careful to do all the words of this law, and that their children, who have not known it, may hear asnd learn to fear the LORD your God, as long as you live in the land which you are going over the Jordan to possess" (Deut. 31:10–12).

I think all of us would hope we might say with Alan Paton's missionary figure in *Cry the Beloved Country,*

> I shall no longer ask myself if this or that is expedient, but only if it is right. I shall do this, not because I am noble or unselfish, but because life slips away, and because I need for the rest of my journey a star that will not play false to me, a compass that will not lie. . . . I am lost when I balance this against that, I am lost when I ask if this is safe. I am lost when I ask if men, white men or black men, Englishmen or Afrikaners, Gentiles or Jews, will approve. Therefore, I shall try to do what is right, and to speak what is true.[6]

In the fourth century Jerome, whose writings issued from a scholarship unsurpassed in the early church and whose greatest achievement was his translation of the Bible into Latin from the original tongues, wrote, "To be ignorant of Scripture is not to know Christ."[7]

[Date and occasion of this speech are unknown.]

---

[6]Paton, *Cry the Beloved Country*, 175.
[7]Knox, *The Holy Bible*, vii.

4

LISTENING

In the sixth century B.C., Seneca wrote of the need for someone to listen:

> For who listens to us in all the world whether he be friend, or teacher, brother, or father, or mother, sister or neighbor, son or ruler or servant? Does he listen, our advocate, or our husbands or wives, those who are dearest to us? Do the stars listen, when we turn despairingly away from man, or the great seas or winds of the mountains? To whom can any man say—Here I am! Behold me in my nakedness, my wounds, my secret grief, my despair, my betrayal, my pain, my tongue which cannot express my sorrow, my terror, my abandonment? Listen to me for a day—an hour—a moment. Lest I expire in my terrible wilderness, my lonely silence. Oh! God, is there no one to listen?[1]

This question is probably being asked more often today by more people than it was in Seneca's day, 500 years before Christ.

Wayne Willis describes the different kinds of listeners he and his wife encountered when they were told that their firstborn son, who was five years old, was diagnosed to have amblyopia, "lazy eye." They were "told, among other things, that vision in the weak eye was so bad (20/100) that he would have to wear a patch for a year and strong prescription glasses for life and even

[1]Willis, "Listen! Hear!" 12.

then might not see well enough to ever obtain a driver's license." They experienced shock, tears, depression, and anxiety as they thought about rearing a handicapped child.

Willis writes of the response he and his wife received from their friends. The first friend said, "Oh, that's nothing. We knew a child who had the same thing and did fine." She then proceeded to describe her own child's problem, which Willis admitted in all fairness was more than lazy eye. On the same day, another friend called to complain about her husband's moodiness. "At the first opening, some quarter-hour into the conversation, my wife blurted out to her" the concern she had for their child. The only response was "I'm sorry"—no questions and no follow-up inquiry the next several times they saw her. A third person offered "advice of the positive-thinking variety: 'Oh, I'm sure it will all work out fine. It's probably not as bad as you think. I'm sure that you'll find out that the physician made a mistake and it's not all that bad.'" A fourth friend, Willis says, "totally unaware that we were plumbing the depths, called and talked for over an hour about a personal problem, and then as she was prepared to sign off politely added, 'All we've done is talk about me. How are things with you?'" Finally, two of their friends did come through for them. They gave them all the time to talk that they wanted, let them cry without trying to cheer them up. They helped by raising questions, reflecting on what they heard, and making a helpful suggestion or two. Willis adds that both friends had earlier leaned on him and his wife for help in their hour of need and thus were highly motivated to serve them.[2]

Why Do We Not Listen?

One of the reasons we talk rather than listen is that we do not like to face negative feelings. However, if I intend to be biblical, honest, and loving, I must listen. In Psalm 77:1 the psalmist admits to all of those negative feelings: "I cry aloud to God, aloud to God, that he may hear me." I must listen because in his love God listens. The Bible is bursting with the words of men

[2]Ibid., 10–12.

and women who pour out their hearts before God. God was not embarrassed or put off by what his people said. Not only did he listen, but he allowed words of anguish and despair to be recorded in writing as in the Book of Psalms and in the Book of Job. The reality of God's love is, in fact, clearer in Scripture because we are also allowed to read of the desperate need men and women have for that love. It is difficult for most of us to accept pain and suffering as integral parts of living. A counseling teacher told me once that it disturbs him that everybody wants to be happy; that's their goal in life.

Another reason we do not listen is that we are all a part of the "me" generation. We had rather hear ourselves talk than to listen to someone else. Perhaps this is true because no matter what else we think, we are actually talking about ourselves.

A third reason is that most of us think that just listening can't possibly be enough. We tend to agree with Phyllis McGinley:

> Sticks and stones are hard on bones,
> Aimed with angry art.
> Words can sting like anything,
> But silence breaks the heart.[3]

We may agree that listening is necessary, but we must eventually do something more. We want to respond with advice, suggestions, reassurance, support, encouragement—something.

Principles of Listening

We must have a genuine interest in the other person. Anne Lindbergh has reminded us that there is nothing so tiring as hypocrisy.[4] If we are not sincerely concerned, we will tire very quickly. Henri Nouwen has said that "if there is any posture that disturbs a suffering man or woman, it is aloofness."[5] Many who need "an attentive ear, a word of support, . . . a firm hand, a ten-

---

[3]McGinley, *Love Letters*, 73.
[4]Lindbergh, *Gift from the Sea*, 32.
[5]Nouwen, *Wounded Healer*, 71.

der smile, or even a stuttering confession of inability to do more, often find" that people "do not want to burn their fingers."[6] We must be willing to become involved, to enter a painful situation, and to take the risk of being hurt. We can't listen to a story of loneliness and despair without experiencing similar pain and even losing some of our peace of mind. In short, we can't take away suffering without entering into it. We must be willing to mourn with those who mourn as well as laugh with those who laugh.

Empathy is a basic element which must be learned and practiced by anyone who is involved in the care of persons. It is the means by which the listener enables the one who is talking to know not only that he has been understood without judgment, but also that the person listening has been able to enter his world and understands what it feels like to be him. Sometimes we have to have had the same experience in order to be able to do this. But sometimes we may have such a sensitivity to the feelings of others that we can truly sympathize with them. We need not have lost the particular member of the family as another to know sorrow; in some ways grief is grief regardless of the nature of the loss. I recently heard a man who had lost his wife years before say to another man who had more recently lost his wife, "I know how you feel." The response he received was, "No, you don't." I do know that in losing a loved one, each person loses something unique. So perhaps we can't honestly say, "I know just how you feel," but rather, "I know something of how you must feel, and I want to share your grief as much as I can."

The men and women who were in the leper colony of Molokai doubtless had many well-meaning would-be comforters, but certainly no word spoken to them before made their hearts leap up as did the two words which one day came from the lips of Father Damien, the priest who had gone to live among them. "We lepers . . . ," he began. Then they knew that nothing they might suffer would be beyond his understanding.[7] Most people will say that listening is the most important part of care.

A second principle of listening is that we have to look beyond

---

[6]Ibid., 72.

[7]Farrow, *Damien the Leper*, 156–59.

the present situation. Cabot and Dicks tell us in *The Art of Ministering to the Sick* that in the case of the very sick we have to look beyond the wasted muscles and the terrifying pallor.[8] In a hospital we have to ignore smells, sights, and sounds; we have to get used to the smell of ether, disinfectants, and the unwashed. We must learn to be at ease with a deformity.

Cabot and Dicks remind us that we also have to learn to look past certain moral facts like sexual immorality when there is nothing we can do about it by direct approach. We fix attention on the better parts of the person's mind which often lie side by side with his worst traits. We must learn painfully that contradictory characteristics lie side by side in many people and affect each other very little. All of us have contradictory qualities. In such people we may need to ignore for months obvious moral deformities. We don't forget them but watch patiently for a chance directly or indirectly to attack them. The cultivation and encouragement of the best that the listener can find is like listening for the clearly articulated words of a stammerer. To look past a chaotic foreground to a background where he can take hold and help is therefore one of the major talents needed in the art of listening.

We may have to remind ourselves that we are included in the "all" who have sinned and that our own justification is only by God's grace. Who among us does not need constant encouragement and admonition?

Another principle of listening is to accept our friend's point of view as being true for him but be willing to state another point of view. Pascal has said that when we wish to influence another person, we must be willing to grant the other person a point of view and then suggest an additional point of view.[9] This approach may help a person to a whole new way of looking at his situation.

Landon Saunders tells the story of a corporate leader who was made head of a large, important, and difficult-to-administer government institution. After a while he realized he was not

---

[8]Cabot and Dicks, *The Art of Ministering*, 21.

[9]Pascal, *Pensées*, sect. I, no. 9.

happy with the way things were going. So for three months he stopped reading papers and listening to news broadcasts. He relied solely on the people he worked with to tell him what was going on. During this period of intentional listening, this wise man received the insights he needed to set the right course.

We need to listen to other people's points of view in the home (and there is where it may be the most difficult), on the job, and in our social and church activities. It is possible that we, as listeners, may change our point of view.

We must refrain from invading the privacy of another's personal pain. If we ask about his feelings and he chooses not to tell us, we should step back, pray, and try to express our concern in another way. Curiosity-seeking has no place in good listening.

We must try to understand what lies beneath the words we hear. Jesus listened for the heart needs of people. When he healed the woman with the flow of blood (Mark 5:25–34), he knew her need was greater than physical healing. Because of her 12 years of hemorrhaging, she had probably been ostracized by her people. By drawing her out and telling her in front of the crowd, "Your faith has made you well," he restored her not only physically but socially and spiritually as well.

Sometimes silence is the best kind of listening. Job's friends sat seven days without saying anything when they went to be with him during his crisis. Although we tend to blame Job's friends for their false accusations against Job, perhaps their silence may be one area in which they should receive our praise.

Another principle of listening is to use Scripture in a helpful way. Martin Lloyd-Jones has said that "every conceivable view of life and of man is invariably dealt with somewhere or another in the Scriptures."[10] The listener is able to direct the person to the One who is able to help and wants more than any human being to help. We believe not only in the Bible's authority but in its power to transform lives. We can echo Paul:

> Blessed be the God and Father of our Lord Jesus Christ, the Father of mercies and God of all comfort, who com-

---

[10]Lloyd-Jones, *Truth,* 20.

> forts us in all our affliction, so that we may be able to comfort those who are in affliction, with the comfort with which we ourselves are comforted by God (2 Cor. 1:3, 4).

As listener, we can offer faith in the value and meaning of life, even in the face of despair and death. We can offer hope because hope offers a vision beyond human suffering and even death. A Christian listener is one whose strength is based not on self-confidence but on a promise given to him. This promise not only made Abraham travel to unknown territory; it not only inspired Moses to lead his people out of slavery; it is also the guiding motive for any Christian who keeps pointing to new life in the face of corruption and death. Hope is very much like the coming of spring. I think of all the parables of Jesus, probably there is none more encouraging than the one of the sower or the four soils, as it is sometimes called. Surely when the sower sowed his field, he hoped for some harvest, and there was that part of the field that brought forth 30-, 60-, and even 100-fold.

Finally, we note that listening takes time and patience, qualities most of us have in short supply. Jesus took the time and had the patience to have a dialogue with the Samaritan woman in John 4. He talked seven times and the woman six times. Each time Jesus talked, he responded directly to the statement that the Samaritan woman had just made. This was not a series of monologues in which each person resumed talking where he or she had left off. It was a genuine dialogue with both persons listening carefully and responding concisely. The exciting aspect of this conversation is that Jesus revealed himself as Messiah to the Samaritan woman, not through a speech but through a dialogue. The first request was, "Give me a drink." The last response was, "I who speak to you am he [the Messiah]."

There are not enough professional counselors to go around, but every Christian can be a listener. Most of us will not take courses in counseling psychology at the Harding Graduate School or the University of Memphis, yet we can be a natural helper motivated by love and willing to work hard at listening.

The finest statement I know on why the Christian must listen and the seriousness of failing to listen is given by Dietrich Bonhoeffer in his *Life Together*:

> The first service that one owes to others in the fellowship consists in listening to them. Just as love to God begins with listening to His Word, so the beginning of love for the brethren is learning to listen to them. It is God's love for us that He not only gives us His Word but also lends us His ear. So it is His work that we do for our brother when we learn to listen to him. . . .
>
> Many people are looking for an ear that will listen. They do not find it among Christians, because these Christians are talking when they should be listening. But he who can no longer listen to his brother will soon be no longer listening to God either; he will be doing nothing but prattle in the presence of God too. This is the beginning of the death of the spiritual life, and in the end there is nothing left but spiritual chatter . . . . One who cannot listen long and patiently will presently be talking beside the point and be never really speaking to others, albeit he be not conscious of it. Anyone who thinks that his time is too valuable to spend keeping quiet will eventually have no time for God and his brother, but only for himself and for his own follies.
>
> . . . There is a kind of listening with half an ear that presumes already to know what the other person has to say. It is an impatient, inattentive listening, that despises the brother and is only waiting for a chance to speak and thus get rid of the other person. This is no fulfillment of our obligation, and it is certain that here too our attitude toward our brother only reflects our relationship to God. It is little wonder that we are no longer capable of the greatest service of listening that God has committed to us, that of hearing our brother's confession, if we refuse to give ear to our brother on lesser subjects. Secular education today is aware that often a person can be helped merely by having someone who will listen to him seriously, and upon this insight it has constructed its own

> soul therapy, which has attracted great numbers of people, including Christians. But Christians have forgotten that the ministry of listening has been committed to them by Him who is Himself the great listener and whose work they should share. We should listen with the ears of God that we may speak the Word of God.[11]

The year I was in Jerusalem, Susan Rubio concluded one of her letters with the passage Isaiah 50:4, 5. I would like to conclude with that passage:

> The Lord God has given me the tongue of those who are taught, that I may know how to sustain with a word him that is weary. Morning by morning he wakens, he wakens my ear to hear as those who are taught. The Lord God has opened my ear, and I was not rebellious, I turned not backward.

I pray that the Lord will open our ears to listen first to God's Word and then to the heart-felt concerns of our brothers and sisters.

[Presented at White Station Church of Christ Retreat, Memphis, Tennessee, 1988; Park Avenue Church of Christ, Memphis, Tennessee, 1988.]

---

[11]Bonhoeffer, *Life Together*, 97–99.

5

SIMPLICITY

I am always impressed with this statement: "For Ezra had set his heart to study the law of the LORD, and to do it, and to teach his statutes and ordinances in Israel" (Ezra 7:10). And in Acts 1:1: "In the first book, O Theophilus, I have dealt with all that Jesus began to do and teach." Always the doing should precede the teaching. Knowing that I teach better than I do, I am hoping by my teaching on this subject to get my priorities in the right order.

I think there are at least two conditions under which one might try to teach on the subject of simplicity. First, there is the story of Barzillai found in 2 Samuel 19:31–39:

> Now Barzillai the Gileadite had come down from Rogelim; and he went on with the king to the Jordan, to escort him over the Jordan. Barzillai was a very aged man, eighty years old; and he had provided the king with food while he stayed at Mahanaim; for he was a very wealthy man. And the king said to Barzillai, "Come over with me, and I will provide for you with me in Jerusalem." But Barzillai said to the king, "How many years have I still to live, that I should go up with the king to Jerusalem? I am this day eighty years old; can I discern what is pleasant and what is not? Can your servant taste what he eats or what he drinks? Can I still listen to the voice of singing men and singing women? Why then should your servant be an added burden to my lord the king?" . . . and the king kissed Barzillai and blessed him, and he returned to his own home.

I dare say that most of us who are older can identify with Barzillai. The cotton candy doesn't taste as it once did; we don't have to see the play or movie or hear the music we once thought we had to; we don't have to see the other side of the mountain. Somebody else's yard sales aren't as appealing as they once were.

The second condition is, you must teach this lesson to a class who is deeply concerned about what the Bible has to say on any subject, including a simple lifestyle. William Wordsworth in 1806 wrote these lines:

> The world is too much with us; late and soon,
> Getting and spending, we lay waste our powers;
> Little we see in Nature that is ours;
> We have given our hearts away, a sordid boon![1]

If that were true in 1806, how much more is it true on the verge of the twenty-first century! I would like to look at two texts: Colossians 3:1, 2, "If then you have been raised with Christ, seek the things that are above, where Christ is, seated at the right hand of God. Set your minds on things that are above, not on things that are on earth"; and Romans 12:2a, "Do not be conformed to this world." We have become so much like the world that non-Christians can't distinguish between the world and us. J. B. Phillips said:

> To the writers of these Letters [the N.T. epistles], this present life was only an incident. It was lived, with a due sense of responsibility, as preface to sharing the timeless life of God Himself. To these men this world was only a part, and because of the cumulative result of human sin a highly infected and infectious part, of God's vast created universe, seen and unseen. They trained themselves therefore, and attempted to train others, not to be "taken in" by this world, not to give their hearts to it, not to conform to its values, but to remember constantly that they were only temporary residents, and that their rights of

---

[1]Wordsworth, "The World Is Too Much with Us," 320–21.

> citizenship were in the unseen world of Reality. Today when all the emphasis is thrown upon making the most of this life, and even Christianity is only seriously considered in many quarters because of its social implications, this point of view is comparatively rarely held.[2]

I think Reuel Lemmons was right when he said, "Jesus said we should be the salt of the earth. I see very few salty churches . . . . We have drawn so heavily upon our culture . . . that there is little about us that is unique except in our own eyes."[3]

Leonard Allen in *The Worldly Church* lists ways in which we see that churches are conforming to our culture—to this world—and concludes that as a church we have lost sight of our biblical identity. If we "offer to the world only basketball and aerobics, counseling and therapy, and sound techniques for building better families and enhancing self-esteem, then we really offer very little that is not provided already by capable experts in fully secular settings. . . . To find our way back home, we must begin with what we have always urged through the years, namely, a return to the Bible."[4]

We probably belong in one of three classes of people. First are those who are frugal with self and frugal with others. We call them misers. We might look at Silas Marner. He wove cloth all day long, and by night he counted his gold. Happily, he changed when a child, Eppie, was brought into his life and he discovered that a human being is worth more than all of the gold in the world. Second are those who are generous with self and frugal with others. We call them selfish people. The Bible condemns selfishness along with other base sins, even though we may consider selfishness as one of the respectable sins. Third are those who are frugal with self and generous with others. I would hope that our study would help us to be the kind of people who are frugal with ourselves and generous with others.

As always, Jesus is our example in this area of our lives as

---

[2]Phillips, *Letters to Young Churches*, xiii.
[3]Lemmons, "Community Should Be Aware," 19.
[4]Allen, Hughes, and Weed, *Worldly Church*, 49.

well as in every other part. In 2 Corinthians 8:9 we read, "For you know the grace of our Lord Jesus Christ, that though he was rich, yet for your sake he became poor, so that by his poverty you might become rich." Jesus was born in a stable and raised in poverty. He worked in a carpenter shop and received no money for his preaching. He had nowhere to lay his head. He had to borrow a boat to cross the Sea of Galilee. His support largely came from women. The price that Judas got for him was 30 pieces of silver—the price of a common slave. He ate the Last Supper in a borrowed room and went out to give his life up. He commended his mother to John, and he gave his garment to soldiers to be gambled for, his peace to his disciples, his forgiveness to the thief on the cross, and his spirit to God.

The Bible refers to prayer about 500 times, to faith less than 500 times, and to material possessions more than 1,000 times. Sixteen of Jesus' thirty-eight parables are concerned with stewardship of material possessions.

Today's citizen of America's Middletown is most interested in food, shelter, and clothing. Jesus knew about these needs and said they would be provided if we put his kingdom first (Matt. 6:25–33). But more than the necessities, we want comforts, luxuries, education, social position, and enjoyment of things. John Wright has said,

> Our society owns the most sophisticated unused equipment in the world. How often do we purchase shelves of books only to have them occupy wall space collecting dust? Or perhaps we buy the most expensive and proved-efficient exercise equipment that is on the market. But after a week or two of sporadic exertion, we never move again except to lift a fork to our mouth. We buy a beautiful piano that never gets played. We equip an enviable workshop that never gets worked in. We select the most efficient study Bible that is never studied.[5]

Jesus tells us not to lay up for ourselves treasures on earth but

[5]Source unknown.

to lay them up in heaven (Matt. 6:19, 20). Richard Foster gives us three good reasons:

1. ". . . this world is a very uncertain place (Matt. 6:19, 20). There simply is 'no hidin' place down here.'" If we do not have moths, rust, and robbers, then we have inflation, which in some countries is making money worth half of what we thought it was worth, and most recently flash floods that have destroyed houses and furnishings. When the spring floods came, an Obion, Tennessee, couple said, "We put our life savings into that home. It's all under water—everything."
2. ". . . whatever we fix as our treasure will obsess our whole life." Our heart and treasure will be brought together. It is not just hard to serve two masters; it is impossible.
3. ". . . provision has already been made. The birds of the air and the lilies of the field all witness to an order in the Kingdom of God, in which adequate provision is made for everyone and everything."[6]

Glover Shipp, in his article "No Room in the Bin," writes:

> The gift-opening was over for another year. Piles of glittering paper, ribbon and empty boxes lay all over the floor. As I began to gather up the remains of Christmas, a mound of trash built up by the door. We stuffed it into bags, ready to carry them to the dumpster behind our son's Southern California apartment. I picked up one of the bags. "Wait," his wife Gina said. "Don't take it out. There is no more room in the bin." . . . The large dumpster was already running over with the season's not-so-merry refuse. Yards and yards of wrapping paper, ribbons, tape, cardboard, styrofoam, tissue, boxes of every size. It represented thousands of dollars spent by just a few families in the shopping orgy called Christmas.

He continues,

> For some reason not clear to us, we Americans have been

---

[6]Foster, *Freedom of Simplicity*, 35–36.

given much to share. Our bin is full and running over in various ways:

1. *Materially*. We have one of the highest per capita incomes in the world. We control much of our planet's wealth. We consume vastly more calories of food than almost any nation. [Yet 750 million people have an annual income of less than 75 dollars per year; 30 million children under five die of starvation each year.]
2. *Educationally*. We have opportunities for education at every level. Most of us have at least some college education. Some of us have nearly drowned by degrees. [Yet Raji Stephan, the Arabic preacher in Jerusalem, had to bring his family to the U.S. last year because the children did not get to attend school the year before. Rocks, bombs, and fear had closed the schools.]
3. *Spiritually*. We have Bibles on every hand, nationwide religious broadcasts, and a great abundance of Christian literature. [Yet one-half of the world's population has never seen a Bible. We have read the stories of people in eastern European countries running after trucks carrying Bibles begging for one.][7]

Shipp concludes his article by calling for a more simple lifestyle.

Throughout history there have been people who have adopted a simple lifestyle, and their stories shout, "It can be done!"

On his twenty-fifth birthday, the famous ex-cricketer missionary C. T. Studd inherited roughly $125,000. Reading the story of the rich young ruler, he gave it all away coolly and deliberately. He sent $25,000 to Dwight Moody to build Moody Bible Institute's original structure. He gave $25,000 to George Müller for missionary and orphanage work, $25,000 to George Holland for work with England's poor, and $25,000 to the Salvation Army in India. He gave the balance to his bride for a wedding

---

[7]Shipp, "No Room in the Bin," 15–18.

present. Not to be outdone, she gave every bit of it away to the Lord's work.[8]

The following examples of stewardship of possessions should inspire us to try harder to be better stewards. The violinist Fritz Kreisler once said:

> I was born with music in my system. It was a gift of God. I did not acquire it. So I do not even deserve thanks for the music. Music is too sacred to be sold and the outrageous prices charged by musical celebrities today are truly a crime against society. I never look upon the money I earn as my own. It is a public money. I am constantly endeavoring to reduce my needs to the minimum. I feel morally guilty in ordering a costly meal for it deprives someone else of a slice of bread, a child perhaps of a bottle of milk. My beloved wife feels exactly as I do about things. In all these years of my so-called success in music we have not built a home for ourselves. Between it and us stand all of the homeless in the world.[9]

Similarly, the Mayo brothers were Christian stewards.

> They believed that money must go back into the service of that humanity which paid it to them. "We try," said Dr. William Mayo, "to take up the medical and surgical education of selected and promising men where the state leaves off. From 1894 onward we have never used more than half of our incomes on ourselves and our families, latterly much less. The very roof of my house goes out of the possession of my family when I die. I wouldn't want my children deprived of the fun and benefit of wanting something and going out to fight for it."[10]

And John Wesley said:

---

[8]Grubb, *C. T. Studd*, 69–70.

[9]Source unknown. See White and Kurtz, *The Biblical Review*, 276.

[10]Schroder, "Ownership Versus Stewardship."

> As our income rises, we are all tempted to let our standard of living rise with it. Simply because we can afford it, does that mean we should buy it? This concept is hard for both children and adults to understand especially if at one time they did not have the resources to buy with.[11]

It is hard to find a man who rendered a better account of his stewardship than John Wesley. When he got 30 pounds a year, he lived on 28 and gave away 2; when he got 60 pounds a year, he lived on 28 and gave away 32; when he later received 90 pounds, he lived on 28 and gave away 62; when he got 120 pounds, he lived on 28 and gave away 92.[12] Wesley said to his sister: "Money never stays with me. It would burn me if it did. I throw it out of my hands as soon as possible, lest it should find its way into my heart."[13]

I want to mention two examples from the Restoration Movement. Barton W. Stone repeatedly admonished his brothers and sisters to care for the widow and the orphan, to minister to the poor and the hungry, to avoid extravagance in dress, and to love one another with pure hearts fervently.[14]

Another pioneer notable in this regard was Joseph Thomas, often known as the "White Pilgrim." He rejected the fashions of the world and embraced a simple, primitive lifestyle for himself. He sold his farm and his horse and rid himself of the garb that was fashionable for preachers of his day. He then donned a long, white robe, which he wore for the rest of his life—a symbol of his rejection of the values of the world and of his commitment to his first and only priority, the proclamation of the scandal of the cross.[15] This was strange, to be sure, but we must admire him for the depth of his conviction.

---

[11]Source unknown. John Wesley (1703–1791) was an Anglican cleric and Christian theologian who founded the Arminian Methodist movement. http://en.wikipedia.org/wiki/John_Wesley (accessed March 23, 2009).

[12]Stevens, *History of the Religious Movement*, 207.

[13]Wesley, *Letters*, 5:108–9.

[14]Hughes, *Reviving the Ancient Faith*, 108.

[15]Thomas, *Life of the Pilgrim*, 253–64.

In the February 25, 1985, *Memphis Commercial Appeal,* there is a story of a retired Atlanta minister and his wife who gave Yale University their life savings of one million dollars to establish the Ivy League's first new chair in 42 years. The preacher's annual salary never went above $15,000. But the endowment was made possible through scrupulous savings and a few wise investments, he said. The endowed chair will be used to help a professor foster more effective communication of the Gospel. How I wish we had such a couple to endow Harding Graduate School!

The U. S. Consultation on Simple Lifestyle began in 1974 at the Lausanne Congress for World Evangelization. This congress summoned Christians to simplify their lifestyles so that the billions who are starving could be fed and the billions who have never heard the Gospel could hear. The congress affirmed that asceticism is not a biblical ideal. This world is a beautiful gift from God, and he intends for us to enjoy and care for it. But those of us who live in affluent circumstances should accept our duty to develop a simple lifestyle in order to contribute generously to both relief and evangelism.

A simple lifestyle is not an end in itself; it is necessary so we can show compassion and so we can evangelize those who are lost. Ron Sider,[16] Richard Foster,[17] Richard Taylor,[18] and Arthur Gish[19] have all made concrete suggestions for us in this effort to simplify the way we live so that the needy can have care and the lost can hear the Gospel:

1. See yourself as a citizen of the planet. Questions of poverty and environment are distorted if we see them only in local and national terms. The Persian Gulf crisis has made us aware that we are not an island. Television has brought starving children to our screen.
2. Seek to be content with what you have. Contentment has always remained elusive, but it is a quality which can be learned. Paul said that he had learned in whatever state to

---

[16]Sider, *Rich Christians.*

[17]Foster, *Freedom of Simplicity.*

[18]Taylor, *The Disciplined Life.*

[19]Gish, *Beyond the Rat Race.*

be content. He knew how to be abased and how to abound; in any and all circumstances he had learned the secret of facing plenty and hunger, abundance and want. "I can do all things in him who strengthens me" (Phil. 4:11-13).

3. Let needs rather than wants govern your choices.
4. Resist obsolescence. I don't know how much longer I can get ribbons for my 40-year-old typewriter.
5. Cultivate silence and solitude. Develop close friendships. Value music, art, books, and significant travel.
6. Walk, jog, and swim. These are among the best forms of human exercise and require a minimum of equipment.
7. Stop trying to impress people with your clothes and impress them with your life. We should reach the point of maturity where we are no longer vulnerable to the opinions of others. George Washington Carver said, "It is not the style of clothes one wears, neither the kind of automobile one drives, nor the amount of money one has in the bank that counts. These mean nothing. It is simply service that measures success." Once when Carver was asked to the White House to meet the president, he was asked if he were not going to buy a new suit of clothes. His response was, "Why? The president wants to see me—not my clothes."[20]
8. Begin a new style of hospitality, simple fare, and a much wider circle of guests. One night we were having company for dinner, and I spent most of the day polishing silver, setting the table, and cooking; but at noon that day Jack called to say he was bringing a former student, his wife, and two children for lunch. Fortunately, I had made a pot of soup. And there was the cheese and fruit. It was as happy a time as the evening meal over which I had fussed.
9. Clothes, shoes, appliances, tools—almost anything can be kept in use with glue, patches, needle and thread, tape, baling wire, and ingenuity. The world is no longer held together by baling wire but by duct tape. I married the master of all of these, so now I don't throw away a nail, a screw, a tiny piece of anything that might belong on something. Leonard

---

[20] Carver, *His Own Words*, 17.

Allen's mother shops at Goodwill and sends her money to missionaries.

10. Watch your thermostat. I admire those hearty souls who can live with the thermostat set on 60 in the winter.
11. Join the resistance movement by claiming, "The price tag is too high."
12. Have a budget book and record expenditures. We would probably be astonished if we knew how much we spent in certain categories in one year. Deficit spending will work no better for us than for the federal government. Ralph Winter has proposed that those who believe in missionary work live as simple a lifestyle as do missionaries.[21] Professional people working abroad earn more money and benefits.
13. Eat sensibly, buying quality food, not non-nutritional junk food. In the 1960s Mrs. George Benson called in her grocery list to Park Avenue Grocery, thereby purchasing only what she needed. Shopping from a list is still a money-saving technique.
14. Do not buy gadgets that are not true time and work savers. I have a mixer I bought with stamps last Christmas, but I still reach for the hand mixer.
15. Listen to G. K. Chesterton: "There are two ways to get enough; one is to continue to accumulate more and more. The other is to desire less."[22] And to Joe Miller of the Amish community: "You can become self-righteous because you dress plain and have a humble life."[23] And to Ralph Winter: "I don't see any point in wasting the Lord's money."[24]

I want to sound two warnings to this matter of simple living. First, simple living is an individual matter; a person chooses before God how best to be a steward of God's gifts in today's world of such gross inequalities. Since we must give an account of ourselves and not of our neighbors, let us not be critical of

---

[21]Foster, *Freedom of Simplicity*, 168.

[22]Ibid., 110.

[23]Source unknown.

[24]Source unknown. Ralph Winter lives in California and works with the Frontier Mission Fellowship. http://www.time.com/time/covers/1101050207/photoessay/25.html (accessed March 23, 2009).

someone else for what they have. Let's look into our own expenditures to make sure we can justify each one. Second, beware of the danger of turning any expressions of simplicity into a new legalism and into arrogance.

Our goal should be that of Henry Martyn, missionary to India, where he worked for seven brief but fruitful years. On arrival to that country he said, "Now let me burn out for God."[25] And he did just that.

I am going to let the inspired apostle John conclude this lesson for us:

> Do not love the world or the things in the world. If any one loves the world, love for the Father is not in him. For all that is in the world, the lust of the flesh and the lust of the eyes and the pride of life, is not of the Father but is of the world. And the world passes away, and the lust of it; but he who does the will of God abides for ever (1 John 2:15-17).

[Date and occasion of this speech are unknown.]

[25]Smith, *Henry Martyn*, 150.

6

WHAT'S MINE?

Steward (1 Cor. 4:1, 2) in its primary meaning is an officer or employer in a large family or on a large estate who manages domestic concerns, supervises servants, collects rent or income, and keeps accounts. He is basically an administrator, supervisor, or manager.

All Creation Belongs to God

I will accept no bull from your house,
    nor he-goat from your folds.
For every beast of the forest is mine,
    the cattle on a thousand hills.
I know all the birds of the air,
    and all that moves in the field is mine. . . .
Do I eat the flesh of bulls,
    or drink the blood of goats? (Ps. 50:9–13).

God does not want or need material things for himself. In reality, then, man owns nothing. God is the owner. Man may possess, but God is the ultimate owner.

A girl relates, "One day after my grandmother's death, Mother brought home a pair of brass candlesticks. My sister and I recognized them as the ones that always sat on Grandmother's mantel. We asked Mother if she owned them now that Grandmother was gone. Mother replied, 'Nearly a hundred years ago Great-grandfather bought them. He thought they were his because he paid for them. But after a while he died, and they came to Grandfather. He thought they were his because his father left them to him. But after a while he died, and Aunt Sue kept them for many years. But she passed away, and they came to your grandmother. Now Grandma is dead, the house is to be sold, and the candlesticks have come to me. Who really owns them?'"

We remember the child's verse:

Back of the loaf is the snowy flour
And back of the flour the mill,
And back of the mill are the wheat and the shower
And the sun and the Father's will.

In Bible times the steward's status was that of a friend, a servant in a high and confidential capacity. Eliezer, Abraham's steward, was responsible for Abraham's house and money, even taking his master's jewels on a trip to find a bride for Abraham's son.[1] But Eliezer didn't own Abraham's house, money, and jewels. He only managed these for Abraham. Joseph was made overseer over Potiphar's house, and all that Potiphar had he put into Joseph's hand (Gen. 39:4–6). But Joseph didn't own his master's money; he used it for him and was accountable for the way he managed it.

A little girl told her teacher that she was going to give her father a pair of bedroom slippers for his birthday. "Where will you get the money?" the teacher asked. The little girl opened her eyes like saucers, "Why, Father will give it to me!" The teacher thought to herself, "The father will pay for his own birthday gift." The little girl hadn't anything in her possession that her daddy hadn't given her. We can't give to God anything but what belongs to him. "For all things come from thee, and of thy own have we given thee" (1 Chron. 29:14b).

Mr. Tenant is a farmer who does not own his land but rents from Mr. Master who lives in the city. Mr. Master pays all the taxes and insurance on the farm buildings. Mr. Tenant has pos-

---

[1]The servant in Genesis 24 is *assumed* to be Eliezer although he is not named there. This assumption is based on the reference to Eliezer in Genesis 15:2.

session for an indefinite term of years, has full charge of the farm, raises the crops he likes best, markets them at his price, and has full use of pastures, springs, and trees from which he may cut fuel for his own use and timber for repair on buildings. On proper notice he is to turn over possession to the rightful owner. Mr. Tenant knows he does not own the farm. It has been in the master's family for several generations. He also knows he must pay rent which may be paid in money, produce, or service.

The parables involving talents, pounds, and vineyards teach that God makes us stewards not of our own possessions but of that which is on loan to us and for which we shall be responsible some day.

We Are Not Our Own

Paul said, "You are not your own; you were bought with a price" (1 Cor. 6:19b, 20a; see also 1 Cor. 7:23). And in his speech to the elders of the church at Ephesus, he said, "Take heed to yourselves and to all the flock, in which the Holy Spirit has made you guardians, to feed the church of the Lord which he obtained with his own blood" (Acts 20:28).

Our First Gift of Self

In 2 Corinthians 8, Paul, speaking of the generosity of the Macedonians in verse 5, said, ". . . but first they gave themselves to the Lord and to us by the will of God." It was Emerson who said, "Rings and jewels are not gifts but apologies for gifts. The only gift is a portion of thyself."[2]

I belong to a rare breed of people who still believe in and practice letter writing. I'm wondering how many of you write letters. I am blessed to have some friends who share that belief and practice. One writes her letters on notebook paper—handwritten, about ten pages long—and encloses pictures and newspaper clippings. When I receive one of her letters, I don't read it hurriedly, but I wait until I have a quiet time, sit down with a

[2]Emerson, "Gifts," 93.

cup of coffee, and savor every word. I feel as though I have had a visit with her. She recently sent me a copy of an article entitled "Letters Sweeten Our Lives." The writer, Alexandra Stoddard, says, "A world of difference separates a phone call from a letter. The phone is a utility—a convenience like a refrigerator or a washing machine. A letter is a gift."[3] She concludes by saying, "I use the telephone when necessary—to discuss business, make and confirm appointments, or check up on a friend—but I let the ink flow from my pen when I want to really connect with another human."[4] Lewis Carroll reminds us, "One of the deep secrets of life is that all that is really worth doing is what we do for others."[5]

In John 12:1–8 we have the lovely story of a woman performing a delightful act of stewardship on Jesus. She was Mary, sister of Martha and Lazarus. It happened at a dinner in Bethany. Mary, sensing the nearness of the cross, wanted to do something to show her faith and love to bring comfort to the heart of Jesus. "Mary took a pound of costly ointment of pure nard and anointed the feet of Jesus and wiped his feet with her hair; and the house was filled with the fragrance of the ointment" (John 12:3). Judas said, "Why was this ointment not sold . . . and given to the poor?" (v. 5). John adds that he said this not because he cared for the poor but because he was a thief. But Jesus' response was, "Let her alone; . . . . She has done a beautiful thing to me. . . . she has anointed my body beforehand for burying" (Mark 14:6–8). Mary's act was beautiful because of the faith behind it. She had learned about God's love, the cross, the grave, the crown. She believed and loved. "You do not always have me" (v. 8). It was beautiful because of its timeliness. Sometimes we wait too long, and our gifts of love arrive too late.

Mary's act was beautiful because of its generosity. She didn't count the cost. She didn't think of it as loss to herself. She knew that nothing could be counted as loss if it expressed love and pleased Christ. We have Jesus' promise that if we do deeds of

---

[3]Stoddard, *Gift of a Letter*, 7.

[4]Ibid., 89.

[5]Foulkes, *Lewis Carroll*, 103.

service for the least of our brethren, it is as though we are doing it for Jesus (Matt. 25:40). It was beautiful because of the example it left. The fragrance of that costly ointment filled the room, and it has never stopped filling human hearts and homes. To the end of time and beyond it, Mary's beautiful act stands as a memorial of her faith and love.

Our Stewardship Demands All

The story of the rich young ruler in Luke 18:22 in the words of Jesus reads, "Sell all that you have and distribute to the poor, and you will have treasure in heaven; and come, follow me." Jesus did not run after him saying, "How about 80 percent or 50 percent?" It was all or nothing. So far as we know, Jesus did not demand this of anyone else.

In the early days of the church, some believers sold their possessions and goods and distributed them to all as any had need (Acts 2:44, 45). So far as we know, this practice was not continued. Only two chapters over, in Acts 5, Peter asks Ananias, "While it remained unsold, did it [the piece of property] not remain your own? And after it was sold, was it not at your disposal?" (Acts 5:4). The sin of Ananias and Sapphira was that of lying. Some (in fact, many) feel if they give God one day in the week, they have the other six to use for themselves. Or if they give one hour on Sunday, they can use the other 23 as they wish. Or, if they give one-tenth, they can spend the rest as they want. It has been suggested that those who resist the tithe on the ground of legalism give 11 percent on the ground of grace. Dr. Francis Pieper suggested that Christians "will also in financial respects do all and more than was prescribed to the people of the Old Covenant by an express command."[6] And yet we are painfully aware that most Christians do not give one tenth. Before you turn in your pledge this year, read 2 Corinthians 8:5, 9 and 2 Corinthians 9:6–15.

James Stewart has said:

---

[6]Pieper, *Christian Dogmatics*, 3:51.

> The reason men do not live as good stewards of their time and talents and possessions is that, although they are members of the Christian Church, the pattern of beliefs on which their lives are based is not really Christian, or only Christian in part. They do not believe that their lives and possessions belong to God so that his right of ownership must be respected in every moment; they believe rather that their own lives and all that they own are theirs to do with them as they will. They call Jesus Lord with their lips but they have no intention of letting him be Lord over their time or their social relationships or their business life or their political decisions.[7]

In Luke 6:46 Jesus asks the question, "Why do you call me 'Lord, Lord,' and not do what I tell you?"

Stewardship is a sign of Christian maturity—a sign that we are growing. The child says, "*my* chair," "*my* spoon," "*my* cup," "*my* toy." The lost son says, "Give me the share of property that falls to me" (Luke 15:12). The rich fool in Luke 12 speaks of "*my* barns," "*my* goods," "*my* grain." He lost sight of God's ownership of all he possessed. But Zacchaeus outgrew his possessiveness and said, "The half of my goods I give to the poor" (Luke 19:8). He came to regard his goods not as "mine" but as "ours."

Matthew left his tax office. Peter and Andrew, James and John left their boats. We sing in the song, "All of self and none of Thee," then "Some of self and some of Thee," and finally, "*None* of self and *all* of Thee."[8] I have difficulty singing that last stanza. The greatest point of dedication is when we can say "Thine."

The Steward Must Be Faithful

God trusts us to administer what belongs to him. The steward's ministry rests upon confidence. In addition to Eliezer and

---

[7]Source unknown. James Stuart Stewart (1896–1990) was a Scottish preacher who taught New Testament Language, Literature, and Theology at the University of Edinburgh. http://en.wikipedia.org/wiki/James_S._Stewart (accessed March 23, 2009).

[8]Theodore Monod, arr., "None of Self and All of Thee," *Songs of Faith*.

Joseph, whom we have already mentioned, Moses was faithful in God's house as a servant (Heb. 3:5). This quality of faithfulness is essential to God's being. Without it he would not be God.

From first to last, the Bible records God's faithfulness. In Genesis 8:21, 22 God said,

> I will never again curse the ground because of man, for the imagination of man's heart is evil from his youth; neither will I ever again destroy every living creature as I have done. While the earth remains, seedtime and harvest, cold and heat, summer and winter, day and night, shall not cease.

In Genesis 9:13–15 God promises, "I set my bow in the cloud, . . . I will remember my covenant which is between me and you and every living creature of all flesh; and the waters shall never again become a flood to destroy all flesh."

Joshua, in his farewell speech to Israel, says that "not one thing has failed of all the good things which the LORD your God promised" (Josh. 23:14). The Psalms are replete with statements about God's faithfulness.

Paul was resting on God's faithfulness when he said in his last letter, "I know whom I have believed, and I am sure that he is able to guard until that Day what has been entrusted to me" (2 Tim. 1:12b).

Finally, in 1 Peter 4:19 we read, "Therefore let those who suffer according to God's will do right and entrust their souls to a faithful Creator."

When David Livingstone returned to Glasgow, the students thought they would have some fun with the missionary. They brought peashooters and rattlers, determined to drown his talk with their noise. But when the great Livingstone walked on the platform bearing in his body the marks of conquests over fever and wild beasts and tropical exploration, the students were hushed into a great silence. Soon the missionary was telling them about his work for "a Gentleman whose word was never broken," and of his following the One who promised him, "Lo, I am with you always even unto the end of the world." Students forgot their precious plans, forgot all else but the matchless appeal of a stewardship life before them.

Cultivate a Pilgrim Mentality

An early pilgrim said, "By the grace of God I am a Christian man, by my actions a great sinner, and by calling a homeless wanderer of the humblest birth who roams from place to place. My worldly goods are a knapsack with some dried bread in it on my back, and in my breast pocket a Bible. And that is all."

The word *pilgrim* in the Greek means "resident foreigner"; that description fits Abraham well. Although God gave Abraham and his posterity the most important piece of land in the world, Abraham never held on to that land as his possession, "For he was looking forward to the city with foundations, whose architect and builder is God" (Heb. 11:10; NIV).

Abraham camped here but was always conscious that his home was heaven. God told Abraham to follow him and he would do great things for Abraham. He left the sophisticated city of Ur to follow the Lord. He gave Lot first choice of the land. He prepared to sacrifice his son as a burnt offering. We read in Hebrews 11:9a, "By faith he made his home in the promised land like a stranger in a foreign country" (NIV).

Abraham is called a "prosperous pilgrim." Abraham had become very wealthy in livestock and in silver and gold (Gen. 13:2). However, he didn't seek riches or make decisions based on personal gain. Even after he risked his life storming into the enemy camp to free Lot and the captives from Sodom, he refused to accept any payment from the king of Sodom. He would make no alliance with that kind of man.

When he allowed Lot first choice of the land, Abraham demonstrated an open-handed disposition that characterized his life. He had great wealth; but unlike the rich young ruler who would not sell his possessions, Abraham would have given it up without question. A man who would not withhold his son of promise would give up anything. Abraham didn't look back to Ur or to Haran. He focused his eyes on the eternal and superior country God had promised.

Moses knew he had better than what Egypt could offer. He chose to be mistreated with the children of God rather than to enjoy the pleasures and privileges of Egypt. "He regarded disgrace for the sake of Christ as of greater value than the treasures of Egypt, because he was looking ahead to his reward" (Heb. 11:26; NIV).

Jesus, too, looked ahead: ". . . who for the joy set before him endured the cross, scorning its shame" (Heb. 12:2; NIV). And Paul said, "I consider that our present sufferings are not worth comparing with the glory that will be revealed in us" (Rom. 8:18; NIV).

It is the long look at eternity that clarifies the ultimate issues of stewardship. We need then to remember these truths when we talk about our stewardship of what has been entrusted to us:

1. All creation belongs to God.
2. We are not our own. We have been bought with the highest price we can imagine—the blood of Jesus.
3. Our first gift must be that of self.
4. Our stewardship demands all.
5. We must be faithful, always remembering God's faithfulness to us.
6. We must remember that we are pilgrims expressed in our song:

    Here we are but straying pilgrims;
    Here our path is often dim;
    But to cheer us on our journey,
    Still we sing this wayside hymn:
    Yonder over the rolling river,
    Where the shining mansions rise,
    Soon will be our home forever,
    And the smile of the blessed Giver
    Gladdens all our longing eyes.[9]

A true-to-life cartoon appearing in a religious publication shows this caption at the top of the grave of Jim Elliot, one of the

---

[9]I. N. Carman, "Here We Are But Straying Pilgrims," *Great Songs*.

missionaries martyred by the Auca Indians: "He is no fool who gives what he cannot keep to gain what he cannot lose." Underneath is the drawing of a fancy, modern home with swimming pool, two late-model cars, a large yard with outdoor equipment, two television sets, modern furniture, and on the patio sitting in a lounging chair a young husband who has just finished reading a letter handed him by his wife. They exclaim, "Another missionary appeal! We gave our tithe. Surely no one expects us to give more!"[10]

I'd like to close with this story: A certain merchant had been called upon during the day by someone for a gift to a needy family. He replied, as some merchants do, "I cannot, for I have so many calls." At night when he got home, and his wife and family had retired to rest, he drew a chair in front of the fire and sat down. As he sat looking into the fire he thought thus:

> I refused that good man an appeal today. I have refused appeals before, and told the people I had so many calls. There was a time when I gave more than I do now. The reason was because I built this new house. The other house was very good, still my wife thought it was not quite the thing. We went to the new house, had to get new furniture, and then got into a new circle. The girls want more for dress, and the boys want more. My expenses have risen, and I am afraid I am entrenching upon what I have been giving to the cause of God.

He is then supposed to fall asleep; whether he did so or not I am not here to say; but as he sat by the fire in came a stranger, a singularly mild and majestic-looking man. He came up to the merchant and said to him presenting a paper, "I am come asking a gift for foreign missions." He asked it very tenderly, and the merchant, with a good deal of hesitance, said, "Really, you must excuse me, I cannot, I have so many calls." The stranger looked very sad. There was no anger in his face, but there seemed great grief. He took out another paper and said, "You do not give any-

---

[10]Elliot, *Through Gates of Splendor*, 172.

thing to foreign missions; will you give something toward home evangelization? There are many heathen at home." The merchant again said, "I can't afford it; besides, I think there is more said about home heathenism than is necessary." "Well," said the stranger, who seemed to look more sad than ever, "there is the Bible Society; will you give something to it?" The merchant was a little vexed and said, "I really do not like to be pressed in this way. I can't give!" The stranger looked sadder than ever, but in a moment seemed to change, and there stood before the merchant one like unto the Son of man. And he said to the merchant: "Five years ago your little child lay sick, near unto death. You went upstairs into your chamber. Your heart was bowed down with bitterness, and you prayed that that dear one might live, your soul being bound up in the life of that child. Who raised your child to life, and spared her to your house?" The merchant covered his face with his hands. "Ten years ago," said the same soft, tender voice, "you lay upon what seemed to be your dying bed. Your affairs were then in a bad state, and if you died you left your children penniless. You turned your face to the wall and prayed that you might be spared until, at least, you might leave your children something. Who heard your bitter cry and raised you up?" The merchant was more confused than ever. "Fifteen years ago, in a certain chamber, you knelt, a broken-hearted sinner, with a weight of sin on your conscience and soul. Filled with bitterness, you cried for mercy. Who came to you and said, 'I have blotted out your sins like a cloud, and like a thick cloud your iniquities,' and opened his heart to wash you from your iniquities?" There was no reply except a sob. "If thou wilt never ask anything of me again, I will never ask anything of thee. Thou shalt not be troubled with my many calls if I am not troubled with thine." The merchant fell on his face before the stranger, "My God, my Lord, forgive me, and take all that I have." And lo, it was a dream—but not a dream, for his life was changed thereby.

May you and I have such a vision and henceforth live unto Christ as those who are alive from the dead.

[Date and occasion of this speech are unknown.]

7

HOSPITALITY

Practice hospitality ungrudgingly to one another. As each has received a gift, employ it for one another, as good stewards of God's varied grace: whoever speaks, as one who utters oracles of God; whoever renders service, as one who renders it by the strength which God supplies; in order that in everything God may be glorified through Jesus Christ. To him belong glory and dominion for ever and ever. Amen (1 Pet. 4:9–11).

I have always been thankful for Peter's second epistle in which he says, "Therefore I intend always to remind you of these things, though you know them" (1:12). I don't propose to tell you anything new but just to remind you of what you already know and hope that we all grow in this Christian grace of hospitality.

Over 150 years ago, Alexis de Tocqueville observed a tendency in the U.S. toward an individualism "which disposes each citizen to isolate himself from the rest of his fellows and to withdraw into the circle of family and friends."[1] In North America and in Europe, hospitality has become increasingly a commercial concept.

Our present period seems preoccupied with individual autonomy and the prosperity of family and friends. This is reflected in our prayer life—"me and my wife, my son John and his wife, we four and no more."

Hospitality may suggest a place of rest from our labors and

[1]Tocqueville, *Democracy in America,* 506.

journeys, a place that is not our home but nevertheless enables us to feel at home as Paul felt in the home of Rufus' mother (Rom. 16:13).

Definition

The Greek word *xenophobia* means "fear of strangers." Ever since school days, we have loved the story of Philemon and Baucis. They kindly received Zeus (Jupiter) and Hermes (Mercury), who traveled in the guise of ordinary mortals. For this favor Zeus rescued them from a flood and appointed them guardians of his temples. He granted them the favor of letting them die at the same moment and metamorphosed them into trees.[2]

We have a true story from modern times of the blessing of entertaining angels unawares. On a stormy night, many years ago, an elderly man and his wife entered the lobby of a small hotel in Philadelphia. "All the big hotels are filled up," said the man. "Could you possibly give us a room here?"

The clerk explained that there were three conventions in town, and that there were no rooms to be had anywhere. "All our rooms are filled too," he said. "Still, I simply can't send a nice couple like you out in the rain at one o'clock in the morning. Would you perhaps be willing to sleep in my room?"

The couple replied that they couldn't do that, but the clerk insisted. "Don't worry about me. I'll make out just fine," he told them.

Next morning, as he paid his bill, the elderly man said to the clerk, "You are the kind of manager who should be the boss of the best hotel in the United States. Maybe someday I'll build one for you." The clerk looked at the man and his wife and smiled. The three had a good laugh over the old man's little joke, and then the clerk helped them with their bags to the street.

Two years passed and the clerk had nearly forgotten the incident when he received a letter from the man. It recalled that night and enclosed a round trip ticket to New York, asking the young man to pay them a visit.

---

[2]Ovid, *Metamorphosis* 8.621.

When the clerk reached New York, the old man led him to the corner of Fifth Avenue and Thirty-fourth Street and pointed to a great new building there, a palace of reddish stone with turrets and watchtowers, like a castle from fairyland thrusting up into the sky. "That," said the older man, "is the hotel I have just built for you to manage."

"You must be joking," the young man said, not quite knowing whether to believe his friend or not.

"I most assuredly am not," said the older man, a sly smile playing around his mouth.

"Who—who are you?" stammered the other.

"My name is William Waldorf Astor."

The hotel was the original Waldorf-Astoria, and the young clerk, who became its first manager, was George C. Boldt.

Although Athens, Greece, was once known for its parks where people sat and talked religion and politics all hours of the day and where sidewalk cafes were busy with chatter on every subject, it is not so anymore. You hardly see a person sitting out anymore. Why? Fear of strangers. There was the case of the conversion to the Christian faith of a Chinese man in Peking. The man, as an act of humility and penance, wanted to walk from Peking to the Vatican. The man said as he walked across Asia, homes were opened to him with warm hospitality. Then he came into the Slavic states; now and then a home would open up with hospitality. "When I came to Europe, I had to sleep in the alleys and in transient shelters." Nobody said, "Come in."

Biblical Basis for Hospitality

Into this atmosphere comes the biblical texts that speak of the love (*philoxenia*) of strangers and the meaning of the New Testament word which is translated "hospitality."

Old Testament Passages

We will look at some of the Old Testament passages treating this subject of hospitality.

1. *Genesis 18*—Abraham and Sarah were sitting out front of the tent, probably with an old funeral home fan like we all used

to use. Three strangers came over the hill. Abraham said, "Sarah, fix three more places for supper. We've got company." In the best of Eastern hospitality, he bowed to them and offered to serve them in specific ways. He offered them shade beneath the tree, water to wash their feet, cakes of meal, curds and milk, and a freshly butchered calf. Abraham and Sarah didn't have a clue that these three messengers were from God. They entertained angels unawares. The writer of the Epistle to the Hebrews refers to this encounter in 13:2: "Do not neglect to show hospitality to strangers, for thereby some have entertained angels unawares."

2. *Exodus 2:20*—Moses, a stranger in the desert, was invited by Reuel, the priest of Midian, to come into his house and eat bread.

3. *Leviticus 23:22*—"And when you reap the harvest of your land, you shall not reap your field to its very border, nor shall you gather the gleanings after your harvest; you shall leave them for the poor and for the stranger." We see this instruction applied when in the Book of Ruth (2:15, 16) Boaz tells his young men to "Let her glean even among the sheaves, and do not reproach her." He goes the second mile and says, "And also pull out some from the bundles for her."

4. *Deuteronomy 10:18, 19*—God "loves the sojourner, giving him food and clothing." Israel is instructed to love the sojourner and given the reason "for you were sojourners in the land of Egypt."

5. *Joshua 2* records the story of Rahab, a woman who sold sexual favors for a living, and she is held up as a model of what hospitality really is. The New Testament doesn't talk about her moral character. Even the strict Book of James (in 2:21–25) says that one knows what justification before God is. He mentions two—Abraham and Rahab, the prostitute of Jericho.

6. *1 Kings 17*—Elijah received hospitality from the widow of Zarephath. In return he gave her an abundance of oil and meal and raised her son from the dead.

7. *2 Kings 4:8–37* records Elisha's story. He went to Shunem where a wealthy woman lived, and she always wanted him to eat some food. Whenever he passed that way, he would turn in and eat food. Finally the wife said to her husband, "Let us make

a small roof chamber with walls, and put there for him a bed, a table, a chair, and a lamp, so that whenever he comes to us, he can go in there" (v. 10). Her reward was a son.

New Testament Passages

1. *Luke 10:38–42*—The setting is the home of Mary, Martha, and Lazarus in Bethany. Jesus taught a marvelous lesson on getting our priorities in order. At that time listening to Jesus' teaching was more important than food.

Mary Ashcroft tells the story of Martha's hospitality in her book *Temptations Women Face*.

> I imagine myself at Bethany one morning. I am Martha. My sister Mary and I have just heard that Jesus will be arriving soon.
>
> "Mary, quick, get the shrimp out of the freezer. . . . Oh no, there the door is now. Mary will you grab that?"
>
> "Hi Jesus, come on in . . . make yourself at home. I'm just throwing together a little lunch. Want some punch? It'll just take a minute."
>
> "Okay, the lemons for the punch, whirl that in the blender with the ice . . . this should be refreshing. . . . I wish I had a starter; I've got that Brie and some chutney . . . perfect. I'll run the punch in and then take in the hors d'oeuvres . . . but first let me get the rice going for the paella, and what about dessert? Oh no! I'm out of ice cream, and I think Lazarus finished off the last of that cake. But that lime dessert is quick to make and on such a hot day, it'd be perfect.
>
> "Okay the chutney on the Brie and the crackers at the edge. . . . Mary's just sitting there, next to Jesus, listening to him as if she has all the time in the world . . . and me in here slaving . . . that's why she has all the time in the world. I hope Jesus realizes that I'm being the servant. Mom would like it . . . but you'd think Mary would at least make the dessert. Where's the butter, and I've got to juice three limes. . . . Why do I do all the work around here when she just sits there? And I'm getting hot, too." . . .

> "Here's something for you to nibble on. . . . But Lord, don't you care that my sister has left me to do the work by myself? Tell her to help me."
>
> "Martha, Martha, you are worried and distracted by many things; but there is need of only one thing. Mary has chosen the better part, which will not be taken away from her" (Luke 10:41, 42).[3]

Afterward, Martha, looking closely at her life, perhaps realized just how much time she was spending on fancy meals and home decorating. We can be sure that Martha then tried to spend time with Jesus—that she listened to Jesus as she had seen her sister do.

2. *Luke 11:2–4*— In Luke's version of the Lord's Prayer, the petition for bread is directly linked with the coming of the kingdom.

3. *Luke 12:16–21*—Only in Luke do we find the parable depicting the rich fool who wants no more than to eat, drink, and be merry. God says, "This night your soul is required of you; . . . So is he who lays up treasure for himself, and is not rich toward God" (vv. 20, 21).

4. *Luke 15:11–32*—The prodigal son experiences the fullness of his repentance at a magnificent banquet.

5. *Luke 18:15–17*—Jesus was teaching one day, and some young mothers came and had their babies in their laps. Matthew and Mark say they had children. A baby whines or cries or has to have his diaper changed, or he drops his pacifier on the floor and you've got to pick it up and wipe it off. The children are causing a disturbance; some people can't hear, and other folks are turning around. The twelve came and tapped the young mothers on the shoulders and said, "We have a nursery for the children." Jesus said, "Let the children come to me, and do not hinder them; for to such belongs the kingdom of God" (v. 16).

6. *Luke 9:58*—In Luke Jesus always enters upon the scene as a guest in need of hospitality. He has nowhere to lay his head.

7. *Luke 7:36–50*—On another level, Jesus is the supreme host.

---

[3] Ashcroft, *Temptations Women Face*, 96–97.

At the home of Simon the Pharisee, Jesus appears first in the role of a guest. But as the story moves on, he is the one who takes charge and hosts the occasion, first by teaching Simon a lesson and then by declaring God's forgiveness to the sinful woman who has anointed his feet. To both he opens the door to new life.

8. *Luke 22:14–38*—At the Last Supper, Jesus gives these instructions to his disciples:

> The kings of the Gentiles exercise lordship over them; and those in authority over them are called benefactors. But not so with you; rather let the greatest among you become as the youngest, and the leader as one who serves. For which is greater, one who sits at table, or one who serves? Is it not the one who sits at table? But I am among you as one who serves (vv. 25–27).

9. *Luke 24*—Two disciples, downcast and heavy of heart, are walking from Jerusalem to Emmaus. Jesus has been crucified. Some women have said, "He's risen from the dead," but they don't believe it. A stranger joins them and asks them what they are talking about. He listens to the men, enters the conversation, and begins to talk about the Scripture. They reach Emmaus. One of the men says, "Well, stranger, we've walked a long way and it's late. We're tired. Won't you stay for supper?" Then they sit at the table. They ask the stranger to say the blessing, and in the breaking of bread he is revealed to be Jesus.

10. *John 21:4–14*—In one of Jesus' post-resurrection appearances recorded in John 21, Jesus tells the disciples where to cast their net in order to catch fish. When the disciples reach shore with their net full of fish, they find Jesus, a charcoal fire with fish on it, and bread. Jesus tells the disciples to bring some of the fish they have caught and invites them to "come and have breakfast." I sometimes say that this is the biblical basis for our potlucks at church. I have also discovered that breakfast is a very good meal to share with others who have a busy schedule.

Acts has an impressive number of references to meals.

11. *Acts 6:1–6*—We see the welcoming of strangers inside the church as well as outside. Hellenists and Hebrew factions of the

Jerusalem church are said to have achieved reconciliation by means of an expanded *diakónia* through which the congregation's material resources were more fairly distributed.

12. *Acts 11:27–30; 12:25*—The delivery of money for food by the Jewish-Gentile congregation in Antioch to the famine-stricken Jerusalem church created a new level of trust between two very different groups of believers. This transaction has been called a banquet of major proportions.

13. *Acts 16:11–15*—Paul enters Europe for the first time, and Lydia asks Paul and Silas to come and stay with her. She must have insisted, since the text says, "And she prevailed upon us."

14. *Acts 16:33–44*—The jailer washed the wounds of Paul and Silas, brought them up to his house, and set food before them.

15. *Acts 27*—On the voyage to Rome, most of the crew and passengers are seasick from the storm and have stopped eating. Paul, after assurance from God, is hopeful. On deck at the dawning of the fourteenth day, Paul urges his shipmates to share some food with him. When they fail to respond, he thanks God and, in the presence of all, breaks a loaf of bread and begins to eat. Then they are encouraged and eat some food themselves.

16. *Romans 16:3–5*—Aquila and Priscilla had the church to meet in their house in Rome and in Ephesus (1 Cor. 16:19). They couldn't have had the church there week after week without wearing out the rug and having wear and tear on the furniture.

17. *1 Timothy 3:2 and Titus 1:8*—In listing the qualifications for an elder, Paul says that the elder must be hospitable, a qualification that probably is not given the emphasis it should be given.

18. *1 Timothy 5:10*—Paul tells Timothy if a woman is to be enrolled as a widow, she must be well attested as one who has shown hospitality.

19. *Philemon*—In the letter Paul writes to Philemon, he tells him to welcome Onesimus no longer as a slave but as a beloved brother. The language of hospitality abounds:

vv. 1, 2: Philemon makes his home available to a house church.

vv. 4–7: He shows love and faithfulness toward all the saints, refreshing their hearts as well as their bodies.

v. 16: Philemon, the expert in hospitality, is bidden to receive his own slave as a guest.

v. 20: Paul states his purpose openly—he wants some refreshment for his own heart.

v. 22: Paul tells Philemon to get a guest room ready for him, "for I am hoping through your prayers to be granted to you."

Paul shows that hospitality by believers takes place on both the spiritual and physical levels.

v. 25: Paul offers Philemon the ultimate refreshment in the close of his letter: "The grace of the Lord Jesus Christ be with your spirit."

The Early Church

Hospitality becomes a prominent feature in the early church[4] although Origen complains of the gap between preaching and practice.[5] Hermas[6] includes hospitality in the list of Christian virtues.

Clement of Rome, during the last decades of the first century, writes a letter to the church at Corinth:

> What visitor among you is there who has not proved your most excellent and firm faith, who has not marveled at your prudent and gentle piety in Christ, who has not proclaimed your magnificent practices of hospitality, and who has not blessed your perfect and sure knowledge? For you did all things without respect of persons and walked in the commandments of God. . . . You were all humble minded, giving more gladly than receiving. You were satisfied with and paid attention to the travel provisions supplied by Christ, and you were storing up carefully in your hearts his words and were keeping his sufferings before your eyes. . . . There was an insatiable desire to do good. . . . You had great concern day and

---

[4] *1 Clement* 1.2.

[5] *Homily on Genesis* 5.1.

[6] *Mandate* 8.10.

> night for the whole brotherhood in order that the number of God's elect might be saved with mercy and conscience (*1 Clement* 1.1, 2).

With missionary increase, organization was needed, and in the fourth century Antioch cared daily for 3,000 widows, sick, and strangers. Bigger churches and sanctuaries later set up hospices, and, where focused on the sick, these developed into hospitals.

What Is Hospitality?

We have looked at the biblical basis for extending hospitality. We have seen some examples, and there are many more from the Old Testament, the New Testament, and the early church. Let's look at what hospitality is and what it is not.

Someone has said we all fall somewhere between Martha Stewart and the person who has the pizza place listed on the speed dial. Entertaining says, "I want to impress you with my beautiful home, my clever decorating, my gourmet cooking." Hospitality says, "This is not mine. It is a gift from God, and I'll use it as he desires." I have a friend who the first time she entertained her Life Group in her home said, "I used my best china, silver, and crystal. They see I have it, and from now on I'll use paper products."

Entertaining always puts things before people. "As soon as I get the house finished, the place settings complete, the housecleaning done, then I will start having people in." Hospitality puts people before things.

Entertaining looks for a payment—compliments, a return dinner invitation, job advancement, esteem in the eyes of friends and neighbors. Hospitality does everything with no thought of reward.

It is possible to both entertain and be hospitable. For several years now, Jo Scott has invited my Outreach class of women to her home for a Christmas luncheon. She has the house beautifully decorated and uses her pretty Christmas dishes. Yet she is showing warm hospitality to strangers (as used in the biblical sense).

Irene Gatewood for most of the 30 years she spent as a missionary in Germany invited the elderly and poor to her apartment for Christmas dinner and always used her Rosenthal china and her sterling silver. Again she was showing hospitality and entertaining.

Who Needs Hospitality?

There are special groups who need to have hospitality extended to them:

New Neighbors

Jerry Jones writes in the January 1992 issue of the *21st Century Christian* about service evangelism. He says a moving van indicates new neighbors. Take over a pot of coffee or a jug of tea or a freshly baked cake. "If the water or utilities haven't been turned on, take a pitcher of ice water" or volunteer the use of your bathroom. He adds, "Most opportunities aren't announced nor do they linger, but if we're willing to risk a trip through an open door, we'll find God there to bless the event. Let's be people who care enough to send our very best—ourselves, Christ's messengers—to our neighborhoods."[7]

Strangers in Church

In the mass migration from the country into the city, many people are looking for a church home. The church might be home away from home for them.

A little boy came home from his first day at Sunday school, and his mother asked him how he liked it. The child replied, "I hated it. They put me in a room full of children all by myself." That is the same feeling of many adults when they attend worship—they are in an auditorium full of people all by themselves. The church can be a very lonely crowd. In one church members were asked what it was that drew them to that particular church. They said it wasn't the theology of the church, or great sermons,

---

[7]Jones, "Service Evangelism," 17–18.

or a terrific youth program, but the overwhelming initial response—"The friendship of the people." When newcomers are visited who do not return, their frequent response is, "We came to the coffee hour between services, and nobody spoke to us."

Some years ago a writer in the *Los Angeles Times* visited numerous churches in the Los Angeles area and rated the friendship experienced. Greeter at the door got 2 points. The prepackaged form letter from the pastor got 3 points. No one spoke, and yet the letter came. The coffee hour got about 5 points. Personal invitations to dinner were around 60 points.

For many people who work all week, Sunday dinner is a convenient time for guests to be brought home from church. I think that is what most of our mothers did. Mrs. L. K. Harding's mother (daughter-in-law of James A. Harding) used to say to the preacher whom she had invited home for Sunday dinner, "If you are a good man, what I have is good enough for you; if you aren't a good man, then it's too good."

If we do issue a dinner invitation, I think it should be as sincere as Lydia's was. Charlie Coil tells the story that in a church where he regularly went for Sunday preaching, there was one woman who always waited until she was sure he had been invited by someone, and then she would offer her invitation. Charlie said that one Sunday he decided he would not accept any other invitation but hers. Then when he went to her home, he discovered she was not prepared for him. I would suppose that episode would have cured her.

Preachers and Missionaries

In John's third Epistle, which is addressed to his beloved Gaius, he tells him,

> Beloved, it is a loyal thing you do when you render any service to the brethren, especially to strangers, who have testified to your love before the church. You will do well to send them on their journey as befits God's service. For they have set out for his sake and have accepted nothing from the heathen. So we ought to support such men, that we may be fellow workers in the truth (3 John 5–8).

It is a blessing for children when preachers and their families and missionaries and their families are in our homes. Many missionaries caught the vision for world missions as young children when their parents had various missionaries stay in their home for a few days. Impressions made in those early formative years yielded rich fruit years later. If Paul came through our city, I think we would all call the church office saying we would like to have him stay with us. Who knows? We may be entertaining Paul unawares.

I think many of our young people who are now going on summer campaigns have had some exposure to missionaries, and now they want to engage in some sort of mission work. Although probably most of these students will not return to do full-time mission work, they return home with a lifetime commitment to support mission work by their concern, their prayers, and their financial support.

When James Baird, former president of Oklahoma Christian, and his wife built their home, they furnished an upstairs apartment to be used by visiting missionaries.

Elderly, Widows, Students, Young Adult Singles, Internationals

Most of these groups have some sort of organized church activities, but these programs do not take the place of inviting them into our homes. A well-known speaker said that he had worshipped for four years as a widower, and only two families ever had him to dinner—one family was a cousin to his late wife, and the other was his preacher.

Cultivate young people. Internationals often complain about Americans and their one-time relationship, opening homes for Thanksgiving or Christmas, then never establishing contact again. Probably one of the richest fields for evangelism is the international student body in various universities.

For Jack and me, it fell our pleasant lot to have a close association with the Japanese students who have come to the Graduate School. They were with us for holidays, birthdays, and Sunday meals. We were also privileged to have their parents and friends when they came for visits. We have had five Japanese students to receive degrees from the Graduate School, and in March two of these students sent us tickets to come to their wedding in Japan. It was a joy to see all five of them engaged in some type of ministry.

I suppose I would have to say that all students are my favorite company. The house does not have to be cleaned. The only requirement is food.

Jesus himself tells us whom we should invite in Luke 14:13, 14. "But when you give a feast, invite the poor, the maimed, the lame, the blind, and you will be blessed, because they cannot repay you." But "You *will be* [italics mine] repaid at the resurrection of the just." We probably need to ask ourselves when we have invited these people into our homes. Jesus ate with outcasts. Paul and Luke took strong stands on behalf of those relegated to the position of second-class citizens in the church. We miss out on this fullness of life if we limit our partnerships to those who most resemble ourselves. Luke 15:1, 2 reports that the tax collectors and sinners were all drawing near to hear Jesus. The scribes and Pharisees murmured saying, "This man receives sinners and eats with them." The marginal Messiah welcomes other marginal people.

Peter Marshall preached a sermon one Sunday entitled "By Invitation of Jesus." He told of a wealthy man who sat before the blazing log fire in his handsome house on a wintry night and happened to turn to this passage from Luke 14. He began to think about the dinner which Jesus described, and then he thought about the dinners and parties in his own home and the sort of people he invited. Most of them were listed in *Who's Who in Washington*, and there were those whose names were household words in business, finance, clubs, and government circles—but *they* were not poor or maimed or lame or blind. What, then, if he should try to carry out something like what Jesus pictured? He determined that he would. He had cards engraved which began this way: "Jesus of Nazareth requests the honor of your presence at a banquet honoring the Sons of Want." Under that was the date for the dinner and the place where the guests were to meet.

A few days later as he went downtown with the invitations

in his hands, he gave them to the sort of people he was inviting this time to his dinner: to an old man trying to sell pencils, to the blind man at the corner newsstand, to any forlorn person he met on the winter street. They looked at the cards with puzzlement and with some disbelief. However, if you are hungry and cold, you don't pass up a possible chance to be fed. So when evening came, men were waiting in line at the Central Union Mission as was printed on the card. What they found there, though, were cars to take them to the home of the man who had issued the invitation; they were received by him and invited to sit down with him to the sort of dinner he would have given his most honored guests. When all the shyness and strangeness had melted away, he read them the words of Jesus and said to them, "If I have given you one evening of happiness, I shall forever be glad to remember it, and you are under no obligation to me. This is not my party. It is His! I have merely lent Him this house. He was your host. He is your friend. And He has given me the honor of speaking for Him."[8]

Much has been said about the lectures of Francis Schaeffer at L'Abri Fellowship in Switzerland. Often overlooked is the behind-the-scenes hospitality of Edith Schaeffer. She says,

> Which shall I do first, go upstairs and write that article that is due, or go out to the garden and pick lettuce and some roses before the frost spoils them? I hesitated, wishing I could go both directions at once. Just then the doorbell rang, and I chose a third direction, the steps down to the front door. "I'm sorry to bother you, but this is an emergency. Can we talk to you now?" My husband was talking to someone in the living room, so I led mother and daughter into the dining room to listen to the problem.
>
> Weeping with those who weep takes time. Two hours later when my husband had come in to join us, I glanced at the clock and realized that everyone needed some food. Slipping out I put together the ingredients for an egg-nog

---

[8]Marshall, *Mr. Jones Meets the Master*, 117–28.

> milk shake and started it whizzing, then dipped out broth from bones on the stove and added chicken bouillon and chopped parsley to give more flavor, then cut pieces of homemade brown bread and topped them with cheese and bacon and tomato slices and slipped them into the oven. A nutritious meal was soon ready for me to carry in on individual trays, without breaking into the flow of the conversation. Not only was the food needed for energy by each of us, but the pleasantness was remembered afterwards, and the beauty of a simple meal treasured, even by someone whose mind was filled with recent disaster and whose eyes were blurred with tears.[9]

Those who visit L'Abri say that much of the biblical teaching and interaction was made effective by Mrs. Schaeffer's loving, sensitive sacrifice. It was her example that made the Gospel come alive. Some people reported, "She made the Gospel believable."

Edith Schaeffer also writes that hospitality is not just praying for a person and forgetting the physical need. "If a brother or sister is ill-clad and in lack of daily food, and one of you says to them, 'Go in peace, be warmed and filled,' without giving them the things needed for the body, what does it profit?" (Jas. 2:15, 16).

"Practice hospitality ungrudgingly to one another" (1 Pet. 4:9). This admonition comes right after the admonition to "keep sane and sober for your prayers" (v. 7). We are not free to avoid inviting lonely people home for dinner after church so that we can have the afternoon free to pray. It is not a question of either/or, but both/and (Col. 1:9, 10).

In Zagreb, Yugoslavia, a local congregation has purchased a residence in the center of the city. In this Marxist land where Christianity until recently was officially discouraged, Christians know the meaning of the exile existence. This house is the place of worship on Sunday, and it is also a place where Christians gather during the week. Here the Christians eat together once a

---

[9]Schaeffer, "Hospitality: Optional or Commanded?" 28.

week. It has the appearance of an extended family. As many as 19 keys to the building are circulating among the members to allow them to come and go as they please. This modern church house must be very similar to the ancient church.

Ways to Show Hospitality

The hospitality we have talked about has largely been in the home but there are many ways to show hospitality:

Life groups: At White Station Sunday lunch is provided for visitors by one Life Group each week. The goal, though not yet reached, is that every member will participate in a Life Group where needs are known and met.

Showers: Some seem to have a gift for decorating and food preparation. We should overcome the idea that if we don't know the person for whom a bridal or baby shower is being given, we won't attend. That's all the more reason to go and give.

The Memphis churches of Christ have a cooperative program to help the disadvantaged. Volunteers, primarily from women's classes, provide lunches every day for those who are involved in educational programs. Other examples of group hospitality include special collections of food for the church pantry, food to the sick and bereaved, or sharing of garden produce and home-made bread and jams. The list is endless.

Now for some practical suggestions, all of which I am sure you know:

1. Keep it simple. During the holidays I was invited to the home of one of our Young Adult Singles. The invitation was for breakfast. She served orange juice, muffins, jam, and tea. It was one of the nicest treats of the holiday season.

One of my young married friends wanted to have an open house for her mother and father's fortieth anniversary. Every anniversary party I have been to has had an array of delectables to eat plus linens, china, and sterling. But she, on a plastic-cloth-covered table, served soft drinks, sandwiches, and cookies. We all had a wonderful time.

Don't be a respecter of persons of those in high position or low position. We are often inclined to neglect those in high places.

Kitty Atkinson, a Harding professor's wife, said, "I wonder how many invitations Dr. and Mrs. Benson have." I was privileged to live in student apartments on campus for 14 years, and some of my happiest times were lunches with students, Sunday night suppers, and sometimes late cups of tea with the wife of a student who was working late hours.

2. Never clean before company. I have a friend who says if you draw the drapes and light the candles nobody notices the rug hasn't been vacuumed or the dusting done.

3. Have company two nights in succession as you already have out the dishes and hopefully the tablecloth can be used again.

4. Sometimes make use of the deli or take people out to a restaurant. It may cost a bit more, but there are times when we have more money than time. On one of our Abilene visits, I commented to Jack's sister that her dinner was delicious. She said, "I bought it all."

5. Don't compare yourself with anybody else. If we do, we are in danger of covetousness. Our hospitality depends on our energy level, our financial resources, and our time. Etiquette is nothing more than making the other person feel at ease.

6. There is no retirement from the Christian grace of hospitality. Jim Woodroof says that his mother in her late 80s cooked Christmas dinner for the elderly (she didn't consider herself one of those) in the church where she worshiped. About 20 people came.

7. All kinds of help are available. Cookbooks are published by the Christian colleges, and *Christian Woman* has a section on foods in every issue.

8. Finally, just begin. That's the first step. Begin with friends, and then add a stranger or two or three.

The most sobering thought and the most powerful motivation for extending hospitality that we have in Scripture is found in Matthew 25:31ff., at the judgment scene:

> Then the King will say to those at his right hand, "Come, O blessed of my Father, inherit the kingdom prepared for you from the foundation of the world; for I was hungry

> and you gave me food, I was thirsty and you gave me drink, I was a stranger and you welcomed me, I was naked and you clothed me, I was sick and you visited me, I was in prison and you came to me." Then the righteous will answer him, "Lord, when did we see thee hungry and feed thee, or thirsty and give thee drink? And when did we see thee a stranger and welcome thee, or naked and clothe thee? And when did we see thee sick or in prison and visit thee?" And the King will answer them, "Truly, I say to you, as you did it to one of the least of these my brethren, you did it to me" (vv. 34–40).

Finally, in Revelation 3:20 Jesus says, "Behold, I stand at the door and knock; if any one hears my voice and opens the door, I will come in to him and eat with him, and he with me."

[Presented at York, Nebraska, June 1992; Sycamore View Church of Christ, Memphis, Tennessee, 1992; Young Adult Singles Retreat, 1992; Freed-Hardeman College, 1998.]

8

Family and Obedience

The text I have chosen for our study is found in Matthew 12:50: "For whoever does the will of my Father in heaven is my brother, and sister, and mother." From this verse I want us to look at two themes in the life and teaching of Jesus—family and obedience. One of the blessings of being asked to teach a Bible class is the chance it provides to study a part of the Bible in order to learn what the book teaches on particular subjects and to look at very familiar material with a new view. In this study I read the four Gospels and wrote down all of the references to these two themes—family and obedience. I found the exercise a delightful one, and I'd like to share with you what I found. I hope that you will go home and read the Gospels, looking for the same themes, and then continue your search for truths found in all parts of your Bible.

Family

The word *family* never occurs in Jesus' teaching, but his emphasis on the family is everywhere evident. He uses the images of family life in much of his teaching. He uses the father/son image often. He uses the symbol of the earthly father in the Sermon on the Mount for the heavenly Father in Matthew 7:9–11.

> Or what man of you, if his son asks him for bread, will give him a stone? Or if he asks for a fish, will give him a serpent? If you then, who are evil, know how to give good gifts to your children, how much more will your

> Father who is in heaven give good things to those who ask him!

He preaches the fatherhood of God; he and his disciples have one and the same Father. He teaches his disciples to pray, "Our Father." In the Garden of Gethsemane, he addresses God as Father and uses the expression "Abba, Father" (Mark 14:36), which is an expression a young child would use to address his father. Nailed to a cross, he interceded for those who would be putting him to death, "Father, forgive them" (Luke 23:34). And as he was dying he prayed, "Father, into thy hands I commit my spirit!" (Luke 23:46).

Mary spent more time with Jesus than did any other person. She was with him in the home, caring for him, looking after his needs. She went with him all the way to the cross.

Jesus encouraged the children to come to him. The innocence of a child is used to explain the meaning of conversion, adding that "whoever does not receive the kingdom of God like a child shall not enter it" (Mark 10:15). Jesus wanted his hearers to depend, like a child, in trustful simplicity on what God offers.

The image of son and sonship is further used in this family imagery found in the Gospels. Both at Jesus' baptism (Mark 1:11) and at his transfiguration (Mark 9:7), God speaks to say, "Thou art my beloved Son." In John 3:16—the Gospel in miniature, according to Martin Luther[1]—we have, "For God so loved the world that he gave his only Son, that whoever believes in him should not perish but have eternal life."

Finally, probably the best-loved story recorded in the Gospels—the Prodigal Son, or the Great Father Heart—makes periodic use of the family image.

Jesus had little to say about relationships between real brothers. Rather, his emphasis was on a new brotherhood of all men. Early Christian writers spoke of Christians as comprising God's family. The church was the family of God. "I will be a father to you, and you shall be my sons and daughters" (2 Cor. 6:18).

In God's wisdom he chose this family image and used it so

---

[1]Sánchez, *The Word We Celebrate*, 111.

widely because: (1) It would be hard to think of a time when a father's care, a wife's fidelity, a child's obedience would not have profound and lasting meaning. It would never lose its relevance. (2) Universally, man can understand these images—China, Africa, Germany. It is in John 14:2 that Jesus uses the home of man to depict the home of his soul. What greater reward could there be than to dwell in our Father's home? Elizabeth Goudge in her novel *The Dean's Watch* has the dean saying to Isaac, "And it is a house not made with hands. . . . Yet when our play is ended and the house lights go up we shall see many kindly faces. It is a house, remember, a friendly place."[2]

Having noticed Jesus' emphasis on family life and his use of images of family life in so much of his teaching, it may come as a surprise to see how very few references we have to his own family. Jesus was born into a family, and his genealogy is given in both Matthew's and Luke's Gospels. For the first 30 years of Jesus' life, he stayed in close relationship with his family. "Throughout his silent years," Barclay says, "Jesus was learning the meaning of family life."[3]

In Luke 2 we have the record of Jesus' accompanying his parents to Jerusalem for the annual Passover Feast. He was 12 years old at the time. When the feast was over and his parents were returning home, they discovered the boy Jesus was missing. After three days of searching, they found him in the temple sitting among the teachers, listening to them and asking them questions. With typical parental concern, they asked him why he had treated them so, for they had been anxiously searching for him.

In John 2 Jesus appeared at a marriage in Cana, and his mother was with him. His mother told him when the wine gave out. Jesus' response was, "O woman, what have you to do with me? My hour has not yet come" (v. 4). She directed her remark to the servants and told them to do whatever Jesus told them to do. After the account of the wedding feast, Jesus went down to Capernaum with his mother, his brothers, and his disciples and

---

[2]Goudge, *The Dean's Watch*, 301.
[3]Barclay, *Discovering Jesus*, 89.

stayed there for a few days.

In John 6 we have the account of Jesus' feeding the 5000 (the one miracle recorded in all four Gospels). The Jews murmured at him because he said, "I am the bread which came down from heaven" (v. 41). Their response was, "Is not this Jesus, the son of Joseph, whose father and mother we know?" (v. 42).

In Matthew 13 after Jesus' teachings in parables, he came into his own country and taught in the synagogue. All were astonished and said,

> Where did this man get this wisdom and these mighty works? Is not this the carpenter's son? Is not his mother called Mary? And are not his brothers James and Joseph and Simon and Judas? And are not all his sisters [though unnamed] with us? Where then did this man get all this? (vv. 54–56).

Jesus says here what we have seen happen in our own towns and homes, "A prophet is not without honor except in his own country and in *his own house*" (v. 57; italics mine). John 7:5 tells us that "his brothers did not believe in him," an illustration of just what Jesus had said.

We have no further information about Jesus' relationship with his own family until he hung on the cross and standing by were his mother and his mother's sister. John records the beautiful scene of Jesus seeing his mother. "When Jesus saw his mother, and the disciple whom he loved standing near, he said to his mother, 'Woman, behold, your son!' Then he said to the disciple, 'Behold, your mother!' And from that hour the disciple took her to his own home" (John 19:26, 27).

A final reference to Jesus' earthly family is found in Acts 1 where after Jesus' ascension, the apostles are gathered in the upper room in Jerusalem. Mary, the mother of Jesus, and his brothers are with them devoting themselves to prayer.

When we think about it, there are a number of great events in the life of Jesus in which his family did not have a part:

1. No brother was chosen to be an apostle, one who would be closest to him in his teaching and life.

2. No family member was present at the Transfiguration—when God declared that Jesus was the One to be heard; his close disciples Peter, James, and John were there.
3. Women ministered to him, but there is no mention of Mary and his sisters.
4. Nicodemus and not his family brought spices.
5. The last sad act we perform for a loved one, his burial, was done by Joseph, who was not a member of his family.
6. Jesus committed his mother to the beloved disciple, not to one of his own family.
7. The first resurrection appearance was not to a member of his earthly family but to Mary Magdalene.

Although Jesus' contacts with his family are few, we have a number of accounts of his contacts with other families—the family in Cana; Peter's home in Capernaum; Matthew's home; the Pharisee's home in Luke 7; Zacchaeus' home in Jericho; the home of Simon the leper; the home of Mary, Martha, and Lazarus in Bethany; and finally the upper room of an unknown householder.

We have noted Jesus' use of images of family life in his teachings and the scant references made to Jesus' own family life. His direct teachings on the family are infrequent, but what he does say is powerful.

In Matthew 15 and its parallel Mark 7, the Pharisees and scribes came to Jesus and said, "Why do your disciples transgress the tradition of the elders? For they do not wash their hands when they eat" (Matt. 15:2). Jesus answered them, "And why do you transgress the commandment of God for the sake of your tradition?" (Matt. 15:3). Jesus illustrates their transgression of God's commandment by quoting from Exodus 20:12, one of the Ten Commandments, "Honor your father and your mother," and Exodus 21:17, "He who speaks evil of father or mother, let him surely die" (Matt. 15:4). Jesus continues, "But you say, 'If any one tells his father or his mother, What you would have gained from me is given to God, he need not honor his father'" (v. 5). Jesus makes unmistakably clear that no gift to the temple could make up for negligence to parents. "Honor" in Jesus' teaching is taking care of family, and that is just what he did at the cross.

In Matthew 19 we have Jesus' strongest statement on the

marriage bond: "Have you not read that he who made them from the beginning made them male and female, and said, 'For this reason a man shall leave his father and mother and be joined to his wife, and the two shall become one'? So they are no longer two but one" (vv. 4–6a). And finally, "What therefore God has joined together, let no man put asunder" (v. 6b).

In Matthew 22 the Sadducees attempted to trick Jesus with their hypothetical case of the man with six brothers all having had the same woman as wife to each of them when they questioned, "In the resurrection, therefore, to which of the seven will she be wife?" (v. 28). Jesus answers that marriage as we know it on earth is not continued in heaven.

Rather than the Bible giving us a detailed account of Jesus' own family life or even of family life in general, the weight of his teaching on family life is putting it in relationship to himself.

This relationship begins very early. In Luke 2 in the Passover Feast incident, in answer to his mother's question, "Son, why have you treated us so?" (v. 48), Jesus says to his parents, "How is it that you sought me? Did you not know that I must be in my Father's house?" (v. 49). The contrast between his earthly and heavenly fathers is not lost to the reader.

In Matthew 10 and its parallel Luke 12, Jesus says that he did not come to bring peace but a sword. He came to set a man against his father, a daughter against her mother, a daughter-in-law against her mother-in-law (v. 35). All of us have seen and known families in which this teaching was fulfilled. Families have been split because of the faith of some members. Jesus further states in Matthew 10:37 that whoever loves father or mother or son or daughter more than him is not worthy of him. Luke's language in 14:26, "If any one comes to me and does not hate his own father and mother and wife and children and brothers and sisters, yes, and even his own life, he cannot be my disciple," is vivid hyperbole reflecting the true meaning of Jesus' intent—love God more.

The cost of discipleship is seen in the three who thought they wanted to follow Jesus but first wanted to take care of home and family responsibilities (Luke 14:15–24). Jesus says that the one who wants to follow him may well be denied that blessing because Jesus demands our first loyalty.

Jesus helps us set priorities straight when in Luke 14:12, 13 as a guest he taught,

> When you give a dinner or a banquet, do not invite your friends or your brothers or your kinsmen or rich neighbors, lest they also invite you in return, and you be repaid. But when you give a feast, invite the poor, the maimed, the lame, the blind, and you will be blessed, because they cannot repay you.

Is our company limited to our family and friends? We can't misunderstand this teaching of Jesus. When have you had someone to eat with you who was poor, maimed, lame, or blind, someone less fortunate who could not repay you?

In Luke 11 in Jesus' teaching that the source of his power to cast out demons was from God and not Beelzebul, a woman in the crowd raised her voice and said to him, "Blessed is the womb that bore you, and the breasts that you sucked!" (v. 27). But Jesus' response was, "Blessed rather are those who hear the word of God and keep it!" (v. 28).

The teachings of Jesus regarding the place of family life may seem hard. Are they too hard? The story of the rich young ruler is found in Mark 10 and its parallels in Matthew 19 and Luke 18. Following the Matthew account, Peter says, "We have left everything and followed you. What then shall we have?" (v. 27). The reward? "And every one who has left houses or brothers or sisters or father or mother or children or lands, for my name's sake, will receive a hundredfold [Luke 18:30 says "manifold more in this time"], and inherit eternal life" (Matt. 19:29).

There is no discrepancy and no inconsistency in Jesus' teaching on family life. It is a matter of setting priorities, and he has set them for us.

Families are broken by death; apparently Joseph died before Mary. We know people who are not now in families, not a part of an immediate family unit. They may not have a father, mother, sister, brother, child, or husband. Yet Jesus said, "Here are my mother and my brothers," establishing a vertical relationship with Jesus, and "He's my brother," thus establishing a horizontal relationship with every child of God.

If every member of our family is taken, Jesus, our brother, is always near. We have his promise to never leave us or forsake us. We ought to read his promises often. He is the one who will finally reunite us with our brother, sister, father, mother, child, husband, or wife.

Who do you first want to see in heaven? Jesus! Why? Because he has made it possible to see all of the others.

Obedience

Having looked at the place of family in Jesus' teachings, we now look at the passage again: "Whoever does the will of my Father"—obedience.

In the very first chapter of Matthew, family and obedience are linked. Joseph was told not to fear to take Mary as his wife, and in verse 24 Joseph did as the angel of the Lord commanded him; he took his wife. Jesus' earthly father knew obedience to God.

In chapter 2 the angel appears a second time in verse 13 and tells Joseph to take the child and his mother and flee into Egypt. The next verse says that he arose and took the child and his mother by night and departed to Egypt. Joseph was obedient. In verses 19 and 20, for the third time the angel of the Lord appeared to Joseph, "Rise, take the child and his mother, and go to the land of Israel." The very next verse says, "And he rose and took the child and his mother, and went to the land of Israel."

Jesus' earthly father was obedient to his heavenly Father. Jesus was born into a home in which obedience was a natural way of life. Today it is no different. Children learn obedience from parents. There will never be a substitute for living by example.

Very early in Jesus' life, we learn of his obedience to his earthly parents. Luke 2:51 says, "And he went down with them and came to Nazareth, and was obedient to them."

In the wilderness temptations of Matthew 4, Jesus was obedient in all three events to the law recorded in Deuteronomy: "Man shall not live by bread alone" (v. 4; Deut. 8:3); "You shall worship the Lord your God, and him only shall you serve" (v. 10; Deut. 6:13); and "You shall not tempt the Lord your God" (v. 7; Deut. 6:16). In not one of the three temptations did he disobey God's law. He, the Son of God, was subject to the law.

The Gospels record Jesus' very specific teaching on obedience. We read in the Sermon on the Mount that the one who does the commands and teaches them will be called great in the kingdom of heaven (Matt. 5:19); that he who does the will of the Father will enter the kingdom (Matt. 7:21); and that whoever hears and does the will of God will be like the man in the song we have so long taught children and perhaps have forgotten as grown-ups—the wise man built his house upon the rock. In Matthew 21:28–31 two sons worked in the vineyard parable. One was obedient, and one was disobedient. Jesus uses the parable to teach obedience.

Jesus pronounces woes on Chorazin and Bethsaida because they did not obey/repent (Matt. 11:20ff.) and on the scribes and Pharisees for their disobedience to God's commands (Matt. 23). In the Gospel of John, belief is equated with obedience: "He who believes in the Son has eternal life; he who does not obey the Son shall not see life" (John 3:36), and "If you know these things, blessed are you if you do them" (John 13:17). The proof of love in John is obedience: "If you love me, you will keep my commandments" (14:15); "He who has my commandments and keeps them, he it is who loves me" (14:21); and "If a man loves me, he will keep my word" (14:23).

The life of Jesus differs from that of all other great teachers of religion and morality in that he lived out his teaching himself to the full. What Jesus taught, he was. What he called men to be, he himself was. T. W. Manson says that everything Jesus does, he does for God, with God, and under God.[4] He is to be in the most complete sense the servant of the Lord, the perfect subject of a perfect King: "My food is to do the will of him who sent me" (John 4:34); "I seek not my own will but the will of him who sent me" (John 5:30); "I keep his word" (John 8:55); "I do as the Father has commanded me" (John 14:31); and "I have kept my Father's

---

[4]Manson, *The Servant-Messiah*, 57, 77.

commandments and abide in his love" (John 15:10).

Finally, in Gethsemane Jesus says, "Not my will, but thine, be done" (Luke 22:42). The cross is his appointed path, and he will go to it certain that this is inside the Father's will.

Christ as the servant was "obedient unto death, even death on a cross" (Phil. 2:8). In turn Christ calls us to be obedient unto death. It is most unlikely that we will have to witness to our faith by dying a martyr's death. Nevertheless, obedience unto death must mean that we live and act out our faith to the very last heartbeat.

In closing I would like to call us back to Jesus' last command. If we are in God's family and we take seriously his teaching on obedience, then we must go and make disciples of all nations or, in the more familiar words of the Mark 16:15 parallel, "Go into all the world and preach the gospel to the whole creation." We do not need to be told that the world may be South Memphis as well as New Guinea and Kenya.

There are, I think, at least two reasons why we have not obeyed this final command of the Lord: (1) We do not appreciate what Jesus has done for us on the cross, and (2) we do not really care about souls that are lost. Creighton Lacy, missionary to China, wrote nearly 15 years ago:

> On the whole we American Christians try to filter out of the gospel any element of sacrifice, of hardship, of positive commitment, leaving only a congenial organization and peace of mind. We often hear it said that the modern generation is lacking in dedication, in courage, in service. Yet many a young person today is dissuaded from the world mission of the church because his or her mother or father or wife protests and urges instead a safer—and a duller—life.[5]

We must commit ourselves to the world mission of the church

---

[5]Source unknown. Creighton Lacy (1919–) is Professor Emeritus of Parish Ministry at Duke University Divinity School. http://library.duke.edu/digitalcollections/rbmscl/ualacyc/inv/ (accessed March 23, 2009).

to participate in the proclamation of the Good News. And the Gospel is good news.

Further, whoever heard of extraordinary news being kept secret? If God has revealed to men the secret of his purpose and the power of his saving grace to remake men into his sons and daughters, then the news must be told! It cannot be done by merely giving money, reading mission study books, or visiting an orphanage. It cannot be done without personal involvement in the Gospel and in the lives of others (see the Parable of the Sower, Matt. 13:3–8, 18–23). We have many examples.

My prayer is that we will have more sons and daughters who want to tell the Good News and more mothers and fathers who encourage their children to be obedient to this, the final command of Jesus. The disciples had no alternative when Jesus told them to go. And we have no other alternative.

The home inlays the very soul of man. William Saroyan tells of three soldiers coming home from World War II to Ithaca, California. One was limping a bit in his left leg.

> The first soldier looked at his friend and said, "Well, brother, this is Ithaca. This is home."
>
> "Boy, let me look at it," the second soldier said. "Just let me look at it. . . . My home, Ithaca! I don't know how *you* feel, but *this* is how I feel." He got down on his knees and began to kiss the brick of the walk again and again, . . .[6]

Home is the climax of all this longing. We never can erase the image of a family out of the mind of man.

[Date and occasion of this speech are unknown.]

---

[6]Saroyan, *The Human Comedy*, 180–81.

9

GOD'S PLAN IN MARRIAGE

We have a fascination for firsts—the first phonograph recording, first car, first transatlantic call, and first man on the moon. How much more for the first person—first man, first woman, and first marriage! Any study of biblical women could easily begin with Eve. The name given her by Adam after the fall (Gen. 3:20) signifies "she was the mother of all living."

God Created Man in His Own Image (Gen. 1:26–31)

Genesis 1 is a panoramic description of creation. On the sixth day God said,

> "Let us make man in our image, after our likeness; and let them have dominion over the fish of the sea, and over the birds of the air, and over the cattle, and over all the earth, and over every creeping thing that creeps upon the earth." So God created man in his own image, in the image of God he created him; male and female he created them. And God blessed them, and God said to them, "Be fruitful and multiply, and fill the earth and subdue it; and have dominion over the fish of the sea and over the birds of the air and over every living thing that moves upon the earth." And God said, "Behold, I have given you every plant yielding seed which is upon the face of all the earth, and every tree with seed in its fruit; you shall have them for food. And to every beast of the earth, and to every bird of the air, and to everything that creeps

> on the earth, everything that has the breath of life, I have given every green plant for food." And it was so. And God saw everything that he had made, and behold, it was very good (Gen. 1:26–31).

Genesis 1:27 should be read in a single breath: "So God created man in his own image, in the image of God he created him; male and female he created them." This verse should be read in a single breath in order that the creation of male and female never be separated from the creation of man in God's image. Adam, the man, is not created standing alone in God's image. He is created for and in personal coexistence with Eve, just as he is created for and in coexistence with God. Just as Adam is the mirror image of God, so Adam and Eve are the mirror image of each other. From the beginning they are created and sustained *together* in relationship to each other. Whatever else their partnership may mean, their basic bond of fellowship consists of the interdependence of maleness and femaleness with which, as individuals, God has ordained them. This bond is important for their being "in the image of God," faithful to the kind of life God commands by creating them in this way. This meaning is confirmed by a later verse which refuses to speak of the male alone as Adam, "the man," but instead reserves this name for them both together. "Male and female he created them, and he blessed them and named them Man when they were created" (Gen. 5:2). Eve was created in the image of God, blessed by God, named by God, and given by God the same responsibility to tend and have dominion over creation.

While Genesis 1 is a panoramic description of creation, Genesis 2 elaborates in detail on that part of the description that is most important for the religious message the writer is attempting to convey, the creation of man.

"Then the LORD God formed man of dust from the ground, and breathed into his nostrils the breath of life; and man became a living being" (Gen. 2:7). "Then the LORD God said, 'It is not good that the man should be alone; I will make him a helper fit for him'" (Gen. 2:18). After the creation of every other form of life, God declared that it was good, and the evening and morning were another day of his handiwork. But after he had made man, God's judgment upon the result was that it was *not* good for man to be alone. It is God who says this, not man. Adam did not complain of his loneliness. But God knew he was alone and knew he could never be himself alone.

God determined to create a helper for man before he ever brought the animals before man to name them. None of the animals could measure up to man's aspirations or satisfy his needs. Chapter 1 leaves the creation of mankind (man and woman) until last to emphasize the importance of mankind in relationship to the rest of God's creatures. Chapter 2 leaves the creation of woman until last to stress the woman's inestimable value to man in contrast to all other creatures.

Helpmeet

In the delightful book *Miss Thistlebottom's Hobgoblins*, Theodore Bernstein discusses the words *helpmate* and *helpmeet*. He says,

> Here we have a comedy of errors. The King James Bible, in Genesis ii, 18, referring to the need for providing a better half for Adam, has the Lord saying, "I will make him an help meet for him." *Help* here meant a person who affords assistance and *meet* meant suitable. Early dictionaries, committing Error No. 1, hyphenated the two words to produce *help-meet*. Later users dropped the hyphen and married the two words. Then came Error No. 2 when some writers apparently thought that *helpmeet* didn't make any sense—which it didn't—and decided the proper word must be *helpmate*. And so today we are stuck with two corrupted words.[1]

The RSV says "a helper fit for him." The NIV says "a helper suitable for him."

Helper Fit for Him

In the Old Testament, the word *helper* has many usages. It

[1]Bernstein, *Miss Thistlebottom's Hobgoblins*, 48.

can be a proper name for a male (Ezer means "help," 1 Chron. 4:4; 12:9; Neh. 3:19). In our story it describes the animals and the woman. In some passages it characterized Deity. God is the helper of Israel. As a helper, God creates and saves. "My help comes from the LORD, who made heaven and earth" (Ps. 121:2). "Our help is in the name of the LORD, who made heaven and earth" (Ps. 124:8). "Happy is he whose help is the God of Jacob" (Ps. 146:5). "O Israel, trust in the LORD! He is their help and their shield" (Ps. 115:9). Thus, *helper* is a relational term; it designates a beneficial relationship, and it pertains to God, people, and animals. The animals are helpers, but they fail to fit Adam.

"So the LORD God caused a deep sleep to fall upon the man, and while he slept took one of his ribs and closed up its place with flesh; and the rib which the LORD God had taken from the man he made into a woman and brought her to the man" (Gen. 2:21, 22). God created one woman for the man. He could have created any number he wished. Man and animals were formed from the ground, but woman was built from man's rib. The writer is emphasizing the special care that God took to make woman the ideal companion and fellow worker of man. Woman is such an important and indispensable creature that a part of the body which God originally formed for man was selected by the Lord so that she could be made from it.

Since woman was taken out of man, she is dependent on him. And since man names his companion, he has authority over her (just as his naming of the beasts and birds demonstrates his authority over them). This is not an overbearing kind of authority, but an authority that woman naturally upholds for the man who provides for her and gives her protection and security. It is true that the Scriptures teach that woman is the subordinate of man in certain respects, again within the context of marriage; but this is not the consequence of her having been created according to God's image to a lesser degree than man. Woman, made in the image of God, is to reflect that image and fulfill her nature in the particular way determined by God which differs in certain ways from that decreed for man; otherwise, one might ask why God made mankind male and female.

Bone of My Bones and Flesh of My Flesh

In Genesis 2:23 after God brought the woman to the man, the man then said, "This at last is bone of my bones and flesh of my flesh; she shall be called Woman." The words *flesh* and *bone* frequently stand together. In Genesis 29:14 Laban tells Jacob, "Surely you are my bone and my flesh!" Then all of the tribes of Israel came to David at Hebron and said, "Behold, we are your bone and flesh" (2 Sam. 5:1). Walter Brueggemann says, "The two terms are used together to speak about a person in his total relation to another."[2]

According to Brueggemann, "Each of these words has a double meaning." The Hebrew term means "flesh" and also means "weakness, empty of power and meaning." This might well be rendered in English "flesh weakness." Brueggemann continues, "It embodies both the physical and psychological. . . . The same is true for the other word in the pair. The term . . . is conventionally translated 'bone' . . . its root meaning [is] 'power' or 'might.' . . . it is useful again to use a hyphen and render it 'bone-power.'"[3]

Brueggemann says that "the poles of 'flesh-frailty' and 'bone-power' mean to express the entire range of intermediate possibilities from the extreme of frailty to power." It is what "we affirm in the marriage formula, 'in sickness and in health, in plenty and in want.' Here the text says, 'in every circumstance from the extreme of frailty to the extreme of power.' A relationship is affirmed which is unaffected by changing circumstances."[4] This relationship is "grounded on shared concerns, loyalties, and commitments which are taken with seriousness. It is not a light, casual relation nor one grounded in a mood or a feeling. It is rooted in an oath of solidarity."[5]

Paul uses the same imagery in Ephesians 5:21–33. Brueggemann suggests, "The relation of Christ and his bride-Church is grounded in a commonality of concern, loyalty and responsibil-

---

[2]Brueggemann, "Of the Same Flesh and Bone," 533.
[3]Ibid., 533–34.
[4]Ibid., 534–35.
[5]Ibid., 542.

ity which is pledged to endure through weakness and strength."[6] In verse 31 Paul quotes Genesis 2:24, "For this reason a man shall leave his father and mother and be joined to his wife, and the two shall become one." Brueggemann says, "It affirms that Christ and his Church are bound by vows which make them 'one flesh,' i.e., one loyalty to endure all circumstances."[7] Christ says to the church, "I will never leave you. I will never forsake you. I will never stop loving you. I will never forget you."

In a nomadic culture, families and clans move around with their flocks and herds; the primary loyalty is to family—to father and to mother. Genesis says that even this loyalty is superseded in marriage. "Therefore a man leaves his father and his mother and cleaves to his wife, and they become one flesh" (Gen. 2:24). God created one woman for the man.

Matthew Henry says that Adam's and Eve's home was a "garden furnished and adorned by nature." Heaven was the roof, "and never was any roof so curiously . . . painted. The earth was his floor." Under the trees were his dining room and his lodging room. His furniture was the work of God—plants and trees.[8]

Perfect existence, however, was short-lived. Sin enters this idyllic home, and its picture is painted in six successive steps:

1. The woman is deeply disturbed by God's command not to eat the forbidden fruit. When the serpent asks her, "Did God say, 'You shall not eat of any tree of the garden'?" (Gen. 3:1), he is emphasizing that God is depriving man of something that would be good for him. Thus, he exaggerates God's hindering him from partaking of everything he has made. The woman says God commands "neither shall you touch it" (Gen. 3:3). God's command in 2:17 contains no prohibition against touching the fruit. Satan fosters within her discontent with her present state. God has given them almost everything, but she wants everything. This is a far cry from the Shunammite woman (2 Kings 4) who, when asked by Elisha what was to be done for her, said, "I will dwell among my

---

[6]Ibid., 541.

[7]Ibid.

[8]Henry, *Commentary on the Whole Bible*, 1:15.

own people" (v. 13).

2. The serpent enforces the woman's desire to eat the fruit by telling her the advantages of eating from this particular tree.
   a. You will not die (physically) immediately (and they did not).
   b. He promises that the eyes of the man and the woman will be opened (and they were).
   c. He promises they will be like God, knowing good and evil (after they ate, God said, "Behold, the man has become like one of us, knowing good and evil" [Gen. 3:22]).
3. Woman's mind dwells on the desirable aspects of the forbidden fruit. She sees that the fruit is good, attractive food and can make one wise. This appeals to the lust of the flesh, the lust of the eyes, and the pride of life—characteristics of the temptations of Jesus (Matt. 4:1–11; Luke 4:1–13) and of all men. "For all that is in the world, the lust of the flesh and the lust of the eyes and the pride of life, is not of the Father but is of the world" (1 John 2:16).
4. The woman takes some of the fruit of the tree. The fruit looks good; but if she touches it, she can find if it also feels good. If she can touch it without being harmed, perhaps she can eat it without being harmed.
5. The woman eats of the fruit.
6. Finally, she gives some to her husband.

The initiative and the decision are hers alone. There is no consultation with her husband. She seeks neither his advice nor his permission. She acts independently (cf. Acts 5 where Ananias, with his wife Sapphira's knowledge, kept back some of the proceeds from the sale of property).

James Weldon Johnson, a gifted black poet, sees the fall in these words:

In the cool of the day—
God was walking—
Around in the Garden of Eden.
And except for the beasts, eating in the fields,

And except for the birds, flying through the trees,
The garden looked like it was deserted.
And God called out and said: Adam,
Adam, where art thou?
And Adam, with Eve behind his back,
Came out from where he was hiding.

And God said: Adam,
What hast thou done?
Thou hast eaten of the tree!
And Adam,
With his head hung down,
Blamed it on the woman.

For after God made the first man Adam,
He breathed a sleep upon him;
Then he took out of Adam one of his ribs,
And out of that rib made woman.
And God put the man and woman together
In the beautiful Garden of Eden,
With nothing to do the whole day long
But play all around in the garden.
And God called Adam before him,
And he said to him:
Listen now, Adam,
Of all the fruit in the garden you can eat,
Except of the tree of knowledge;
For the day thou eatest of that tree,
Thou shalt surely die.

Then pretty soon along came Satan.
Old Satan came like a snake in the grass
To try out his tricks on the woman.
I imagine I can see Old Satan now
A-sidling up to the woman.
I imagine the first word Satan said was:
Eve, you're surely good looking.
I imagine he brought her a present, too,—

And, if there was such a thing in those ancient days,
He brought her a looking-glass.

And Eve and Satan got friendly—
Then Eve got to walking on shaky ground;
Don't ever get friendly with Satan.—
And they started to talk about the garden,
And Satan said: Tell me, how do you like
The fruit on the nice, tall, blooming tree
Standing in the middle of the garden?
And Eve said:
That's the forbidden fruit,
Which if we eat we die.

And Satan laughed a devilish little laugh,
And he said to the woman: God's fooling you, Eve;
That's the sweetest fruit in the garden.
I know you can eat that forbidden fruit,
And I know that you will not die.

And Eve looked at the forbidden fruit,
And it was red and ripe and juicy.
And Eve took a taste, and she offered it to Adam,
And Adam wasn't able to refuse;
So he took a bite, and they both sat down
And ate the forbidden fruit.—
Back there, six thousand years ago,
Man first fell by woman—
Lord, and he's doing the same today.

And that's how sin got into this world. . . .[9]

Man Seeks to Evade His Responsibility (Gen. 3:7–13)

The first thing man does is to try to hide his guilt by covering

[9]Johnson, *God's Trombones*, 31–33.

his physical nakedness. The serpent is correct in stating if they eat the fruit their eyes will be opened, but his insinuation that this will enrich man's life is wrong; the truth is that it makes him miserable. Knowing that they are naked in 3:7 is the antithesis of not being ashamed that they are naked in 2:25. In 3:7 they are ashamed that they are naked. On their own initiative, they make aprons out of fig leaves. These are not adequate, so God, in his own characteristic goodness, makes them garments of skins with his own hands (there's something very special about handmade gifts). Like a tender and loving father, he provides for them.

They attempt to hide from the presence of God among the trees of the garden. "Am I a God at hand, says the LORD, and not a God afar off? Can a man hide himself in secret places so that I cannot see him? says the LORD" (Jer. 23:23, 24). Psalm 139:7–10 has the answer to this rhetorical question.

> Whither shall I go from thy Spirit?
> Or whither shall I flee from thy presence?
> If I ascend to heaven, thou art there!
> If I make my bed in Sheol, thou art there!
> If I take the wings of the morning
> and dwell in the uttermost parts of the sea,
> even there thy hand shall lead me,
> and thy right hand shall hold me.

Adam and Eve shift the blame to someone else. Man blames the woman and God because God gave woman to man. Woman blames the serpent. This is the first case of rationalization of which we have now become masters. It is heartwarming, whether it comes from the lips of a child or a mature adult, to hear "I did it" with no attempt to rationalize or to fix blame.

If we notice God's manner of dealing with the man and the woman, we see:

1. He makes them aware of his presence.
2. He asks man and his wife a series of questions designed to help them see themselves as they really are. The purpose of the questions is to make them feel the full weight of responsibility for their actions. Only then can he help them.

3. God punishes them to make them realize the seriousness of their sin.
4. Finally, he provides for the new needs that they have in the situation which they have brought upon themselves. He does not abandon them.

God's Punitive Curses (Gen. 3:14–19)

Punishment for the Serpent

1. The serpent will be forced to go on its belly and eat dust all the days of its life.
2. God will put enmity between the serpent and his seed and the woman and her seed.
3. Serpents will harm people, but people will dominate and exterminate them. This would suggest that before the fall there was a harmonious relationship between man and other creatures. The woman is Eve, and her descendants are the human race. As long as time will last, there will be a continuing hostility between snakes and people, but people will prevail (when we walk in the woods and are warned of snakes, there is no joy in the walk). Spiritual hostility exists between mankind and the devil. Ultimately, man will prevail, and the devil will be conquered. The only echo in the New Testament to this passage is found in Romans 16:20. Paul makes God the subject. "Then the God of peace will soon crush Satan under your feet."

God's Curse on the Woman

1. Woman will suffer pain in childbirth. God intended for man and woman to have children from the very first. "And God blessed them, and God said to them, 'Be fruitful and multiply and fill the earth and subdue it'" (Gen. 1:28). Having children is not a curse; children are from the Lord. It seems that before the fall, the woman could have given birth to children painlessly; as a result of the fall, giving birth to a child will be painful.
2. And the woman's desire shall be to her husband. Her wishes shall be subject to those of her husband. In matters of ulti-

mate concern, it is the husband's decision that must prevail. Woman's place is not that of slave; instead, the husband is to rule lovingly but firmly, always in the best interest of his wife. Again, this is the same picture as that of the marriage relationship in Ephesians 5:22, 23.

Punishment of Man

1. He must work especially hard for his food. Work is not a curse placed on man as a result of the fall because God commanded the man to till and keep the garden before he sinned. Work is a blessing. The curse consists of the difficulty of the work and the hindrances man has to overcome to procure his food.
2. Man must die physically. One probably should never read this without reading Paul's statement in 1 Corinthians 15:22, "For as in Adam all die, so also in Christ shall all be made alive."

This first sin vitiates all relationships: between animals and human beings, mothers and children, husbands and wives, man and the soil, man and his work. In creation man and woman know harmony and equality; in sin they know alienation and discord.

God Enables Man to Begin Again

In Genesis 4:1 we have the birth of Cain; there is always something very special about the birth of the first child simply because it is the first. Then, of course, the birth of the second child is special because he is the second, and so on. So the second child, Abel, was born.

Genesis 4:1 represents a typical way of telling about the birth of a child in the Old Testament. The man knew his wife, the wife conceived, she bore or gave birth to a son or daughter, and she or her husband named the child. The verb *knew* is a euphemism meaning "had sexual relations with." "I have gotten a man with the help of the Lord."

This is the first of many biblical texts that teach that conception and birth are a cooperative enterprise involving man, woman, and God. If God closes a woman's womb, a couple cannot have children. We will see this later in Genesis 20:18. It is only if he opens the womb that they can have children. We will see this in Genesis 29:31 when the Lord opens Leah's womb and in 30:22 when he opens Rachel's womb. Children are God's gifts to man and woman. "Lo, sons are a heritage from the LORD, the fruit of the womb is a reward. Like arrows in the hand of a warrior are the sons of one's youth. Happy is the man who has his quiver full of them!" (Ps. 127:3–5).

Then a brother kills another brother. It is impossible to imagine the grief that this would bring to parents. Our hearts are torn when one child accidentally kills another. But for a brother to plot the death of another is unthinkable to us. I once heard a very godly woman say that there was no sorrow that could compare with that of a mother whose children did not get along—but not getting along is not murder. I can't imagine the grief that came to Adam and Eve when one son murdered another.

The following are parallels in the life of this older son and the life of his parents. They highlight for us the fact that parents are models for their children, whether it is a small boy imitating his father's walk or committing a grievous sin or persevering in the faith.

1. They each committed sin. Adam and Eve sinned against God by eating the forbidden fruit. Now their son Cain becomes angry with his brother and murders him.
2. Like Adam and Eve, Cain tries to evade the responsibility for sin by telling God he does not know where Abel is.
3. As in the case of Adam and Eve, God's way of dealing with Cain reveals great truths concerning man's rebellion and God's nature. God asks Cain what he has done—the same question the Lord asked Eve in 3:13. The Lord is trying to get Cain to see himself as he really is. Robert Burns said, "O wad some Power the giftie gie us / To see oursels as ithers see us!"[10] Better far to see ourselves as God sees us.
4. As with Adam and Eve, God decrees that Cain will be cursed from the ground.

---

[10]Burns, "To a Louse," 494.

   a. The ground will cease to give him its produce, and thus he will no longer be able to cultivate it.
   b. The ground will not make Cain feel he is a welcome inhabitant so that wherever he goes, he will be a fugitive and a wanderer.
5. God drives Adam and Eve from the Garden of Eden, and he drives Cain away from the ground. A change in their geographical locations does not mean that they are literally separated from the Lord. However, they do not enjoy the kind of relationship with the Lord that existed before their sinning. Probably no Scripture better pictures this than Psalm 51:11, 12, David's confession and his plea: "Cast me not away from thy presence, and take not thy holy Spirit from me. Restore to me the joy of thy salvation, and uphold me with a willing spirit." There is no real joy apart from the presence of God.
6. When God drove Adam and Eve out of the garden, they established a new home east of the Garden of Eden (Gen. 3:24). Now that God drives Cain from his home, he sets up a new home east of Eden.

At the age of 130, Adam knows his wife again, and she bears a son and calls his name Seth ("to appoint," "to establish"). "God has appointed for me another child instead of Abel, for Cain slew him" (Gen. 4:25). It is through this son that the ancestry of Jesus is traced. Other sons and daughters are born to them, but their names are not given. In chapter 5 we have the descendants of Adam. Adam lived 930 years, and he died. There is no record of the death of Eve.

New Testament Allusions

When Jesus described marriage as it should be, it was to the creation narrative in Genesis 2 that he appealed. Mark 10:6–8 tells us that "from the beginning of creation, 'God made them male and female.' 'For this reason a man shall leave his father and mother and be joined to his wife, and the two shall become one.' So they are no longer two but one."

In 1 Timothy 2:11–14 Paul argues that woman's place in the

church should be one of silence and submissiveness. He refers to the Genesis story to establish creation order and to prove vulnerability. In 2 Corinthians 11:3 Paul uses Eve as an illustration of how easily one can "be led astray from a sincere and pure devotion to Christ."

Our task now, so it seems to me, is to return to the Genesis story of Adam and Eve for God's plan in marriage, the "one man, one woman, one flesh" concept of Genesis 2:24, and to recognize God's marvelous love in applying that same imagery to the Christ and the church in Ephesians 5:21–23, 28.

[Presented at York College, 1982.]

10

A Woman's Influence

For as long as I can remember, when I have read the story of Ananias and Sapphira, I have wondered what would have happened if Sapphira had said, "Ananias, we can't do this thing that we are planning to do; we can't be dishonest. We can't cheat the church; that's the very body of our Lord who so recently gave his life so we could be saved. How could we ever have thought of doing such a thing? We can give a part of our property and tell the apostles that we are giving a part of what we own to take care of the needy among us. I know Peter and the other apostles will understand. But we must not lie to God. That's serious business. We may lose our very souls. I know we would like to be thought of as a generous couple, as generous as Barnabas; but we can't sell our souls to the devil for that kind of recognition. Besides, we are so blessed to be a part of this most exciting work, the very beginning of the church, and we want to be a good example to those around us. People need to see that, without our saying a word, we are not so attached to the farm we own."

This story set me to thinking about how we may influence or be influenced by others either to do good or to do wrong. We probably all are who we are because of the various influences in our lives—parents, grandparents, brothers, sisters, uncles, aunts, teachers, students, preachers, and friends. We may not have realized their influence until late in life, and perhaps we never let them know that they influenced us.

There are so many books now on women's self-esteem. The New Testament emphasized the influence of women a long time ago. The annunciation about the birth of Jesus was first given to

Mary, and it is Elizabeth who first recognized the mother of the Messiah and counseled her before the birth. Anna proclaims Christ's birth "to all who were looking for the redemption of Jerusalem" (Luke 2:38). Jesus' longest recorded conversation was with a woman, and he first revealed to her that he was the Messiah (John 4). He first proclaimed himself as "the resurrection and the life" (John 11:25) to Martha, and Jesus wept with the sisters at the tomb of Lazarus. Women accompanied Jesus on his preaching mission and on his final journey to Jerusalem.

Mary of Bethany first grasped the fact of his impending death. The only voice raised in protest during his trial was that of a woman, the wife of Pilate. Women stood at the foot of the cross. Women first discovered the empty tomb. The risen Lord appeared first to Mary Magdalene and commanded her to tell "my brethren" (Matt. 28:10).

Paul remembered with gratitude the many women with whom he shared his ministry of reconciliation. "For they have labored side by side with me in the gospel" (Phil. 4:3).

It has been said that woman is the rock where man either anchors or is wrecked. Today I want to concentrate on how wives may be able to influence their husbands. But the matter of influence can apply to any human relationship. We will look at biblical examples, both good and bad, at a second-century Jewish couple, at a wife of the Restoration period, and at a modern woman who so greatly influenced her husband and enabled him to do the great work he did for the Lord.

We begin, as always, with Scripture. Proverbs 19:14 tells us that "a prudent wife is from the LORD." And in that most familiar passage in Proverbs 31, we read:

> A wife of noble character who can find?
>   She is worth far more than rubies.
> Her husband has full confidence in her
>   and lacks nothing of value.
> She brings him good, not harm,
>   all the days of her life.
> She selects wool and flax
>   and works with eager hands.

She is like the merchant ships,
bringing her food from afar.
She gets up while it is still dark;
she provides food for her family
and portions for her servant girls.
She considers a field and buys it;
out of her earnings she plants a vineyard.
She sets about her work vigorously;
her arms are strong for her tasks.
She sees that her trading is profitable,
and her lamp does not go out at night.
In her hand she holds the distaff
and grasps the spindle with her fingers.
She opens her arms to the poor
and extends her hands to the needy.
When it snows, she has no fear for her household;
for all of them are clothed in scarlet.
She makes coverings for her bed;
she is clothed in fine linen and purple.
Her husband is respected at the city gate,
where he takes his seat among the elders of the land.
She makes linen garments and sells them,
and supplies the merchants with sashes.
She is clothed with strength and dignity;
she can laugh at the days to come.
She speaks with wisdom,
and faithful instruction is on her tongue.
She watches over the affairs of her household
and does not eat the bread of idleness.
Her children arise and call her blessed;
her husband also, and he praises her:
"Many women do noble things,
but you surpass them all."
Charm is deceptive, and beauty is fleeting;
but a woman who fears the LORD is to be praised.
Give her the reward she has earned,
and let her works bring her praise at the city gate
(Prov. 31:10–31; NIV).

Finally, 1 Peter 3:1 says, "Wives, in the same way be submissive to your husbands so that, if any of them do not believe the word, they may be won over without words by the behavior of their wives, when they see the purity and reverence of your lives" (NIV). I daresay almost every woman has known of a husband who has been won to Christ not by a word spoken by his wife but by her behavior.

Biblical Examples

Eve (Gen. 1; 2)

As you would expect, we turn to that first wife, Eve. God determined to create a helper for man before he ever brought the animals before man that he might name them. None of the animals could measure up to man's aspirations or satisfy his needs. Genesis 1 leaves the creation of mankind (men and women) until last to emphasize the importance of mankind in relation to the rest of God's creatures. Genesis 2 leaves the creation of woman until last to stress the woman's inestimable value to man in contrast to all other creatures. A unique opportunity was given to Eve to become an example to every wife who followed her, but she ate of the fruit forbidden by God and gave some to her husband. She acted on her own initiative, and the decision was hers alone. There was no consultation with her husband. She did not seek either his advice or his permission. She acted independently. And so although in creation man and woman knew harmony and equality, in sin they knew only alienation and discord.

Rebekah (Gen. 27)

No matter how we may try to justify Rebekah's actions in planning for Jacob to receive the blessing that rightfully was Esau's, we must say she was deceptive and bent on accomplishing her own objective. She broke a serious social prohibition which in a later period was to become law: "Cursed be he who misleads a blind man on the road" (Deut. 27:18), and "You shall not curse the deaf or put a stumbling block before the blind" (Lev. 19:14). It is wrong for a wife to conspire against her husband. In doing so Rebekah paid a dreadful price. She lost Esau.

She drove a wedge between her two sons. Jacob had to flee for his life, and she died without ever seeing him again. She had said to Jacob, "Let the curse fall on me" (Gen. 27:13); by her scheming, she did bring a curse on herself.

Job's Wife (Job 2)

With wealth gone, with children gone, with everything gone except the woman who had shared life with him, Job hears his wife's advice, "Curse God and die" (2:9). It was not her love that had gone to pieces but her faith in God. However, Job came back with, "You speak as one of the foolish women would speak" (2:10). This woman was foolish because she thought pain and suffering were inconsistent with the love of God. She thought that by getting rid of God, she could get rid of the evil that God seemed to have sent, and she renounced hope when she renounced God. Someone has said of marriage, "It's us against them." A husband and wife together can bear untold suffering, but apart it is almost unbearable.

Samson's Wife and the Other Woman—Delilah (Judg. 14–16)

Samson's wife was a Philistine woman of Timnah whose name we do not know. She badgered him to tell the answer to the riddle he had posed: "Out of the eater, something to eat; out of the strong, something sweet" (14:14; NIV). She used the age-old tactic, "You don't love me." But then when that failed, she used that tactic which almost no husband can resist—she cried. Samson relented and told her the answer to the riddle.

Then Samson fell in love with the prostitute Delilah. She nagged him for days to tell her the secret of his strength. Finally she said to him, "How can you say, 'I love you,' when you won't confide in me? This is the third time you have made a fool of me and haven't told me the secret of your great strength" (Judg. 16:15; NIV). Then the text says, "With such nagging she prodded him day after day until he was tired to death. So he told her everything" (Judg. 16:16, 17; NIV). She sold him to the Philistines for 1,100 shekels of silver given by each lord. Through her influence Samson lost his power and his vision, and he became a slave.

Jezebel (1 Kings 21)

Probably the most familiar story of the evil influence of a wife on a husband is that of Jezebel on Ahab. The outstanding feature in Ahab's reign of 27 years was the persistent effort of Queen Jezebel to oust the worship of Jehovah and to establish that of Baal. She established Phoenician worship at the court of Ahab and refused to acknowledge the sovereignty of Jehovah. She wanted and tried to destroy that great prophet of God, Elijah. But Ahab, the king, despite his many cities and famous palaces of ivory, had his heart set on one vineyard, and that was one he could not have. Israelite law made it very difficult to alienate landed estates and provided for their retention by the family of their holders. Any attempt to seize an estate by violence was to be resisted since the land was considered to belong to Jehovah. In keeping with the law, Naboth refused to sell his patrimony. Ahab took to his bed, turned his face to the wall, and refused food. His wife entered, learned the cause of his sullenness, and scoffed at him. She said, "Is this how you act as king over Israel? Get up and eat! Cheer up. I'll get you the vineyard of Naboth the Jezreelite" (1 Kings 21:7; NIV). So she wrote letters in the king's name charging Naboth with treason. Sentence was pronounced. That evening Jezebel received the message, "Naboth is dead." Then Elijah gave the Lord's message, "Dogs will devour Jezebel by the wall of Jezreel" (1 Kings 21:23; NIV). She was thus denied a common burial, for the hungry dogs had already eaten her.

By this time you may well be wondering if there are any wives in the biblical story who exerted a good and noble influence on their husbands. There are indeed, and we begin, as you might know, with Sarah.

Sarah (Gen. 11–23)

Sarah's influence on Abraham was not so much that of assertion but that of submission. She left her home and her friends in Ur. She left her home, which may well have resembled the Arab houses found today in Baghdad, Iraq, and the conveniences of the day to live in a tent or, since Abraham was wealthy, several tents. There is nothing in Scripture to suggest that she was ever unwilling to go where Abraham wanted to go or that she in any way hindered his progress. She made the move from Ur, to Haran, to Canaan, to Egypt, and back to Canaan. There is no record of her complaining about having a father-in-law and a nephew in her family circle. We may perhaps wonder why she didn't refuse to go along with Abraham's plans for deceiving both Pharaoh and Abimelech. She was the first woman to extend hospitality to guests. But the outstanding quality by which she lives in our memory is the steadfastness of her devotion to Abraham. Prosperity does not divorce them; adversity does not divide them. At her death we are told that Abraham mourned and wept for Sarah.

Abigail (1 Sam. 23)

Described as an intelligent and beautiful woman, Abigail was the wife of Nabal, the Carmelite. After Nabal's death, she married David. Nabal was an ill-tempered, drunken man. When David was hiding from King Saul, he asked Nabal for food for himself and his men. Nabal's response was, "Who is this David?" and he refused to aid him. David threatened to plunder Nabal's possessions and to kill him. When Nabal's servants told Abigail what had happened and asked her to see what she could do because disaster was hanging over the whole household, the text says she lost no time. She took 200 loaves of bread, two skins of wine, five dressed sheep, five seahs of roasted grain, 100 cakes of raisins, and 200 cakes of pressed figs, loaded them on donkeys, and went to David. She asked David to hold her responsible for what had happened, and she took upon herself the blame which belonged to Nabal. She told the truth about her husband, that he was both irresponsible and worthless. She explained to David that had she seen the young men when they came, a much different answer would have been rendered. She dissuaded him from taking violence against Nabal since it was the Lord who kept him from shedding blood and avenging himself. It is wonderful when God keeps us from foolish acts and sins which we almost commit. She reminded him of the great destiny in store for him.

> And when the LORD has done for my master every good thing he promised concerning him and has appointed

> him leader over Israel, my master will not have on his conscience the staggering burden of needless bloodshed or of having avenged himself (1 Sam. 25:30, 31; NIV).

Abigail has tact, and tact has a wonderful power in smoothing out tangled affairs. In the home it is a most indispensable ingredient. It will speak the soft word. It is silent when silence is better than speech. Abigail was the instrument of the Lord, and through her David came to know that it is best to leave vengeance in the hands of God.

The Shunammite Woman (2 Kings 4)

One of my favorite Old Testament characters is the Shunammite woman. As she saw Elisha pass her door day after day, she urged him to stay for a meal. Elisha's stopping became a habit. I have an idea that Elisha timed his journey in order to arrive at her house at mealtime. Finally, this well-to-do woman said to her husband, "I know that this man who often comes our way is a holy man of God. Let's make a small room on the roof and put in it a bed and a table, a chair and a lamp for him [all the necessities]. Then he can stay there whenever he comes to us" (2 Kings 4:9, 10; NIV). If you were fortunate to have been brought up in a home where there was indeed a preacher's room, then you can understand why this woman wanted to have Elisha as a frequent guest. I doubt if the husband would have ever thought of extending this kind of hospitality; however, when she suggested it, her husband evidently agreed, for we find that her plan was accomplished.

Although there is much said in the Bible about extending hospitality, wives are usually the ones who invite guests into the home. And in the qualifications for elders, Paul tells Timothy that the elder must be hospitable (1 Tim. 3:2). This Shunammite woman possesses a quality seldom seen in women today, that of contentment. When asked by Elisha's servant what could be done for her, she replied, "I have a home among my own people" (2 Kings 4:13b; NIV). If more wives cultivated this quality of contentment, it just might be that homes would be happier places for husbands to return to at the end of the day.

Priscilla

Priscilla is another wife who moved around with her husband—from Pontus, to Rome where they were expelled by Claudius, to Corinth, to Ephesus, to Rome, and back to Ephesus. That's a lot of packing and unpacking to do. She and Aquila were one in the Lord; they are never mentioned apart. Three times her name is mentioned first, and twice Aquila's is. The church met in their house both in Rome and in Ephesus. Someone has said they couldn't have had the church in every Sunday without wearing out the carpets and making the furniture threadbare. They were personal evangelists. Although Apollos was an eloquent man and well-versed in Scriptures, he knew only the baptism of John. They took him and expounded to him the way of God more accurately. They didn't criticize him; they didn't ostracize him. They taught him. Their teaching fell into good soil so that he powerfully confuted the Jews in public, showing from the Scriptures that Jesus was the Christ. He became such an influence that he was put in the class with Paul and Peter in 1 Corinthians 1. Aquila and Priscilla were truly one in the Lord, and whatever service they rendered, they rendered it together.

Second-Century Examples

Akiba's Wife

Student wives at Harding Graduate School often need to work outside the home so that their husbands can attend graduate school. I have an example of encouragement for you from second-century Judaism. According to legend Akiba was a shepherd in the employ of the rich Kalba Sabu'a, whose daughter took a liking to Akiba. She consented to a secret engagement on the condition that he devote himself to study. When her father heard of this secret engagement, he drove both Akiba and his daughter from his house. They lived in such poverty that the wife had to sell her hair, reminiscent of one of O. Henry's short stories. By agreement with his wife, Akiba spent 12 years away from her pursuing his studies. Returning home at the end of that time, he overheard a neighbor censuring him for his long absence. The Lord might have said to him or her what he said to Peter,

"What is that to you?" But Akiba's wife said, "If I had my wish, he should stay another 12 years at the Academy." Akiba didn't enter the door but went back to the Academy and did study another 12 years. I doubt that any wives at the Graduate School have been asked to work for 24 years while their husbands attend school! The second time when Akiba came back, he came as a most famous scholar accompanied by 24,000 disciples. When his poorly-clad wife was about to embrace him, some of his students, not knowing who she was, sought to restrain her. But Akiba said, "Let her alone; for what I am and for what we are, to this noble woman the thanks are due."[1]

Tertullian's Tribute to His Wife

Also from this same second century comes this lovely tribute that Tertullian, the Latin church father, gives to his wife:

> Whence are we to find words enough fully to tell the happiness of that marriage which the Church cements, and the oblation confirms, and the benediction signs and seals; which angels carry back the news of to heaven, which the Father holds for ratified? For even on earth children do not rightfully and lawfully wed without their fathers' consent. What kind of yoke is that of two believers, partakers of one hope, one desire, one discipline, one and the same service? Both are brethren, both are fellow servants, no difference of spirit or of flesh; nay, they are truly "two in one flesh." Where the flesh is one, one is the spirit, too. Together they pray, together prostrate themselves, together perform their fasts; mutually teaching, mutually exhorting, mutually sustaining. Equally are they both found in the Church of God; equally at the banquet of God; equally in straits, in persecutions, in refreshments. Neither hides ought from the other; neither shuns the other; neither is troublesome to the other. The sick is visited, the indigent relieved, with freedom. Alms are given without danger of ensuing torment; sacrifices attended

[1]Finkelstein, *Akiba*, 79, 136.

> without scruple; daily diligence discharged without impediment: there is no stealthy signing, no trembling greeting, no mute benediction. Between the two echo psalms and hymns; and they mutually challenge each other which shall better chant to their Lord. Such things when Christ sees and hears, He joys. To these He sends His own peace. Where two are, there withal is He Himself. Where He is, there the Evil One is not.[2]

A Restoration Period Example

If ever we feel that we are giving up anything for the Lord, we need to read the story of the wives of some of the Restoration preachers, those nineteenth-century preachers who blazed trails for New Testament Christianity without any creeds. Among the most colorful figures of this period was Raccoon John Smith, so nicknamed because he lived among the raccoons. To pay a debt that he had incurred, he decided to dispense with hired help and cultivate his farm with his own hands. But then there came the day when he threw down his ax, came into his house, and exclaimed to his wife, "Nancy, I shall work no more! Get whom you please to carry on the farm but do not call on me! In all the land, there is not one soul to open his mouth in defense of the best cause under the sun! I am determined from this time forth to preach the Gospel and leave the consequences to God."[3]

Nancy Hurt Smith quickly caught his spirit and cheerfully accepted the responsibilities of carrying on the farm and providing for the family so her husband could be relieved of every temporal care and devote himself wholly to the preaching of the Gospel. Her zeal was no less than his; her sacrifices, perhaps, were as many and as great. She had made him promise that he would look in on his home, if possible, every week. But sometimes his schedule of preaching did not allow him to keep his promise. He would be at "a distant place, preaching and baptizing till the week was nearly gone and then, dismissing the people at a late

---

[2]Tertullian, *To His Wife*, 8.

[3]Williams, *Life of Elder John Smith*, 192.

hour, ride hurriedly home through darkness, sometimes through mud and cold and storms, in order to keep that promise."[4] Sometimes he would pass by his house, too hurried to stop and rest, but he would linger awhile at the gate to hear her words of cheer. Once he stopped as he was passing and without dismounting from his horse called her to the gate.

> "Nancy," he said, giving her the saddlebags in which he carried his clothing, "I have been immersing all the week. Will you take these clothes and bring me some clean ones right away? for I must hurry on." "Mr. Smith," she said pleasantly . . . , "is it not time that you were having your washing done somewhere else? We have attended to it for a long time." "No, Nancy," said he. "I am much pleased with your way of doing things, and I don't wish to change."[5]

Smith's biographer wrote that except for her noble self-sacrifice, perhaps the labors of her husband would have been lost to the church; it was through her heroic but unrecorded struggles with poverty and care that he was at last known in the gates, when he sat among the elders of the land. On her tombstone are inscribed these words: "In all his sacrifices and service, his companion shared. She gave her life to God, and her death was precious in his sight."[6]

A Modern Example

Finally, I have chosen the person of Laura Catherine Keeble as a model for all wives of men who pioneered in Christian education and who endured hardships we find almost impossible to believe. Sandra Humphrey's interview with her appeared in the premier edition of *Christian Woman*.[7]

For 34 years she worked with her husband, Marshall Keeble,

---

[4]Ibid., 238.

[5]Ibid.

[6]Ibid., 578.

[7]Humphrey, "Laura Catherine Keeble," 18–19.

and never cared who got the credit, only that God was glorified. She helped her husband establish and operate Nashville Christian Institute, a school for young black people. Often Brother Keeble would be gone for extended meetings, sometimes lasting more than a month. But she said that no matter what time of day or night he returned, "they knelt together in their living room and thanked God for keeping them both safe and prayed that the trip would be fruitful." When asked if she felt lonely when Brother Keeble was gone for such a long time, she said, "I really never was alone." She kept seven teenage girls in her home; she "was 'banker' for all the students; . . . I was counselor and 'momma' to the boys. I cleaned, did the boys' laundry and sometimes even had to get them to take baths." She "did not waste time feeling sorry for herself and waiting for Brother Keeble to return from his trips to make her life fulfilled. . . . Until she was 81 years old, she worked delivering meals for the senior citizens' program. . . . Many of the people she took food to still call her when they are not feeling well." She said, "You have to learn to take on responsibility. Some women keep a beautiful home, but they never learn to be *responsible* for things like paying taxes and insurance."

When asked if she had just one piece of advice to give to today's Christian women, this is what she said: "Marry in the church! If you can't get somebody just stay [single] like I did for 35 years. Any time somebody says, 'I *used* to be a Christian,' you nearly always know that they married out of the church." With such a wife beside him, we do not have to wonder how Marshall Keeble accomplished so much in his lifetime and in his generation baptized more people than any other man. On the other hand, if he had not had a wife who believed in his mission and who refused to complain about living in cramped college quarters and about having all of the responsibilities, he would never have been able to accomplish what he did in his service to the Lord.

Conclusion

Finally, although the term *co-dependency* has fallen into disfavor, it does describe an ideal, when husbands and wives influence each other for good. One lifts up the other who is downhearted. One has an insight into biblical truth that the other has not seen and can tell the other what he has gleaned from Bible study. They pray together. One doesn't see that opportunity to serve, and the other does. One wants to increase his or her giving to the Lord, and the other agrees. Both love the Lord with all their souls, minds, and strength. When the Lord is lord of both, then both, because they influenced each other for good, can look forward to an eternity together where they can praise and serve God in a more perfect way than they could on earth and where they can enjoy the fellowship of all the saints.

[Date and occasion of this speech are unknown.]

11

EVANGELISM

When we were children, we sang at Vacation Bible School, "Jesus Loves the Little Children of the World." As adults we sing, if we have a visiting missionary, "Of One the Lord Has Made the Race" and the more lively "Send the Light."

We have no difficulty understanding the vision that Peter had on the housetop because the explanation is given to us. We have no difficulty understanding the significance of Jesus' conversation with the woman of Samaria. We have no difficulty understanding James' teaching that we are not to be respecters of persons. Our difficulty comes in translating these teachings into our lives. How easy it is to teach our lessons, and how hard it is to follow those truths we are teaching others!

In whatever way we may have reasoned and justified our failure to make friends of and to teach God's salvation message to people who are different from us, in those moments when we read God's message with a desire to know and live by it, we know we condemn ourselves. If ever we can bring ourselves to a recognition of our own sin and an honest confession of our sin, there may yet be hope for us.

Outside of the Bible, I think no writing has so moved me as Alan Paton's novel *Cry the Beloved Country*. Among the papers found in the desk of the Englishman Arthur Jarvis after his murder by a native was that one which read:

> I shall devote myself, my time, my energy, my talents, to the service of South Africa. I shall no longer ask myself if this or that is expedient, but only if it is right. I shall do

> this, not because I am noble or unselfish, but because life slips away, and because I need for the rest of my journey a star that will not play false to me, a compass that will not lie. I shall do this, not because I am a negrophile and a hater of my own, but because I cannot find it in me to do anything else. I am lost when I balance this against that, I am lost when I ask if this is safe, I am lost when I ask if men, white men or black men, Englishmen or Afrikaners, Gentiles or Jews, will approve. Therefore, I shall try to do what is right, and to speak what is true.[1]

The giant step for us all is the decision to do God's will—to have the mind of Christ as our own in the treatment of races different from our own. We must decide, as did Jarvis, not to ask what is expedient, safe, and man-approved, but only to ask what is right in God's view of right.

How can we know if our resolve is sincere, one that can find application? We must make a beginning, however small that beginning may be. Begin by finding a minority family—minority in social, economic, educational, or racial areas—and determine that you will become involved in the life of that family. You will be concerned with the daily as well as the Sunday activities of that family, with the present and the future of that family, with their hurts and their joys.

The rewards will far outweigh the frustrations of that involvement. Among the rewards are these:

1. You will increase your dependence on God because you see all too clearly how helpless you are.
2. You will recognize in a new way the manifold blessings of God and will come to ask, "Why have I been so blessed?"
3. You will know the sheer delight of obedience to God with no conditions or rationalizations attached.
4. You will know that the real power of conviction belongs to God. This awareness will keep you from the extremes of discouragement and pride.
5. You will experience the boundless joy that comes from see-

---

[1]Paton, *Cry the Beloved Country*, 175.

ing one buried with Christ and rising to walk in a new life.

6. You will know the anticipation of living with that new life in all eternity where the deprivations and hardships will not even be a memory.
7. You will increase your own faith by sharing it with one who must be taught very simply and very clearly about God's plan for us all.
8. You will have your sympathies deepened for those whose lot has not fallen into pleasant places and who have not had a goodly heritage.
9. You will become a better steward of whatever material means the Lord has entrusted to you. You will never again be able to spend your money in an irresponsible way.
10. You will learn to be a better steward of your time.
11. You will know the joy of giving when the gift will most likely not be returned.

Just as many Samaritans believed in Jesus because of the woman's testimony, so teaching one minority family will result in their leading many to believe on the Savior of us all.

Ever since I was a child and we had missionaries visit in our home and tell of their stories in overseas mission work, I have thought that would be such a wonderful work to do. I especially remember Dr. and Mrs. Benson and their children and the stories they told of their life in China.

When high school days were over and I was a student at Harding College, we had numerous opportunities to listen to missionaries as they came home and related their stories of mission work. One of my classmates, Orville Brittell, decided that he couldn't wait until graduation to go to Africa, so he left after his junior year and went. Georgia and Alvin Hobby left soon after their graduation for mission work in Africa. I graded English papers for Mrs. Zelma Lawyer while I was a student at Harding and listened with fascination to her telling of her life and that of her family in Africa. Myrtle Rowe returned from Africa, and we never tired of the stories she told us about her work with native girls. Forever engrained on my memory are the wonderful stories of that master storyteller J. D. Merritt. I remember in a chapel speech one day he said, "Africa is my theme song." He would tell us about the native preacher Bicycle, and we thought we knew him personally.

One of my dearest friends, Irene Johnson, decided to go to Germany as a missionary. She could not get a visa after her graduation from the University of Missouri, so she came to Harding to teach a year until she was able to go. She went with my roommate, Dot Baker, so I felt a very personal interest in their work. They wrote detailed letters of their language study in Switzerland and finally of their beginning work in Frankfurt, Germany. At first their work consisted in the distribution of clothes to the needy, and then from that benevolent program came the opportunity to teach children's and ladies' classes. They were, in a sense, pioneer missionaries to post-war Germany.

I was still thinking how wonderful it would be to be a missionary! But school administrators thought I should stay at Harding and be a teacher and librarian instead. For 37 years I did just that, first on the Searcy campus and later on the Memphis campus at the Graduate School. During my 21 years at the Graduate School, we had a close association with students who were preparing to be missionaries and visiting missionaries who spoke in chapel. In one year's graduating class, there were eight men and their families preparing to go to the mission field. One of the delights of overseas travel is the chance to visit with our former students and to see firsthand the results of their training and their dedication.

I correspond with a number of missionaries—most of them former students at the Graduate School—and it is thrilling to read their newsletters recounting the number of Bible studies and conversions among the people with whom they work. We are inclined to think, "If I could just cross the ocean, then I would be a personal worker, and I could perhaps send such newsletters home." Alas, most of us will stay in the continental United States. But souls that are lost are within a stone's throw of most of the houses where we live. The teaching of the Bible to the lost may not be so glamorous in our own neighborhood or in a government housing project, but lost souls are there as well as in Kenya, New Guinea, France, Italy, Sicily, and Brazil—countries where our congregation is supporting full-time missionaries.

With that kind of background, it was natural that my keen interest in missions has not faded but has become more intense. Through this interest came my involvement in the Outreach Ministry at the White Station Church of Christ. It is not a story of successes (there have been countless more failures) or of how to do it, but just the experiences of one person.

In the winter of 1973, we announced that we would begin a class for the mothers of the children who rode the buses; the children had been coming for about a year. We had no idea whether anybody would come. I prepared my lesson and waited. That first Sunday one person came; she walked with crutches and with great difficulty. But I keep her name—Esther Pratcher—in my Bible so I'll never forget she was the first and only one who responded to that first invitation. The next Sunday two more came. From that point one or two more came until the highest number was around 14. The class has always been open to anyone attending White Station; but it began primarily as a class for mothers in the Outreach program, and the teaching was directed to them.

No single teaching in the Bible has been of as much encouragement to me in this class as the Parable of the Sower or the soils. We have had those represented by the path whom the evil one snatched away. We have had many represented by the rocky ground who heard the Word and immediately received it with joy, who endured for a while and then fell away. The greatest number were those represented by the thorns—those who heard the Word, but the cares of the world choked the Word. The cares of these mothers are many. With one exception (and her husband is disabled), they all represent single-parent homes. Mothers must work outside the home to support their families, have sole responsibility for seeing their children have clothes and transportation for school attendance, must face the teachers alone when there are problems, must discipline alone, and on and on their burdens go. Sheer weariness takes its toll.

But then finally there is the good soil—those who hear and understand the Word and bear fruit. Those who are faithful over a period of years have a far-reaching effect on their extended families, who may have no church affiliation. They demonstrate in their lives a different way of talking, acting, and being. That very difference enables them to have an influence for good on friends and families about them. These families are able to see Christian behavior when their loved ones suffer hardships, serious illness, and death. They also see a sweet spirit of sharing in times of joy.

In addition to influencing families, I see another blessing in the forming of meaningful friendships. Some women who never had a friend on whom they could depend or on whom they could call without expecting some kind of reimbursement now are finding solid relationships in the church. The one who has a car may take others grocery shopping or by Kentucky Fried Chicken on the way home from church. The burdens of these women have not been lifted, but they are beginning to know that as Christians, no matter how enormous their own responsibilities, they must have a concern for the welfare of others.

After an involvement of 15 years in an outreach program, I would like to pass along to you some of the convictions which first drew me to such a program and to which I still fervently hold:

1. The Great Commission did not have a terminal date; it is still in force. Matthew 28:19 is for all time.
2. Realize it is God's work. We may plant and water, but it is God who will give the increase. We are fellow laborers with God, and it is not possible to have a better partner.
3. We must reach out to people who are not like us. Jesus did—Nicodemus, the Pharisee who came by night; the Samaritan woman married five times and now living with a sixth man; the lepers; the Roman centurions, symbols of foreign oppression; the demoniacs; the publican, Matthew. The cultural, economic, educational, and social background of the poor will most likely be different from yours; but then nobody, not even the most faithful apostle, was just like the Lord.
4. We must not give up, no matter what the frustrations and disappointments. We are all too familiar with the retreat, the seminar, the Ladies' Day that recharges our batteries and makes us think that when we go back home we really are going to be concerned about our neighbor (near or far) who

doesn't yet know the Lord. Our enthusiasm may last for a few weeks, but then it wanes and we need another retreat. We need that staying power. More than 30 years ago, Irene Johnson decided to go to Germany and spend her life there as a missionary. At one point her parents, now aged and ill, needed her. When she told the German brethren that she must go home to help care for her parents, they were all concerned she wouldn't come back. She promised she would, and she kept that promise. After her long illness with cancer, she was coming home for a visit. Again, the people thought she would not return. She told them, "But I have bought a round-trip ticket." She continued to be a missionary in Europe, but after her marriage to Otis Gatewood moved her base of operations to Vienna.

We need to be reminded of E. Stanley Jones' remarks when asked about his return to India. He said, "It is not your business whether you succeed or fail—it is your business to be true to the call of God as you know it."[2]

5. Do not despise the day of small things. No one makes us so aware of the one person as Jesus in his parables of the lost sheep when there were 99 that were not lost, the lost coin when 9 were not lost, and the lost boy.

The society in which we live has so engulfed us with numbers—dollars and people—that we hardly blink an eye over an expenditure of a billion dollars on a government project or thousands of people who are killed in an earthquake tragedy. The person who takes seriously the Bible message must concentrate on the one.

The Laubach Literacy Program has as its theme, "Each one teach one." If we look at the 27 million adults in America, 80,000 in Shelby County, who can't read or write, then we may ask, "What difference will my teaching one person to read make?" A Laubach tutor tells this story:

> An old man walking down a Spanish beach at dawn saw what he thought to be a dancer in the distance. The

[2]Jones, *Victorious Living*, 215.

dancer, a young man, was running across the sand rhythmically bending down to pick up a stranded starfish and throwing it far out into the sea. "Why," said the old man, "do you spend so much energy doing what is a waste of time?" The young man explained that the stranded starfish would die if left until the morning sun. "But there must be thousands of miles of beach and millions of starfish. How can your effort make any difference?" The young man looked down at the small starfish in his hand and as he threw it to safety said, "It makes a difference to this one."[3]

Finally, in a very concrete way, I am indebted to Dale Pauls for this reflection on 1 Corinthians 13:

Evangelism is patient.
Evangelism is kind.
It does not envy; it is not competitive.
It does not boast;
It points away from self to God.
It is not proud.
It is neither arrogant nor self-righteous.
It is not rude;
It does not approach people gracelessly;
It is courteous, respectful and sensitive.
It is not self-seeking;
Its purpose is not personal aggrandizement;
Indeed it surrenders personal rights.
It is not easily angered, or exasperated.
It keeps no record of wrongs, or rejection, or failure.
Evangelism does not delight in evil but rejoices with the truth; it finds no pleasure in worldly techniques of persuasion, but is confident that truth honestly proclaimed will prevail.
It always protects others, their vulnerabilities, and their confidences.

[3]Gupta, "Valedictory," 8, col. 3.

It always believes the best.
It always hopes the best.
It never gives up.
Such evangelism never really fails.[4]

[Presented at Battle Creek, Michigan, August 1987; Ladies Class, Fall 1988]

[4]Pauls, "The More Excellent Way," 1, 4.

12

Women in Leadership Roles in the Church

I believe this subject may be the most crucial one the church will face in the next century. If you visit bookstores, you will see an array of titles on women, on feeling good about yourself, and on self-esteem. My study of the biblical role of women leads me to think that we should feel very good about ourselves, that we have no cause for low self-esteem.

In the fall of 1895, a young lady intent on being a foreign missionary sought admission to J. W. McGarvey's Bible classes at the College of the Bible. McGarvey would not admit her. However, because of a recognized agreement that students who enrolled in Kentucky University might also enroll for courses in the College of the Bible, McGarvey had to relent. The young lady might attend his classes if she would enter the classroom only after the men had arrived and had begun their recitations; if she would sit on the back row near the door; if she would speak to none of the men; if, as the class was about to end, she would leave before the men were dismissed; and if on certain days she would not attend if the discussion for that day was not appropriate for female ears.[1] In 1904, however, women were allowed to enter formally the College of the Bible. McGarvey later explained, "Someone remarked after we have admitted some of these women, that we will soon be turning out female preachers; but I replied that by the time they study the Scriptures with us, they will learn that women are not to be preachers."[2] We have

---

[1]Stevenson, *Lexington Theological Seminary*, 125–26.
[2]Ibid., 127.

come a long way since this incident.

The first part of this paper will deal with biblical principles for women's role in the church, and the second part with the specific applications of these principles.

First, the Bible is God's Word, trustworthy and true, and can be relied upon and believed in every detail. Second, Scripture does not contradict Scripture. All Scripture is profitable and God-breathed. Since God is its author, all of Scripture works together to present God's truth to us.

Martin Luther said,

> If I profess with the loudest voice and clearest exposition every portion of the truth of God except precisely that little point which the world and the devil are at that moment attacking, I am not confessing Christ. Where the battle rages, there the loyalty of the soldier is proved, and to be steady on all the battlefront besides is mere flight and disgrace if he flinches at that point (*Briefwechsel* 1523, 3:81f.).[3]

So if we believe all of the Bible but reject 1 Corinthians 11:2–16, 1 Corinthians 14:33–36, 1 Timothy 2:8–15, and Titus 2:3–5, we fail in our loyalty to the Word of God. These are the passages in the New Testament that deal with woman's role in the church, and we will study them later.

Women in the Old Testament

In the Old Testament, the Lord called all Israel to hear, to learn, and to obey the law. Moses commanded the reading of the law to the entire population. "Assemble the people, men, women, and little ones, and the sojourner within your towns, that they may hear and learn to fear the LORD your God, and be careful to do all the words of this law" (Deut. 31:12). As morally responsible persons, women received God's promises and came under his judgment as well (Deut. 31:12, 13; 13:6–11).

---

[3]In Schaeffer, *The God Who Is There*, 18.

In private worship women were free to approach God in prayer (Hannah, 1 Sam. 1:10; Rebekah, Gen. 25:22; Rachel, Gen. 30:6, 22). He responded to their prayers and appeared to them. Women were able to participate in sacrifices and offerings. Men, as heads of households, brought many of the sacrifices; but the families shared in the eating of them (1 Sam. 1:4, 5). It appears Hannah was the bringer of the sacrifice in the year that she brought Samuel to Eli (1 Sam. 1:24). In cases of purification, a woman was not represented by her husband but brought her own sacrifice to the priests (Lev. 12:6; 15:29). The Nazarite vows were open to both men and women (Num. 6:2–20).

Women appear to have had certain roles in public worship. The bronze basin used in Moses' tabernacle was made from the mirrors of the women who served at the entrance to the tent of meeting (Exod. 38:8), although we do not know what their service was. We have records of women who participated in the worship of God by singing. Miriam and the women of Israel are reported to have sung and danced at the great victory over Pharaoh (Exod. 15:20, 21). Women evidently had a place among the choirs of the temple as well (1 Chron. 25:5, 6; 2 Chron. 35:25; Ezra 2:65).

It would appear that the patriarchal leadership role extended not only over the personal and domestic affairs of his family but also over the religious matters as well. He served as representative before God in public worship.

Significant changes came about with the Mosaic legislation. The sons of Levi were chosen to replace the others in the service of God in the tabernacle and temple (Num. 3:12, 13). The priesthood itself was also restricted under Moses. Males of the levitical house of Aaron were singled out to serve as priests (Exod. 28:1–3).

The Mosaic provision stands on a historical continuum and continues the practice of having representative males officiate in public worship functions. Women were not known to have served as elders of tribes, villages, or cities in Israel. They did serve as prophetesses, and Deborah was a judge.

In the Old Testament, the father was the center of the Jewish family. He was master, but he was not a despot. The wife had limited rights. Her marriage had been agreed upon by a trade between her father and her husband. She was first and foremost a sexual being. Home was her realm and also her glory. As mother she was to be honored (Exod. 20:12), and she was to be revered (Lev. 19:3).

The Old Testament offers a number of examples of women who were far wiser than their husbands. Abigail shows herself wiser than her husband, Nabal (whose name means "fool"), and more concerned for the honor of God than was David (1 Sam. 25). Zipporah, Moses' wife, showed her responsiveness to the Lord by circumcising her son when Moses had failed to do so (Exod. 4:25, 26).

The daughters of Zelophehad (Num. 27) provide information about a modification of the usual rule of male inheritance. They complained that they were the sole heirs of their father and that his name should not be done away. Moses ruled that in the absence of sons, the daughters should next inherit followed by the man's brothers and then others as usual (27:8–11).

The ideal for the woman held up by both Jews and the church is that of Ruth. She is loyal, submissive, and agreeably dependent, and she relies only on marriage and children for status and fulfillment.

Deborah (Judg. 4:4–6) holds several roles at once. She is a prophetess and manifestly speaks for God, passing on his commands to others. She is also a judge to whom Israelites willingly submit, many evidently traveling some distance to reach her. She is also a wife. The three roles do not seem to have appeared incongruous to the author of Judges. Deborah's authority extended not only to the cases brought her as judge but was readily accepted by the fearful Barak, who wishes not only her command but also her physical presence.

Two unnamed women are identified only as wise women. The wise woman of 2 Samuel 14:2 was sent for by Joab to intercede for Absalom with his father, David. She presented a hypothetical case to the king. Then she revealed herself and her real mission to persuade him to bring back the banished Absalom. She was successful in her mission.

In 2 Samuel 20:16–22 Joab, David's army commander, had

been pursuing a man named Sheba, who instigated a revolt against David. The man had fled to one of the northernmost cities in Israel. As Joab and his army made preparations to lay siege to the city, a wise woman from the city asked to speak with Joab personally. She made her case for the preservation of the city. Joab replied that he was persuaded to leave the city intact, but he must have his prisoner. She agreed, "His head shall be thrown to you over the wall." She went to the people and spoke to them "in her wisdom." Convinced, they did what was required. Joab blew the trumpet signal to send the army away, and the city was saved.

During the repair of the temple, the law book was discovered and brought to King Josiah (2 Kings 22:3–20). When the law was read, the sins and neglect of the people became clear to them. They wondered if there was any hope for the nation. Josiah sent his scribe, high priest, and close advisers to find out. They went to Huldah, the prophetess. She told them all that the Lord had spoken to her; on the basis of her message, Josiah set about stamping out all traces of idolatry.

Rizpah is an example of raw courage and tenacity (2 Sam. 21:10–14). She stayed by the slain bodies of her sons and grandsons, guarding them day and night until the rains came and King David was shamed into giving them a decent burial.

Esther is an example of a Jewish woman in an important public role. Her love of her people and her willingness to risk her life for their sake have made her a heroine everywhere her story has been read.

The longest passage of teaching material that we are sure is from a woman is found in Proverbs 31. This ideal wife is capable of prodigious achievements. She is tremendously valuable to her husband (v. 10). He has confidence in her. She makes a fine profit from her business ventures (v. 11). In the running of her prosperous household, she is involved in the manufacture of clothing for her family and servants at both the level of purchase and of sewing (vv. 13, 14, 19, 21, 22). Her long hours (vv. 15, 18) and careful supervision of the servants bring blessing and honor to her husband and to herself (vv. 23–31). This woman goes well beyond the confines of her private dwelling. She is likened to a merchant ship bringing cargo from afar (v. 14), and she is involved in real estate and agriculture (v. 16). Her activity in purchasing a field and in planting it herself is noteworthy as land was of tremendous importance to the Israelites, being an inheritance from God as well as a means of livelihood.

These examples and others such as Jochebed, Miriam, Rahab, Naomi, and Jael give strong support to the wisdom, courage, competence, and ingenuity of women in the Old Testament story.

Women in the Ministry and Teachings of Jesus

Jesus treated women as they should be treated. Dorothy Sayers summarized his attitude:

> They [women] had never known a man like this Man—there never has been such another. A prophet and teacher who never nagged at them, never flattered or coaxed or patronized; who never made arch jokes about them, never treated them either as "The women, God help us!" or "The ladies, God bless them!"; who rebuked without querulousness and praised without condescension; who took their questions and arguments seriously; who never mapped out their sphere for them, never urged them to be feminine or jeered at them for being female; who had no axe to grind and no uneasy male dignity to defend; who took them as he found them and was completely unselfconscious. There is no act, no sermon, no parable in the whole Gospel that borrows its pungency from female perversity; nobody could possibly guess from the words and deeds of Jesus that there was anything "funny" about woman's nature.[4]

Jesus treated women as people. The foundation stone of Jesus' attitude toward women was his vision of them as persons to whom and for whom he had come. He did not perceive them

---

[4]Sayers, *Unpopular Opinions*, 121–22.

primarily in terms of their sex, age, or marital status; he seems to have considered them in terms of their relation, or lack of one, to God. It is this axis which explains how Jesus was unaffected by the prejudices of his day toward the poor, the lepers, the Samaritans, the prostitutes, the tax collectors, and women in general. "For whoever does the will of my Father in heaven is my brother, and sister, and mother" (Matt. 12:50).

Jesus' encounter with the Samaritan woman in John 4 is a good example of his willingness to dismiss conventions of men which stood in opposition to his purpose. From the perspective of the rabbis of the day, the woman had three points against her: she was a Samaritan, she was a woman, and she was immoral. This nameless Samaritan woman made no effort to keep her relation to him secret but announced to all that he knew all she had done, in contrast to Nicodemus who came under cover of night.

A persistent woman came to Jesus crying out, "Lord, Son of David, have mercy on me! My daughter is suffering terribly from demon-possession" (Matt. 15:22; NIV). The Canaanites were considered unclean, and the disciples want her sent away; Jesus, however, responded to her persistence.

Luke 7:36–50 reports an incident at the home of Simon the Pharisee in which a repentant woman who was a sinner entered the dinner chamber and anointed Jesus' feet. Jesus used her as an example of faith and love. It is she, not the Pharisee, who exemplifies godly faith in action. Jesus dealt with her as a person without reference to her sex.

Mark 5:24–34 records the story of a woman who for 12 years had had a flow of blood. She had suffered much under many physicians, spent all of her money, and still was no better. In fact, she was worse. But she trusted Jesus to heal her just by touching his garment. Immediately the hemorrhage ceased. Jesus met people as individuals and responded to them according to their need whether they were lepers, Samaritans, tax collectors, or women with bleeding.

Luke 13:10–17 reports Jesus' healing of a crippled woman in a synagogue on a Sabbath day. She had been bound by Satan for 18 years. Jesus made her back straight and also called her a daughter of Abraham.

The parables portray women in natural activities. A woman kneading yeast into flour illustrates the hidden but pervasive work of the kingdom (Matt. 13:33). A woman looking for a lost coin illustrates the concern of God for lost sinners (Luke 15:8–10). Prepared and unprepared bridesmaids are examples of readiness for the Lord's return (Matt. 25:1–13). A persistent woman confronting a lazy judge teaches about the need for faithful prayer (Luke 18). And a poor widow who gives the little that she has shows that devotion is not measured by the magnitude of our gifts but the commitment of our hearts (Mark 12:41–44).

The women of Luke 8:1–3 are Jesus' traveling companions and appear to be a part of his close circle. They contributed to the support of his ministry.

In the account of the crucifixion and resurrection, Matthew and Mark comment on the presence of Mary Magdalene and Mary the mother of James the younger and Joses. Also mentioned is Salome, thought to be the mother of the sons of Zebedee (Mark 15:40; see also Matt. 27:55, 56; Mark 15:47; 16:1). Mark in his description of the women adds, "In Galilee these women had followed him and cared for his needs" (Mark 15:41; NIV). We learn of their continuing care in the account of the removal of Jesus' body after the crucifixion. Mary Magdalene and Mary the mother of James and Joses returned after the Sabbath to anoint his body, becoming the first witnesses to the resurrection (Matt. 27:61; 28:1–7). John's account notes that Jesus appeared to Mary Magdalene directly (John 20:1–18). It is ironic that Jewish law prohibited women from acting as witnesses, and yet it was women who became the first witnesses to the resurrection.

Mary the mother of Jesus is presented as a woman of faith and a follower of Jesus. She was present when Jesus performed his first miracle (John 2:1–11). Matthew 12:46–50 places her on a level with all others who do the will of God. Her Magnificat in Luke 1:46–55 is perhaps the most famous outpouring of praise in the Bible.

What can we say about Jesus' behavior toward women? Women were active workers for his kingdom and valued disciples, but the specifics of their activity are not revealed in the Gospels. We know Jesus taught women about himself, and a corollary of knowing about the Lord is witnessing to him, as did Mary Magdalene and the woman with a flow of blood.

Early Church

A large number of prominent women in the Roman Empire became Christians. Women greatly assisted in the extension of Christianity. Women, too, suffered martyrdom. They displayed no less degree of fortitude and heroism than did the men, nor did the church expect from them any inferior response.

The apostles who had watched Christ's ascension returned to Jerusalem to await the Holy Spirit (Acts 1:12–14). After the list of the apostles, we are told of another group which joined together with them in prayer—the women, Mary the mother of Jesus, and his brothers. Then Pentecost came. Peter, quoting Joel, said, "Your sons and your daughters shall prophesy, . . . and on my menservants and my maidservants in those days I will pour out my Spirit; and they shall prophesy" (Acts 2:17, 18).

Acts 5:14 says, "And more than ever believers were added to the Lord, multitudes both of men and women." In Acts 8:12, when the Gospel is taken by Philip to Samaria, we read, "But when they believed Philip as he preached good news about the kingdom of God and the name of Jesus Christ, they were baptized, both men and women."

As Paul set off on his missionary journeys, he understood the Gospel was for all persons, Jews and Gentiles, men and women. We read in Acts of women participating in church after church. In Philippi (Acts 16:13–15) Lydia, a seller of purple, became the first convert in Europe. She had a household to support. In Thessalonica (Acts 17:12), "many of them therefore believed, with not a few Greek women of high standing as well as men." In Athens (Acts 17:34) we meet Damaris. The letters of Paul reflect the same state of affairs. In Romans 16 approximately one-third of the 25 persons Paul salutes are women.

Women are fellow workers. Outstanding among the women is Priscilla. She and her husband enter the biblical narrative in Acts 18:2 as acquaintances of Paul. They sailed with Paul from Corinth to Ephesus where they worked as tentmakers. She, no less than her husband, instructed the gifted Apollos (Acts 18:24–28), made their home the setting for a house church in Ephesus and Rome (1 Cor. 16:19; Rom. 16:3–5), and was a fellow worker of Paul (Rom. 16:3, 4).

In Philippians 4:2, 3 we learn of Euodia and Syntyche. Paul warmly identifies them as persons who have labored side by side with him and whose names are in the Book of Life. Whatever quarrel there is between them needs to be resolved. Acts 21:9 mentions the four daughters of Philip the evangelist who were prophetesses. We see the activity of the early church in caring for the widows in Jerusalem (Acts 6:1) and in Joppa (Acts 9:36–43). In 1 Timothy 5:3–16 there is a lengthy discussion of provision of support for widows in need. In verse 10 a widow should be well attested for her good deeds, should have brought up children, shown hospitality, washed the feet of saints, relieved the afflicted, and devoted herself to doing good in every way.

Deaconesses

Phoebe (Rom. 16:1, 2) is the most controversial female figure in Paul's letters. Paul commended her to the Romans as a representative of the Cenchrean church who had helped many, himself among them, and asked that she be assisted as necessary. *Diakonos* is the common Greek word for "servant." In the RSV the word is translated "deaconess"; in the NIV as "servant"; and in the majority of modern English translations, the word has been translated "minister" or "deacon." The term applied to men but not to women. Phoebe served in some very special and significant capacity of service in the church, but she was not a deacon in the official sense of the term. Phoebe is called a *prostatis* in Romans 16:2. This means she was a helper, a patroness, probably in the sense that she shared her wealth with the saints at Cenchrea.

We have ample evidence of there being elders and deacons in the second-century congregations, but it is not until one gets to the Church Orders of the third century that he encounters female appointees as a part of the church organization. This is far too late to claim scriptural authority for the arrangement.

In the third century[5] and in the fourth century,[6] the function of the deaconess is described. She was to assist the clergy in the baptism of women, minister to the poor and sick, particularly women, and help in the instruction of female catechumens; she was to act as an intermediary between the clergy and the women in the congregation. She was also to visit women in pagan households. She did not preach and teach publicly. It would seem that the office of deacon is an office for men only, but at the same time women are to be involved in the diaconal or service area. There is no clear scriptural evidence for women occupying the office of deacon.

Galatians 3:28; 1 Corinthians 11; 14; 1 Timothy 2

Galatians 3:28 is the cornerstone text for women's liberation movements. This verse addresses the question, "Who may become a son of God and on what basis?" The context is faith in contrast to law as the means of salvation. Paul's point is that without respect to nationality, social status, or sex, all are justified by faith (v. 24), all are children of God (v. 26), all have put on Christ (v. 27), all are heirs according to promise (v. 29). The point of Galatians 3:28 is not equality in Christ but oneness in Christ. Peter shares Paul's view when in 1 Peter 3:1–7 he speaks of the unity of the male and female marriage partners as "joint heirs of the grace of life."

The words *subordination* and *submission* have fallen into disrepute in our time. But the principle of subordination pervades the universe. Jesus was subject to Joseph and Mary (Luke 2:51). Paul says that God has subjected all things under Christ (1 Cor. 15:27), and Peter says that this includes angels, authorities, and powers (1 Pet. 3:22). God the Father is excepted from this submission, but ultimately the Son himself will be subject to the Father (1 Cor. 15:28). If everything is under Christ, the church is subject to him (Eph. 5:24). In James 4:7 we read that we should submit ourselves to God. In the church the younger

[5]*Didascalia* 16.
[6]*Apostolic Constitutions* 8.28.

ones are to submit to the older ones (1 Pet. 5:5); the flock is to submit to the shepherds (Heb. 13:17); each Christian is to be subject to every other Christian out of reverence for Christ (Eph. 5:21). In the social order, submission is to be given to every human ordinance (1 Pet. 2:13). Wives are to be subject to their husbands (Eph. 5:22; Col. 3:18). Women in the assembly are to learn in all submissiveness, and they are not to teach men (1 Tim. 2:11, 12). In the Timothy passage, Paul grounds his case on the created order: Adam was first formed, then Eve, with the additional thought that it was Eve who was deceived, not Adam (1 Tim. 2:13, 14).

At times when God's unchanging Word clashes with man's changing culture, the passage in 1 Peter 1:24, 25 reminds us that the Word of the Lord stands forever. Passages in 1 Timothy 2:11–15 and 1 Corinthians 14:33b–37 are not illustrations, but commands. The reasons given are not time-bound, historically and culturally relative arguments that grow out of or apply only to the first century. Rather, they describe the way God created man and woman and the relationships that God commanded that they should sustain to one another.

Older women are called on to teach and train young women in reference to their responsibilities to their husbands and children (Titus 2:3, 4). When Priscilla and Aquila, that inseparable wife-and-husband team, expounded to Apollos the way of God more accurately (Acts 18:26), they took him aside; they did not correct him in the synagogue. Lois and Eunice taught young Timothy from childhood (2 Tim. 1:5; 3:15). A mother's teaching may influence the whole direction of a person's life, as it did for Timothy.

Paul's antidote for the confusion in the Corinthian church is that all things are to be done for edification (1 Cor. 14:26). In 1 Corinthians 12:7 Paul, in the section on gifts, says, "To each is given the manifestation of the Spirit for the common good." Chapter 13, that most marvelous exposition on love, is central to Paul's thought. If our overriding concern for the church is edification or building up the body, we will not spend our time and energy on particular cases, either in practice or in our fertile imaginations, which the Bible simply does not address.

In the role of women in the practice of the New Testament church, then, we see that women were integral members, attended worship, sang, were taught, learned of the faith, and shared it with others. They also played an active part in the daily life of the community, teaching one another and caring for the poor. In the mainstream of the church, however, women are taught to stay at home and to be submissive to their husbands. Their duties are within the house, not outside. There are no female apostles, evangelists, or elders. There are no examples of women engaged in public teaching.

Women in Leadership Positions Today

We need first to look at definitions. I think we normally have no problem identifying who women are. Yet in a Los Angeles airport this past summer, I was hard put to know whether I was looking at a woman or a man. Her head was shaved on one side, and the other side was colored purple.

The term *leadership*—the dictionary definition is "the office or position of a leader," and a leader is "a person who leads"—is given to one who guides someone along the way, especially by going in advance.

The church, the whole body of Christians, is composed of those who are called out not just on Sunday at 11:00 and 6:00, on Wednesday night at 7:30, and on Tuesday morning at 10:00 when many ladies' Bible classes meet. Today we are not talking about what is done in the confines of the building, but we are looking at what Christians can and should be doing wherever they are. In my Outreach class on Sunday morning, I have Lucy Alexander, a divorced mother with four children. Lucy takes part in all church activities. One day she related this story. By mistake she received double her supply of food stamps. She said at first she thought how lucky she was. She needed them, and here they were. But then she said she had recently read an article in *Power for Today* that if you are not a Christian all of the time, you are not a Christian any of the time. She said, "I knew what I had to do. I got on the bus and returned the stamps that were not due me." That is church work, and it's outside the building.

Some Principles of Leadership That Need to Be Observed

1. The most crucial principle is that of servanthood. Six times in the Synoptics we read that the greatest must be the servant (the least) of all (Matt. 20:26–28; 23:11; Mark 9:35; 10:43–45; Luke 9:48; 22:26, 27). Jesus was the greatest leader of all; he simply said, "Follow me." Sometimes he didn't say anything; he taught, healed, and lived in such a way that people followed. He was the greatest servant of all.

2. No one makes us so aware of the value of one person as Jesus in his parables of the lost sheep, when 99 were not lost; the lost coin, when 9 were not lost; and the lost boy.

The Laubach Literacy Program has as its theme, "Each one teach one." If we look at the 27 million adults in America who can't read or write, we may ask, "What difference will my teaching one person to read make?" A Laubach tutor tells this story:

> An old man walking down a Spanish beach at dawn saw what he thought to be a dancer in the distance. The dancer, a young man, was running across the sand rhythmically bending down to pick up a stranded starfish and throwing it far out into the sea. "Why," said the old man, "do you spend so much energy doing what is a waste of time?" The young man explained that the stranded starfish would die if left until the morning sun. "But there must be thousands of miles of beach and millions of starfish. How can your effort make any difference?" The young man looked down at the small starfish in his hand and as he threw it to safety said, "It makes a difference to this one."[7]

Most of what Jesus did was with one or just a few. He moved through a throng of people and reacted to the timid touch of a needy woman.

3. We must rid ourselves of the mindset that some services

---

[7]Gupta, "Valedictory," 8, col. 3.

are superior and others inferior. Paul dispels that concept in his graphic comparison of the church to the human body. There are different functions in the church but not categories of superior and inferior services. I don't think saving foreign stamps for International Bible Correspondence School or getting together a group of women to write letters to missionaries or taking that nourishing meal to a shut-in or washing and mending clothes for the clothes closet are little things. I recently read of a psychology professor who turned janitor on his retirement. His response to the curious was, "It doesn't matter, just so the school goes on." That attitude should be the pattern of thought from which all Christians operate.

I noticed that the articles in the July-August 1987 *Christian Woman* were written by a professor of pediatrics at the University of Tennessee, a curriculum specialist for the Alabama Department of Mental Health, an instructor at Western Michigan University, a radio talk-show host, a ladies' Bible class teacher, a professor and director of the Dietetics Consortium for the University of North Carolina, a food writer for the *Nashville Banner*, a junior high speech and drama teacher, a medical director for American General Life, and a homemaker. These are all women, and not one of the occupations is more important than another.

4. We must leave to each Christian the freedom to choose that service that he or she may wish to perform and recognize that it may be different from the one I choose. Because I have a special interest in the Outreach program, I must not expect everyone else to have that interest. This is easier said than done. I have a friend who has a burning desire to enroll every member of the congregation in the work of World Bible School.

5. Finally, there is a limit to the services we can do and do well. I have never thought it a virtue to volunteer for every service with the result that all of the tasks are haphazardly performed. We are limited by responsibilities in the home and by children, by jobs, by physical health, by energy, and by time. Jesus did not heal every blind, deaf, lame, and paralyzed person. He did grow weary and resorted to drawing away from the crowds. As one writer has aptly said, "We are not meant to die on every cross."

A Woman's Involvement in Ministry

In my home congregation, we have recently adopted a rather complex Involvement Ministry system patterned after the Richland Hills church in Fort Worth, which I suppose has been a leader in this area. Omitted, however, from this list is the ministry which I want to first speak to—that of homemaker. Titus 2:4, 5 and 1 Timothy 5:14 support the woman's responsibility for home management with the reason given that the Word of God will not be discredited. Carl Spain has said that we have put down work in the home as not being church work.[8] A woman, however, is not limited to working only at home. The virtuous wife of Proverbs 31 illustrates the meaning of home worker. Her activities include travel, commerce, agriculture, and charity; but she does not neglect her household. She sees that the needs of her husband and children are met.

Phyllis Alexander worked in the library for me while her husband was a student at the Graduate School. She is an artist, has three children, and is a homemaker. I saw her recently, and she said, "A homemaker is all I have ever wanted to be." She does her art work at home. Her daughter told her, "I'll be so glad when I grow up and can stay at home like you." Phyllis is providing leadership in that most important of all tasks—homemaking.

The church fellowship hall is a poor substitute (although a necessary one) for showing hospitality. John Mark's mother opened her house as a gathering place for prayer (Acts 12:12). Lydia urged her hospitality upon Paul and his company when he went to Macedonia (Acts 16:15). Homes provide places for Bible studies, entertainment of Christian workers, and entertainment of lonely people. We still need to invite those Jesus said we should—the poor, the maimed, the lame, the blind (Luke 14:12–14).

The following 21 major areas of involvement represent over 200 tasks. There isn't a single major area in which women can-

---

[8]Source unknown. Carl Spain (d. 1990) was a professor of Bible at Abilene Christian University, Abilene, TX. http://www.acu.edu/centennial/profiles/carl_spain.html (accessed March 23, 2009).

not be involved. No committee structure is indicated in the Bible; the committee itself is an expedient. I have chosen some of the tasks to list under each one of these major areas:

Beautiful Grounds and Buildings. Unless you have a landscape artist in your congregation, I daresay that women know more about flowers, shrubs, and tree planting than men do.

Being There. This group visits delinquent members, the hospitalized, shut-ins, nursing homes, elderly, bereaved—and not just once.

Financial Management. With the number of women graduating from colleges with accounting majors, I am more willing to trust some of the budget preparation and financial counseling to them than to someone who is untrained in these areas.

First Impressions. These serve as greeters before and after services, they visit newcomers, and they give baptismal assistance. In the early church, this was one of the primary functions of women.

Good Samaritans. Food and clothing is distributed. Our senior high group has been involved in delivering Meals on Wheels, and I have two friends who deliver meals every Monday morning.

Graphics. This group works on the church bulletin and directories. Some of our women may now be seen carrying cameras to capture meaningful events in the life of the church.

Junior High, Senior High, Single Young Adults. All of these age levels have girls and women participating in their programs. One woman whose husband is a doctor with an unpredictable schedule completely decorated the senior high room and has spent countless hours counseling those in this group.

We Need You. These coordinate various volunteer needs. They are people who at a moment's notice will give up a planned schedule for the day to transport a sick person to the doctor, will help with a special mailout in the office, will make phone calls in emergency situations.

Keeping Up with the Spiritual Family. Our three secretaries have computers and can tell you in a moment about a person's attendance record.

Life Groups. Every member of the congregation belongs to a Life Group. Who takes food, sends cards, makes phone calls, and visits the members of the Life Group? Women.

Love Feasts. Two women in our congregation provide leadership, whether it's a tea for a new bride, a baby shower, a ham breakfast for blood donors, or a full-blown fellowship meal for 900 people. Every time you see a punch bowl, you know that one woman, Lyda, can't be far behind. I am amazed at how smoothly all of these affairs are carried out.

New Horizons. This committee evaluates the use of buildings, including community use of buildings. Many church buildings in Memphis house elementary grades and care centers for Harding Academy.

Outreach. These members visit in Outreach homes, prepare the Bus Journal, and help with out-of-class activities.

People Helpers. Dietrich Bonhoeffer said that "the first service one owes to others in the fellowship consists in listening to them."[9] Counseling the divorced, the depressed, and the discouraged takes time and patience. Some congregations have full-time women counselors on their staffs.

Reaching Out. This ministry includes home Bible studies and World Bible School.

Spiritual Helpers. These members serve as big brothers and sisters and plan women's retreats.

Strong Family Beginnings. Care of children and purchasing and maintenance of nursery equipment are some of their services. Recently two classes, one on Sunday morning and one on Wednesday night, have been started for new mothers.

Tender Loving Care. This ministry provides classes for the deaf, both beginning and advanced, interpreting for the deaf, and literacy and tutorial programs.

Teaching and Learning. Janice Baker, a Baltimore public school teacher, recently said, "If you love some area of knowledge and you'd love to bring other people around to thinking about what you love, then teaching is a great job." If you love the Bible and you would love to bring other people around to thinking about what you love, then teaching the Bible is a great job.

Many of these activities of teaching and learning will be

---

[9]Bonhoeffer, *Life Together*, 97.

within the confines of the church building—teaching, supervising, working in the library or media center, planning teacher workshops, editing Bible school newsletters, and arranging attractive bulletin boards. Outside the building and in vocations women have chosen, teaching and learning is a daily activity. I note that Dr. Joyce Hardin has been named to the position of assistant academic dean at Lubbock Christian College. She has written *Three Steps Behind*, a history of her family's missionary years in Korea, and has recently written a missions curriculum for fifth and sixth grades. Betty Bates, one of my former students, for many years served as academic dean of Harding Academy of Memphis, the largest private school in the country. Although I have recruited two young men to pursue librarianship, I have been more successful in steering young women into this special interest field. We would be the poorer if it were not for Sandra Humphrey's editing *Christian Woman*, Joy McMillon's journalism skills in serving as managing editor for *Christian Chronicle*, Billie Silvey as associate editor of *20th Century Christian*, Helen Young as consulting editor for the same magazine, Emily Lemley as co-editor of *Power for Today*, Bobbie Holley as editor of *Mission*, and many other women who serve as staff writers for other church publications.

We all need role models. In the teaching area, I know of no woman who can better serve as a role model than Dr. Marie Wilmeth, head of Abilene Christian University's Home Economics Department from 1953 until her retirement in 1974. Wherever she worked, she left a trail of giving and sacrifice, whether it was as a county home demonstration agent showing rural citizens how to grow, prepare, and can food and how to take care of their homes and themselves, or guiding students through their programs of study at Abilene Christian University.

At Abilene she knew that some children somewhere in that town went to bed hungry. She called a local elementary school and told a school administrator, "I'd just like to do something special for them." The official led her to a poverty-stricken family with seven children. Marie arranged to pay for the children's school lunches. She took them to church, entertained them at basketball games, and brought them into her home. She took the mother grocery shopping and taught her to buy nutritious food for her children. In 1953 she built a modest home and began taking in needy students. She kept about 30 students altogether. The first girl to live with her was Dr. Marianna Rasco, who later became chairman of the Home Economics Department at Abilene. Because of Wilmeth's frugal and unselfish life, she was able to give the school $15,000 in 1964 to build the Child Development Center.

In recognition of her lifetime of service to students and to needy children wherever she found them, the university established the Marie Wilmeth Endowed Scholarship for Home Economics. Dr. Rasco, her former student, noticing her age (she was nearly 80 then), said it was time to honor Marie. She said, "Somehow the more I thought about honoring Dr. Wilmeth, it had to be something that would last. And buildings don't last. We have to look at what her life has been a testimony to." The scholarship will continue to do what she has done all of her life—help others. At this point, more than $100,000 has been raised by her friends and former students.

Worship Enrichment. This group makes video tapes, has special occasion singers, does hymn book maintenance, plans children's worship, and has a caroling ministry. We have two current-day Fanny Crosbys in our congregation.

World View. Women have had an important part in mission work since the first century when Priscilla and her husband explained the faith to Apollos (Acts 18:24–28). Today women outnumber men on the mission field. The disparity in numbers continues to grow because more and more single women are serving overseas. It is appropriate for women to serve on missions committees and not just as secretaries. In our own time, Irene Johnson Gatewood has been the woman missionary known to most of us. In one newsletter she told about attending a board meeting of the camp she started many years ago. A group from Frankfurt was also there. She wrote, "Imagine my great joy when out of the 12 who were there, 10 had been in my kindergarten. Most of them had sat on my lap as little children, and I taught all of them to pray, sing, and learn the Bible. Now they are Christians, planning their own devotions, teaching others the Bible, helping in camp and church work, doing personal work, even converting their own parents."

There are other Irenes now. They are serving as nurses or other medical assistants, teachers in missionary operated schools, and social workers. A Christian couple from Florida has established a fund at Harding University—The Student Missionary Loan / Grant Fund for Single Women—and many university students have been awarded grants to work in places such as Haiti, Costa Rica, and Scotland. *Strategy*, a mission bulletin of the ACU Center for Missions Education, in its June-August 1986 issue gave reports from four single women who worked as Mark apprentices for two years. Another report was given by a widow who, after the death of her husband and with no formal training in missions, served in a work with abandoned women in Costa Rica. She wrote that the language proved to be such a problem for her that the only way she could teach was by example. So she began teaching the women to make things to sell in order to augment their income. Men evaluating her work said that her work was as important as any program in the congregation.

Becky Amole, a graduate of Harding Graduate School, worked with Health Talents International in Belize. Among her activities were assisting in mobile clinics, holding Bible studies, teaching health education, working with the local congregation, teaching literacy classes for adults, tutoring children in school, counseling teenage girls, teaching older women crafts, and coordinating a month-long VBS. I would challenge any person—man or woman—to meet Becky's schedule.

Missionary wives around the world, in addition to being homemakers and mothers, are doing many of the tasks that Becky and other single women perform. A crucial ministry of the wives is the constant encouragement they give to their husbands.

Betty Paden went to Italy in 1949 and along with her husband, Harold, helped establish the beachhead from which the work there has expanded into all of that nation. She was a missionary in her own right. She studied diligently, and her Italian became excellent. She worked with ladies' classes and with children. For 17 years they labored until a malignancy forced them to come to America for treatment. She died in 1967.

Her husband paid the following tribute to his wife:

> She was not attached to things in this world, neither asked for new clothes nor comforts. Here she suffered many a winter's storm with an ill-fed and ill-clad post-war Italian people just to witness for Christ where there was none. I recall mid-winter, 1949, when her feet were frostbitten because we had no heat at Frascati; when her teeth decayed when she was carrying "Hoppy" because there was no milk after the war; when she slept on straw mattresses without springs without ever complaining; when she washed our clothes by hand for years and later cried because the old washing machine wouldn't work nor could be repaired; when she walked miles to teach a ladies' Bible class; when the sad news of her grandparents' death reached Italy (they had raised Betty from the time she was three); when she braved a journey over 9,000 miles with three pre-school children all alone; when she continued to teach her little Italian children in her kindergarten for months even though she already had fever; ad infinitum. Yet she never complained once.[10]

You probably have your own list of heroines, but we desperately need these role models who in every generation show us by their lives that there is a higher ground on which to live.

Conclusion

We need to remind ourselves periodically that the Great Commission did not have a termination date; it is still in force. Whether it's teaching your own child in the home, teaching informally your next-door neighbor across a kitchen table, participating in organized personal work programs, going on campaigns, serving as a missionary here or overseas—wherever—we

---

[10]Source unknown. Harold Paden was a missionary in Italy along with his brother, Cline Paden. http://en.wikipedia.org/wiki/Cline_Paden (accessed March 23, 2009).

must be telling the Good News to somebody who has not yet heard it.

In our study we have seen women at work from biblical times to the present. We have seen there is no shortage of good works to be done by women. The only question I need ask myself is, "When the Lord comes back, will he find that I have been a faithful steward of what he has entrusted to me?"

[Presented at White Station Church of Christ, Memphis, Tennessee, no date; Wooddale Church of Christ, Memphis, Tennessee, no date.]

13

TRANSLATING THE BIBLE

You may have often wondered, "What would a man give in exchange for his life?" The answer may take many forms; but for John Wyclif, William Tyndale, John Rogers, and others involved in the early translation of God's Word into English, the answer was, "The English Bible." We owe an unpayable debt to these men who gave their lives to make available the Bible in the English language. With the Bible in its multiple translations available in almost every home, it is difficult for today's reader to conceive of a time when the English Bible was a rarity.

In this century the demand for a more appropriate Bible in contemporary English has so far produced over 75 translations. There are three basic answers to the question, "Why so many Bible translations?" The first is the discovery of new biblical manuscripts resulting in a more accurate text. Erasmus, who in 1516 gave us the first printed Greek New Testament, had only six manuscripts available to him. Now there are over 5,000 manuscripts available to scholars in New Testament textual criticism. The Dead Sea Scrolls, discovered in the Wilderness of Judea by twin Bedouin boys in 1947, gave us our earliest known copy of the Hebrew Book of Isaiah. All of the Old Testament books except Esther are represented in this find. The second reason is advancement in biblical scholarship. The various forms of pottery or dishes used by the people in biblical days are known to us through excavations. Since it is now known that candles were unknown in biblical days, modern translations use "lampstand" or "lamp." The discovery of numerous secular manuscripts has increased our understanding of biblical Greek, and we now know that the Greek of the New Testament was that used by the average man throughout the Roman Empire. The inscriptional material recovered by archaeologists has provided important helps in understanding the Hebrew vocabulary since comparison can be made with other ancient related languages. Among the most familiar inscriptional discoveries are the famous Moabite Stone, written by Mesha, king of Moab (2 Kings 3:4), first known in 1868, and the Siloam inscription found in 1880 in the tunnel of the water system thought to be that mentioned in 2 Kings 20:20. The third reason for new translations is that of language changes. Words are vehicles of thought, and the passing of time automatically renders obsolete many words that once were in acceptable usage. The *Oxford English Dictionary* has just completed its supplement to the original edition with 75,000 entries of words which have come into use in this present century.

The aims of all translations have been noble. To see how well they have lived up to their aims requires a detailed examination of the text from which the translation was made, the exegesis of the text, cultural features, and kind of translation (whether literal or one modified by sentence structure, context, and style). Omitted from this discussion are recent Jewish and Roman Catholic translations. Paraphrases (*The Living Bible*; now called *The Book*) have also been omitted since this category does not claim to be a translation but a restatement of the author's thoughts using different words.

The King James Version, 1611

Perhaps most of us who were first taught to love the Bible were taught through the King James Version (KJV). The literary beauty of this translation remains unchallenged after three and one-half centuries. Authorized by King James I of England, the Bible was to be a revision of existing translations and was to be done by "54 learned men." The version we read today is not the version of 1611 since this Bible has been revised many times. An extensive revision was published in 1762 and another in 1769, and it, in general, represents the version as it is known today. Although this first edition did not enjoy a kind reception, it was finally accepted because it was a superior translation to anything else then available. Its major handicap is that the English language has changed so much over the years that today's young people find that it is difficult to understand. A book by Ronald Bridges and Luther A. Weigle has articles on 827 KJV words and phrases which have become archaic or have changed their meanings so that they no longer give the sense intended by the translators.[1] The translators of 1611 did a remarkably good job in their day, but the greatest advances in archaeological discovery in the Middle East and in understanding of biblical languages have taken place in the present century.

American Standard Version, 1901

This version is a revision of the English Revised Version, 1881–85, the initiative for which came through the Church of England but included an interdenominational group of translators. The translators did not propose a new translation but only a revision of the KJV, seeking to clarify meaning and to attain greater uniformity in translating parallel passages. Cooperating with the English revisers was an American committee. The initial reception of the English Revised Version went beyond expectation. The *Chicago Tribune* reprinted the entire New Testament in its May 22, 1881, edition, employing for the purpose 92 compositors and 5 correctors and completing the whole book in 12 hours.

The American committee realized a need for publishing a version that would incorporate changes they thought were necessary and which were not included in the English Revised Version. The American Standard Version (ASV), 1901, is the result of their labors and is considered to be a superior translation to the English Version. Maintaining a greater consistency of translation where the Hebrew or Greek word had the same meaning, the ASV is a meticulously literal translation. Certain archaisms of vocabulary and diction were dropped. This version represents an important step in the progress of Bible translation and has been widely used for college and seminary study.

---

[1]Bridges and Weigle, *The Bible Word Book*.

Revised Standard Version, 1946, 1952

The New Testament of the Revised Standard Version (RSV) was published in 1946, the Old Testament in 1952. The RSV Bible Committee is an ongoing committee, and its annual meetings are devoted to a study of new manuscripts and ways in which the original text may best be rendered. A second edition of the New Testament was issued in 1977, and the second edition of the Old Testament was published in 1989. In both Testaments the archaic second personal pronoun *Thou* and its correlative forms *Thee*, *Thy*, and *Thine* were eliminated. This change more accurately reflects the usage of Hebrew and Greek texts since the original languages make no distinction between address to God and to a person. Also eliminated were the corresponding verbal endings -est (-edst, -st, -t).

The translators saw their task as "the revision of the present American Standard Bible in the light of the results of modern scholarship, this revision to be designed for use in public and private worship, and to be in the direction of the simple, classic style of the King James Version."[2] An effort has been made to bring punctuation, quotation marks, paragraphing, and capitalization into accordance with modern usage. The text of prose passages is arranged in sense paragraphs as in the ASV instead of being broken up into separate verses as in the KJV. The RSV has extended the practice of the ASV in printing poetic passages in poetic form.

New American Standard Bible, 1971

The New American Standard Bible (NASB), a publication of the Lockman Foundation, states in its Preface, "The producers of this translation were imbued with the conviction that interest in the American Standard Version should be renewed and increased." The twofold purpose of its Editorial Board was "to adhere as closely as possible to the original languages of the Holy Scriptures and to make the translation in a fluent and readable

---

[2]Weigle, *An Introduction*, 11.

style according to current English usage." Textual, translational, explanatory, and doctrinal notes have been provided.

As admirable as are the goals of the Editorial Board, the translation does not consistently follow its announced procedures. The NASB remains the most literal recent translation, but it does not reach its stated goal of putting the Scriptures in a "fluent and readable style according to current English usage."

New International Version, 1978

Sponsored by the New York Bible Society International, the New International Version (NIV) is a translation by a committee composed of 115 scholars representing more than a dozen evangelical groups. The NIV is a new translation made directly from the original languages and is in no sense a revision of any of the other English versions.

The Preface states:

> They have striven for more than word-for-word translation. Because thought patterns and syntax differ from language to language, faithful communication of the meaning of the writers of the Bible demand frequent modifications in sentence structure and constant regard for the contextual meanings of words.

Edwin Palmer, executive secretary of the NIV, gave as the four goals of the translation: accuracy, clarity, contemporary idiom, and dignity.

The NIV has enjoyed a wide popularity among evangelicals, and the prediction by some reviewers is that it is one of the few current translations that will endure.

Good News Bible (Today's English Version) 4th Edition, 1976

This translation was prepared by the American Bible Society to meet the needs of new readers and for educated persons who are not familiar with the archaisms of early versions. The revisers did not try to make a literal translation but asked the question, "What does the biblical text mean?" Then they tried to find the equivalent meaning in contemporary English. Because of its readability, this translation has been widely used on the mission field and by readers with a limited level of formal education.

The text is illustrated with line drawings, and the helps in the GNB are outstanding—notes, word list, maps, subject index, introductions, and outlines for each book.

Conclusion

Finally, two conclusions may be drawn from this brief overview of selected translations: (1) There is no single perfect translation; each one has its strengths and weaknesses, and (2) there is no seriously unreliable translation; basic Christian truths can be found in all of these translations. The crying need, dear reader, is to take up your Bible and devote yourself to its reading, study, meditation, and obedience.

[Originally published in *Christian Woman* 3 (Jan./Feb. 1987): 15–19. Reprinted with permission, Gospel Advocate Co., Nashville, Tennessee.]

THE WAY IT IS

"Our state is not so important. What is crucial is that we resolve to be God's person whatever our state—teenager, young adult, middle-aged adult, older adult, single, married, widowed. I can serve God whatever my state if I believe he will fulfill his purpose for me."

Annie May Alston Lewis

Photo by Rebecca J. Johnson, Jackson, Tennessee

Annie May Alston Lewis
June 23, 2000

14

Whatever Our State We Will Serve Him

Because our state may change by the day (sometimes very suddenly and unexpectedly), the particular state we are in is not terribly important. Except in cases of sudden death, often by accident, in most families one partner will precede the other partner to the grave. Lynn Caine has written a book entitled *Widow,* and in chapter 9 she has as her first sentence "Now I had a new role. Widow."[1] Before the introduction to the book, she quotes Edna St. Vincent Millay's poem "Lament":

> Life must go on,
> And the dead be forgotten;
> Life must go on,
> Though good men die;
> Anne, eat your breakfast;
> Dan, take your medicine;
> Life must go on;
> I forget just why.[2]

Although Jesus honored marriage in his ministry, again and again he asserted that full, complete, dedicated service is possible apart from earthly relationships. The single woman has problems, but so does everyone else. Most of her problems are simply human problems not specifically rising out of her marital status. Frank O'Malley of Notre Dame, a dedicated teacher and

---

[1]Caine, *Widow*, 73.
[2]Millay, "Lament," 65.

bachelor, said, "Whether you get married or not, you live to regret it"[3]—a wry way of saying that every kind of life has its difficulties. Paul Tournier has a chapter in his book *A Place for You* entitled "Our Places Change,"[4] and so they do.

The status of one of my very close friends changed this past year. She said in a visit during Christmas, "I've decided I'm probably going to spend the rest of my life in this apartment, so I had the superintendent of maintenance come and drive all the nails I want in the walls." Then in less than three months, she called to say, "Annie May, I'm going to get married." I think the change in her status was as much a surprise to her as it was to everyone else. A former college roommate had died, and she was marrying her former roommate's husband. In the marriage she also acquired two children.

The biblical story of Ruth brings to mind a number of different changes in state. Naomi, a wife and mother when she goes to the country of Moab, returns to the land of Judah without her husband and her sons. In Ruth 1:19 the women said, "Is this Naomi?" She said to them, "Do not call me Naomi, call me Mara, for the Almighty has dealt very bitterly with me. I went away full, and the LORD has brought me back empty. Why call me Naomi, when the LORD has afflicted me and the Almighty has brought calamity upon me?" (Ruth 1:20, 21). The change in her status was from pleasant to bitter. In the same story, we see the role of Ruth change from that of widow to wife and mother, and Naomi becomes a grandmother. According to Ruth 4:17, "The women of the neighborhood gave him a name, saying, 'A son has been born to Naomi.' They named him Obed; he was the father of Jesse, the father of David."

Our state is not so important. What is crucial is that we resolve to be God's person whatever our state—teenager, young adult, middle-aged adult, older adult, single, married, widowed. The

---

[3]Source unknown. Frank O'Malley (1909–1974) taught classes on modern Catholic writers, Catholic philosophy in literature, and the philosophy of literature at the University of Notre Dame, Notre Dame, IN. http://ethicscenter.nd.edu/inspires/fomalley.shtml (accessed March 23, 2009).

[4]Tournier, *A Place for You*, 53–65.

age and the marital status are secondary factors.

I am not interested in listing off specific acts you can do. Every one of you could come up with a list a mile long of services that you know need to be performed without any committee assignment. I am, however, very much interested in some biblical principles that will make you want to be involved whatever and wherever the need.

Contentment in Our State at Any Given Time

The Shunammite woman of 2 Kings 4:8–13 is a giver; she is so hospitable that she urges Elisha to eat with her every time he passes her house. She needs no man's favor. When Elisha asks, "What is to be done for you?" she replies, "I dwell among my own people."

Paul said that he had "learned, in whatever state I am, to be content" (Phil. 4:11). Contentment isn't a state in which we are born or which we inherit or which we come to have by our surroundings. We *learn* it. And no learning is easy. In 2 Corinthians 6:10 he speaks of having nothing and yet possessing everything.

Jeremiah Burroughs describes Christian contentment as "that sweet, inward, quiet, gracious frame of spirit, which freely submits to and delights in God's wise and fatherly disposal in every condition."[5]

Wives are reminded in 1 Peter 3:4, "Let [yours] be the hidden person of the heart with the imperishable jewel of a gentle and quiet spirit, which in God's sight is very precious."

God's Purpose for Me

Look at the St. Vincent Millay poem again:

Anne, eat your breakfast;
Dan, take your medicine;
Life must go on;
I forget just why.

---

[5]Burroughs, *Rare Jewel*, 19.

If you believe that the Lord will fulfill his purpose for you, then you won't forget why life must go on. Read Psalm 57:2: "I cry to God Most High, to God who fulfils his purpose *for me*" (italics mine). Or read Psalm 138:8: "The LORD will fulfil his purpose *for me*" (italics mine). Job says to God, "I know that thou canst do all things, and that no purpose of thine can be thwarted" (Job 42:2). Paul, in Romans 8:28, said, "In everything God works for good with those who love him, who are called according to his purpose." Paul had dreamed of planting Christianity in distant places where the name of Christ was unknown; but when he found himself surrounded by prison walls, he was happy that he could pray, write, and teach.

Always God's purpose is filled with compassion and mercy (Jas. 5:11). François Fénelon said, "From the moment you wish nothing more according to your own judgment, and that you wish everything which God wishes without reserve, you will have no longer so many uneasy returns and reflections to make over what concerns you."[6] He has a purpose for my life as much as he did for the lives of Sarah, Rachel, Deborah, Mary, and Dorcas.

Waiting on God is an important aspect of God's purpose. "Wait on the LORD" is a constant refrain in the Psalms (27:14; 37:34; 40:1; 130:5), and it is a necessary phrase. It is hard to wait for God. He has eternity to accomplish his purpose, and our concern is for the present time.

God Knows Me

In a family with several children, the mother knows the dispositions, the temperaments, the attitudes, the moods, the abilities of each child. No mother likes for comparisons to be made among her children because she recognizes these differences and in love deals with each different child.

But God knows these differences better than any mother can. He knows when I get up or sit down, he is acquainted with all of my ways, and he knows my words before I speak (Ps. 139:1–6 and

---

[6]Fénelon, *Christian Perfection*, 90–91.

13–18). He knows all men and "needed no one to bear witness of man; for he himself knew what was in man" (John 2:25). During the course of daily life, we may easily forget God. Our lives are varied, but he knows every activity, every word, and every intent of the heart even when we do not know ourselves. Joe Hacker, former head of the Bible Department at Harding University, once said, "I am graven on the palms of his hands. I am never out of his mind. There is not a moment when his eye is off me or his attention distracted from me and no moment when his care falters."[7]

How I Can Serve God Whatever My Status

I would like to suggest six areas in which I can serve God whatever my status if I believe he will fulfill his purpose for me.

1. Be an example.

God sets every person down in a network of relationships where he must be some kind of link between the generations and, whether he knows it or not, leave his particular touch on the lives of those around him. We don't very easily learn by listening to someone giving instruction; we're constantly saying, "Show me." Recently, my library assistant and I were working on a listing in correct form for our journals for a computer printout. Even before reading instructions, we told our vendor, "Do a sample for us."

One of the most touching stories of the power of example was reported in the Memphis newspaper. Joseph Hardy Miller, a 17-year-old Central High student, president of the student body, son of a neurologist, grandson of a well-known Baptist preacher, was appointed commissioner of sanitation at Central High School when he was a freshman. One of his duties was to see that the cafeteria was clean. After two hospitalizations and surgery for a

---

[7]Hacker (speech, Harding Graduate School of Religion, Memphis, TN, n.d.). Used by permission. Email from Joe Hacker, Searcy, AR, to Don Meredith, Memphis, TN, August 29, 2007.

malignancy, the principal found him stacking trays in the cafeteria. "The students have gotten messy while I was gone. I thought if they saw me doing this, they would be better."

God knew there was no power like that of example, so he sent Jesus in order that we could actually see him with the woman taken in adultery, with the woman at the well, with the woman in Simon's house. If it were not for this last incident, how could we know that love grows out of forgiveness?

Why do you think we have Hebrews 11? The Bible gives definitions of faith—but we can't fully know what faith is until we see Abraham leave his home, not knowing where he was going, just because God said for him to; or Abraham ready to offer Isaac, his only son; or Moses leave Egypt and not be afraid; or Rahab protect the spies. But these accounts seem far away and long ago.

Is it possible for us to be a modern-day example to our students in school, in Bible study, to our family, our friends, our associates at work? We talk a lot about our contemporary world and its culture to which we must adapt, but what this contemporary world would take note of is plain Christian living.

2. Really believe with Paul that you are a debtor to all men.

Paul was indebted to Aquila and Priscilla. "Greet Prisca and Aquila, my fellow workers in Christ Jesus, who risked their necks for my life, to whom not only I but also all the churches of the Gentiles give thanks; greet also the church in their house" (Rom. 16:3–5b). "Aquila and Prisca, together with the church in their house, send you hearty greetings in the Lord" (1 Cor. 16:19). They were some of the earliest personal workers with Apollos but were also active in their church life (Acts 18).

Once when Jim Bill McInteer was asked why he continues his strenuous schedule, he gave a one-word answer—debt. The Lord has been so kind. It takes a lifetime to thank him. Then we need an eternity to praise him.

Part of God's purpose for us is that we teach his truth—whether it's in kindergarten, summer camps, a Bible study in the home, or wherever we can find people who have not yet been told of his grace.

3. Be steadfast.

"Be steadfast, immovable, always abounding in the work of the Lord" (1 Cor. 15:58). "And let us not grow weary in well-doing" (Gal. 6:9). You can name your own list of Christian services and endeavors which had no difficulty getting started with all kinds of promotion and fanfare. How many times have we heard, "I'm excited about . . ."? From mission work abroad, to mission work here in difficult places, to ministry to long-neglected groups of people, the ministry begins with excitement. Then we grow weary in our visitation and benevolent work. We grow tired of giving our energy and time to a program of work that everybody else, including perhaps church leaders, has lost interest in; we decide to give up too.

Irene Johnson did essentially the same work for more than 35 years in Germany. She was involved in teaching children's classes, teaching others to teach, visiting, encouraging, loving, praying, working with her hands. She added new works, including Bible camps and women's retreats, but she did not give up the earlier call to service. She just kept doing the good she started and for which she went to Europe so many years ago. Others came and went, but she stayed.

She had to wait for the children to grow up to see the fruit of her labor. Now preachers all over western Germany who were in her children's classes rise up to call her blessed. She married Otis Gatewood in the twilight of her life and continued her good works in Vienna, Austria, as long as she was able.

W. E. Sangster in his description of a saint gives this comment: "The saint never gives up. He goes on serving, loving, helping. . . . He aches for souls. Neither indifference nor slander, nor injury can stop him. He does not make a motive of gratitude. His great motive is his utter love for God."[8] A saint "is kind to the ungrateful and selfish" (Luke 6:35).

"May the God of steadfastness and encouragement grant you to live in such harmony with one another, in accord with Christ Jesus, that together you may with one voice glorify the God and Father of our Lord Jesus Christ" (Rom. 15:5, 6).

---

[8]Sangster, *Pure in Heart*, 104.

4. Be one in whom the love of God has made all people one family.

To so many of us, the phrase "the brotherhood of man" is just a pious phrase. When we practice rather than preach James' teaching on not being a respecter of persons, when we teach and show hospitality and minister to the needs of those who are different from us no matter what the pressures are from family, friends, or church community, we will be able to say with Alan Paton's mission figure in *Cry the Beloved Country,*

> I shall do this, not because I am noble or unselfish, but because life slips away, and because I need for the rest of my journey a star that will not play false to me, a compass that will not lie. . . . I am lost when I balance this against that, I am lost when I ask if this is safe, I am lost when I ask if men, white men or black men, Englishmen or Afrikaners, Gentiles or Jews, will approve. Therefore I shall try to do what is right, and to speak what is true.[9]

Paton is saying essentially what George Müller said earlier: "There was a day when I died; utterly died to George Müller, his opinions, preferences, tastes and will; died to the world, its approval or censure; died to the approval or blame even of my brethren and friends and since then I have studied only to show myself approved unto God."[10] According to 1 Corinthians 4:1–4, only in Christ can we solve the problem of living together with all of our differences.

5. Be one who believes that life does not consist in what one has.

The tyranny of things is more than a well-turned phrase. We won't ever have any impact with our teaching on sacrificial living unless we can demonstrate it in our lives. As long as silver, china, antiques, and collectors' items have priority over whether somebody gets to hear the good news about Jesus, we lose our

---

[9]Paton, *Cry the Beloved Country*, 175.
[10]Sangster, *Pure in Heart*, 141.

influence. Treasures are not confined to money or to what money will buy but to whatever stops with this life and this world.

6. Believe that we are strangers and exiles (Heb. 11:13).

Today I'm nearer my home than I've ever been before. Even today Christ might come to receive his own. We need desperately to keep alive that hope and to rekindle it in the lives of others. J. I. Packer likens the meeting of the redeemed in heaven with their father God and their brother Jesus as a family gathering like the day "the sick child is at last able to leave the hospital, and finds father and the whole family waiting outside to greet him."[11]

Jesus is coming, and all of the excuses for failing to teach others, all of my lack of steadfastness (holding out to the end), all of my involvement with things, all of my failure to do whatever I could have done to break down the barriers that separate—all of these excuses will seem so feeble when I by myself stand before Jesus who spent his life teaching others, who held out to the end doing his Father's will, who didn't own anything material, and who by his life and teaching made us know that the brotherhood of man could be a reality.

I hope we can all pray the prayer of Thomas à Kempis in complete submission of our lives to the God who made us and beyond whose love and care we cannot stray (Ps. 139:7–12):

> O Lord, Thou knowest what is best for us, let this or that be done, as Thou shalt please. Give what thou wilt and how much Thou wilt and when Thou wilt. Deal with me as Thou thinkest good, and as best pleaseth Thee, and is most for Thy honor. Set me where Thou wilt and deal with me in all things just as Thou wilt. . . . Behold, I am Thy servant, prepared for all things; for I desire not to live unto myself; but unto Thee; and O, that I could do it worthily and perfectly![12]

[Date and occasion of this speech are unknown.]

---

[11]Packer, *Knowing God*, 198.

[12]Thomas à Kempis, *Imitation of Christ* III, 15.

15

WE LIVE IN A WORLD OF CHANGE

A casual observer today has only to glance around to see technological, scientific, and moral changes. I was made aware of the technological change when an IBM representative came to the library one day to service one of our electric typewriters. She glanced in my office to see an old Royal standard that I had bought second-hand over 30 years before and asked, "What is that?" She had never seen a non-electric typewriter. The computer age is here, and no amount of resistance will ward it off. We all grant that it is here to stay. We applaud what it can do when it's working and lament when it's down instead of up.

Even our houses reflect the changes we have seen in our generation. In my hometown there are streets lined with two-story houses, usually occupied by one person, and yards too large for that one person to keep. You are familiar with one house there—the home of Alex Haley's grandmother, probably the finest house in town in its day and the home where Alex and his brothers visited every summer. Alex was buried in the front yard. In those old houses, there was a basement and an attic where people could get away from each other. Children were not always under foot, and adults were not always around to evaluate and adjudicate. I remember my mama used to say, "You just can't see everything a child does." But in the crowded surroundings in which we live today, a child doesn't have a place to hide. Although houses built around the turn of the century had some inconvenient features such as deep, narrow closets, nooks and crannies that were wasted spaces, and full attics that invited clutter, still it was a haven for children. When Robert Louis Stevenson wrote his poem

"A Good Play," he began it with the lines that are all but incredible today: "We built a ship upon the stairs / All made of the back-bedroom chairs."[1] In the first place, who has a back bedroom and with chairs besides? And furthermore, who would permit children to build a boat on the stairs? But Stevenson was describing the life of children in an old Victorian house that had lots of bedrooms and a back stairs to the upstairs for the children as well as the adults. This made it possible for the children to submerge themselves in make-believe with little or no interference from the adult world housed under the same roof.

Changes in the world of moral values are as evident as in the technological and scientific areas. I cannot remember a single divorce among the friends of my parents. I can remember one pregnancy outside of marriage in my high school. To tell today's youth about life without cars and designer clothes seems like a fairy tale; unlike the small child who has just heard his favorite story, he doesn't say, "Tell it again." Only the unusual child wants to hear the stories of the long ago and far away.

How often do you find yourself saying, "It's a different generation"? Yet listen to this statement attributed to Socrates, who lived around 400 years before Christ: "Our youth today love luxury. They have bad manners, contempt for authority, disrespect for older people. Children nowadays are tyrants. They contradict their parents, gobble their food, and tyrannize their teachers." That sounds as current as today's newspaper.

But we all do recognize the truth of Heraclitus' statement, "You cannot step in the same river twice."[2] In a world of change, there is no wonder that we ask, "Whom can we believe?" and "What can we believe?"

Whom Can We Believe?

Steve Riser has well said,

> A person's concept of morality is directly related to a per-

---

[1]Stevenson, *Child's Garden of Verses*, 17.
[2]Heraclitus, *Fragments*, 94.

> son's concept of God. It is a direct outgrowth of their faith—their core values—their religion. For example, if you are a consistent atheistic evolutionist, then it is OK to act like an animal because that is all you believe you are. On the other hand, if you believe that you are a unique creation of an infinite personal God and as a Christian your body is the temple of the Holy Spirit, then you will desire to honor God in your body by conforming to the moral teachings of the Bible.[3]

Our lives are manifestations of what we think about God.

A. W. Tozer, in *The Knowledge of the Holy*, has this beautiful prayer:

> O Christ, our Lord, Thou hast been our dwelling place in all generations. As conies to their rock, so we have run to Thee for safety; as birds from their wanderings, so have we flown to Thee for peace. Chance and change are busy in our little world of nature and men, but in Thee we find no variableness nor shadow of turning. We rest in Thee without fear or doubt and face our tomorrows without anxiety.[4]

The immutability of God appears in its most perfect beauty when viewed against the mutability of men. In God no change is possible; in men change is impossible to escape. Neither man nor his world is fixed; they are in constant flux. In this world where men forget us, change their attitude toward us, revise their opinion of us for the slightest cause, it is wonderful to know that God does not change. His attitude toward us now is the same as it was in eternity and will be in eternity to come.

In coming to him in prayer, we don't have to wonder if he is in a receptive mood. He is always receptive. He does not keep

---

[3]Riser, "Christian World View" (sermon, Raleigh Presbyterian Church, Memphis, TN, date unknown). Used by permission. Email from Dr. Steven C. Riser, Memphis, TN, to Jean Saunders, Memphis, TN, March 24, 2009.

[4]Tozer, *Knowledge of the Holy*, 55.

office hours or set aside periods when he will see no one. Today he feels toward his creatures just as he did when he sent his only begotten Son into the world to die for us.

His attitude toward sin is the same as when he drove out the sinful man and woman from the garden, his attitude toward the sinner the same as when he said, "Come to me, all who labor and are heavy laden, and I will give you rest" (Matt. 11:28).

In the first place, God is immutable in his counsel, his plans, and his will. Some of the Bible translations use the word *repent* for God's actions, and that word conveys to us a change in the direction of one's life, a meaning that doesn't apply to God. "And it repented the Lord that he had made man" (KJV) is better translated in the NIV, "The Lord was grieved that he had made man" (Gen. 6:6). In 1 Samuel 15:35 we have, "And the Lord repented that he had made Saul king over Israel." The NIV reads, "And the Lord was grieved that he had made Saul king over Israel." In Jonah 3:10, "God repented of the evil which he had said he would do to them" (the Ninevites). The NIV translates, ". . . he had compassion and did not bring upon them the destruction he had threatened." In all three cases, the idea is not that God needed to change his behavior but that he was grieved over man's sin.

In Jeremiah 15:6 the KJV reads, almost in a spirit of desperation, "Thou hast forsaken me, saith the Lord, thou art gone backward: therefore will I stretch out my hand against thee, and destroy thee; I am weary with repenting." The NIV translates, "I can no longer show compassion." In every case, though, it is man who has changed, not God.

The familiar story of the potter and the clay is told in Jeremiah 18:1–10.

> This is the word that came to Jeremiah from the Lord: "Go down to the potter's house, and there I will give you my message." So I went down to the potter's house, and I saw him working at the wheel. But the pot he was shaping from the clay was marred in his hands; so the potter formed it into another pot, shaping it as seemed best to him.

> Then the word of the Lord came to me: "O house of Israel, can I not do with you as this potter does?" declares the Lord. "Like clay in the hand of the potter, so are you in my hand, O house of Israel. If at any time I announce that a nation or kingdom is to be uprooted, torn down and destroyed, and if that nation I warned repents of its evil, then I will relent and not inflict on it the disaster I had planned. And if at another time I announce that a nation or kingdom is to be built up and planted, and if it does evil in my sight and does not obey me, then I will reconsider the good I had intended to do for it" (NIV).

God is perpetually the same. He *only* can say, "I AM WHO I AM" (Exod. 3:14).

In the second place, God is immutable in his attributes. His power is unabated; his wisdom undiminished. His truthfulness is unchangeable, for his word is "for ever . . . settled in heaven" (Ps. 119:89; KJV).

His love is eternal. "I have loved thee with an everlasting love" (Jer. 31:3; KJV). "His steadfast love endures for ever, and his faithfulness to all generations" (Ps. 100:5). It is interesting that God closes the Old Testament with a statement of his unchangeable quality, "For I the LORD do not change" (Mal. 3:6).

The same emphasis on the unchangeable nature of God is brought over into the New Testament, as James 1:17 reads, "Every good endowment and every perfect gift is from above, coming down from the Father of lights with whom there is no variation or shadow due to change." The closing chapter of Hebrews, emphasizing the superiority of Jesus (13:8), states that "Jesus Christ is the same yesterday and today and for ever."

In this quality of immutability, we see the vast difference between God and us. Words to Reuben apply to us: "Unstable as water" (Gen. 49:4). Israel's faithlessness is described by the psalmist as, "They twisted like a deceitful bow" (Ps. 78:57). The children of Israel wanted to leave a life of slavery in Egypt and then wanted to return for the onions, leeks, and garlic (Num. 11:5). The multitude who cried, "Hosanna to the Son of David" (Matt. 21:9), changed to, "Away with him, crucify him!" (John

19:15). When Paul was at Lystra (Acts 14), the people wanted to make him a god and then later stoned him, leaving him for dead. But no matter how unstable I may be and how fickle my friends may prove, God changes not. His purpose is fixed, his will stable, his Word is sure. Here is a rock on which we may fix our feet and an anchor to which we can hold.

Will your anchor hold in the storms of life,
When the clouds unfold their wings of strife?
When the strong tides lift, and the cables strain,
Will your anchor drift, or firm remain?

It is safely moored, 'twill the storm withstand,
For 'tis well secured by the Savior's hand;
And the cables, passed from His heart to mine,
Can defy the blast, thro' strength divine.

It will surely hold in the floods of death,
When the waters cold chill our latest breath;
On the rising tide it can never fail,
While our hopes abide within the veil.

When our eyes behold thro' the gath'ring night
The city of gold, our harbor bright,
We shall anchor fast by the heav'nly shore,
With the storms all past for evermore.

We have an anchor that keeps the soul
Steadfast and sure while the billows roll,
Fastened to the Rock which cannot move,
Grounded firm and deep in the Savior's love.[5]

What Can We Believe?

We can believe the very simple statement, "Thy word is truth" (John 17:17). The 176 verses of Psalm 119 are the most beautiful

---

[5]Priscilla J. Owens, "Will Your Anchor Hold?" *Great Songs.*

and detailed meditation on the law of God that we have in the Bible. Verse 89 tells us, "For ever, O LORD, thy word is firmly fixed in the heavens." Ever since that time when Jehoiakim, sitting in his winter house, cut off with a penknife the columns of the scroll containing the words of Jeremiah against Israel and Judah (Jer. 36:23), men have attempted to destroy, not with a penknife but with their critical views, the Bible. Yet the Bible still stands. It is the anvil against which the hammers striking it are worn out.

A classic in literature is a classic because it stands the test of time. It is timeless; it does not go out of date. So Shakespeare, because his works are classics, is still studied in public schools and colleges and universities throughout the world. His plays are still performed on stage and television 400 years after Shakespeare wrote them. The Bible is the greatest classic of all time and year by year continues to be the number-one best seller.

In today's world we see moral values crumbling, but God's Word on the purity of life for the Christian has not changed.

Biblical Truths Which Have Not Changed

The biblical truths which have not changed range from Genesis through the last chapter of Revelation, but I have chosen some basic ones in keeping with the theme of this study.

Will of God First

As important as the family is, it is subordinate to the kingdom of God. The supreme demand of life is that one do the will of God. If family obligations hinder a person from doing the will of God, then those obligations must give way to more important ones. When during the great Galilean ministry Jesus' mother and brothers came looking for him, Jesus stated publicly that his disciples were his mother and his brothers (Matt. 12:46–50). Where loyalties clash, one must devote oneself to the kingdom of God.

Fornication

Fornication was an ever-present danger in the first-century world. Paul deals with the problem in 1 Corinthians 6:9, 10: "Do not be deceived; neither the immoral, nor idolaters, nor adulterers . . . will inherit the kingdom of God." He said the same thing, in other words, to the Galatians (5:19–21), to the Ephesians (5:3–5), and to the Colossians (3:5, 6). Today the argument against fornication on the basis of fear of disease or fear of pregnancy is losing its force because of the advances of medical science. But Paul's argument is timeless; fornication is wrong because it is a violation of the basic purposes of sex.

Divorce

The ancient Hebrew law regulating divorce is found in Deuteronomy 24. As in all patriarchal societies, divorce was the prerogative of the man. A man was permitted to divorce his wife if "she finds no favor in his eyes because he has found some indecency in her" (24:1). The rabbis did not agree on defining the indecency. Shammai allowed divorce only on the grounds of unchastity; his pupil Hillel allowed divorce on the most trivial grounds, such as the wife's burning her husband's bread.[6] Today, the most common cause of divorce seems to be "irreconcilable differences," a term completely unknown to the biblical writers.

In reporting the final journey to Jerusalem, Matthew, Mark, and Luke record that the Pharisees interrupted Jesus' journey, testing him on his attitude toward divorce. Jesus attributed divorce under the law of Moses as a concession to "hardness of heart" and pointed them back to God's original intention of one man and one woman for life. Matthew records, "And I say to you: whoever divorces his wife, except for unchastity, and marries another, commits adultery" (Matt. 19:9).

Abortion

We read with shock and dismay the stories of parents in China who expose their infant girls, leaving them out in the elements to die, since the government imposes harsh measures on families with more than one child. Limited to one child, the parents want that child to be a boy. Yet abortion clinics in Texas advertised for young women to "bring ten of your friends and get your

---

[6]*Mishnah*, Gittin 9:10.

abortion free." Scripture speaks to the question of abortion: mankind is made in the image of God (Gen. 1:26, 27); "whoever sheds the blood of man, by man shall his blood be shed" (Gen. 9:6); "You shall not murder" (Exod. 20:13; NIV); God hates hands that shed innocent blood (Prov. 6:17).

The enormity of the problem is seen in the fact that 16 million abortions have been performed in the 13 years since the Supreme Court legalized abortion. At a recent area meeting of elders and preachers in Texas, a young girl who had had an abortion while she was a leader in a church youth group urged church leaders to teach their young people about abortion. She said, "Please do not leave here thinking it is only the bad kids facing this problem. Please do not leave here thinking that abortion is not present in the church."

Be Subject to One Another (Eph. 5:21)

We live in a day when any kind of subjection is considered degrading. However, in our rational moments, we know we live by laws of subjection. I don't know of anyone who wants to test the law of gravity by jumping off a skyscraper or test the traffic laws of the U.S. by traveling streets on the left-hand side of the road. Although subject to all manner of civil laws, still there is something in us that finds distaste in the idea of being subject.

But Paul's opening words in that marvelous passage in Ephesians 5:21 on the family are, "Be subject to one another out of reverence for Christ." The phrase "out of reverence for Christ" sheds an entirely new light on the reason. The wife is urged to be subject to the husband, who is the head of the family (1 Cor. 11:3). The subjection of women within the family, says W. O. Carver in *The Glory of God in the Christian Calling*, is the ordering of their lives "in voluntary adjustment to their husbands as rightful head of the family."[7]

Exhortation also applies to the husband. The same selfless love which Christ has for his church, the husband is to have for his wife. According to Paul, the relationship of husband and wife is a reciprocal one. Although there are differences, they are dif-

---

[7]Carver, *The Glory of God*, 168.

ferences of function rather than of worth or importance.

Paul's emphasis in this passage is upon the responsibilities of the husband and wife rather than upon the privileges of each. If the woman is concerned with self-assertion or the man is concerned with maintaining his authority, the family is in danger of disintegrating. But if the two are subject to one another out of reverence for Christ, they have achieved that unity of which both Jesus and Paul spoke when they quoted the creation account.

My favorite author, Jack Lewis, recently wrote an article entitled, "I Wish She Would Stay Here with Me," reflecting on probably the saddest statement to come out of the indescribably awful space shuttle tragedy. When the five-year-old daughter of Christa McAuliffe was asked if she wanted her mother to go into space, she said, "No. I wish she would stay here with me."[8]

Jack writes that "without wanting to put a special 'guilt trip' on anyone, without wanting to stand in judgment on anyone, or wanting to set standards for anyone, I do register some questions about priorities which seem to me to be losing out in our present struggles. There are passages whose application puzzles me in the midst of the drive for achievement."[9]

He quotes, "So I would have younger widows marry, bear children, rule their households, and give the enemy no occasion to revile us" (1 Tim. 5:14), and "Bid the older women . . . to . . . train the young women to love their husbands and children, to be sensible, chaste, domestic, kind, and submissive to their husbands, that the word of God may not be discredited" (Titus 2:3–5). That last clause furnishes a happy motivation for our behavior.

Jack writes, "In our society many people seem to have the drive to discharge multiple functions. It may be that they are able to discharge credibly all of the things the apostle was talking about and have their achievements too; however, the crime problem and the breakdown in morals suggests that in many cases something has gone wrong."[10]

---

[8]Lewis, "I Wish She Would Stay Here with Me," 1, 3.

[9]Ibid., 3.

[10]Ibid.

He concludes,

> When our mothers have become presidents of the corporations, have become president of the country, have set the world records in all sorts of competitive activity, have gone to the moon and back, have climbed the highest mountain and then some more; when they get to where they are headed, there still will be the haunting picture of that little girl saying, "I wish she would stay here with me."[11]

Sandra Humphrey, editor of *Christian Woman,* conducted an interview with Laura Catherine Keeble, the wife of Marshall Keeble, the beloved black preacher who baptized more people than any other man in his generation. If you had the chance to hear him preach, you were greatly privileged. When asked if she had just one piece of advice to give to today's Christian women, she offered, "Marry in the church! If you can't get somebody, just stay like I did for 35 years. Anytime somebody says, 'I used to be a Christian,' you nearly always know that they married out of the church."[12]

Children, Obey Your Parents

Finally, the last of the teachings of the Bible in our lesson is that which speaks forcefully of the obligation of children to their parents. The fifth commandment of the Decalogue enjoins, "Honor your father and your mother" (Exod. 20:12). It is significant that no age limit is placed on this commandment. We are to honor, which implies taking care of their needs as long as they live. The Letter to the Ephesians (6:3) adds the promise "that it may be well with you and that you may live long on the earth."

Faith for the child is still best learned from the home. Timothy's faith was learned from his grandmother and his mother, and it was probably their early teaching that enabled Paul in the

---

[11]Ibid.

[12]Humphrey, "Laura Catherine Keeble," 19.

last years of his life to say that he had no one like Timothy so genuinely anxious for the Philippian Christians (Phil. 2:20). The church, with the most talented and dedicated youth minister and with all of the programs developed from a fertile imagination to try to keep young people faithful to the Lord and active in his service, can never do what devoted Christian parents with obedient children can do.

Some Change May Be Good

We have talked about the timeless truths found in the Bible given by a God who does not change. Yet we recognize that some change may be good and work for the good of men.

The very ability to change is a gift from God. For human beings the whole possibility of redemption lies in their ability to change. To move from one sort of person to another is the essence of repentance; the liar becomes truthful, the thief honest, the proud humble. The whole moral texture of the life is altered. The thoughts, the desires, the affections are transformed, and the man is no longer what he was before. So radical is this change that the apostle calls the man who used to exist "the old man" and the man who now exists "the new man" who is renewed in knowledge after the image of God, who created him (Col. 3:9, 10).

A son of thunder wanting to bring down fire on a Samaritan village (Luke 9:54) became the apostle of love; Peter, denying his Lord, wept bitterly and preached the first gospel sermon; Paul, the persecutor of the church, became its most zealous missionary to the Gentile world.

Always, when Jesus dealt with sinners or the lost, his concern was for the redemption and the reconstruction of their lives. After the accusers left the woman taken in adultery (John 8:3–12), Jesus asked, "Woman, where are they? Has no one condemned you?" Her reply was, "No one, Lord." Jesus responded, "Neither do I condemn you; go, and do not sin again." Jesus was not excusing the woman for what she had done. When he said, "Neither do I condemn you," he was saying that he was not seeking to enforce the Mosaic law which prescribed death as the penalty for adultery. He was not concerned with punishment but with redemption. He urged her to give up forever her sinful life.

Paul's words are as true today as when he penned them: "All have sinned and fall short of the glory of God" (Rom. 3:23). It is still true that all sin has consequences. In the cases of Achan, Uzzah, Nadab and Abihu, David and Bathsheba, and Ananias and Sapphira, that consequence was death. But thanks be to God, there is no condemnation for those in Christ (Rom. 8:1); and his promise that "neither death, nor life, nor angels, nor principalities, nor things present, nor things to come, nor powers, nor height, nor depth, nor anything else in all creation, will be able to separate us from the love of God in Christ Jesus our Lord" (Rom. 8:38, 39) will continue to give hope to the child of God until Jesus returns to take us to that perfect home which he is now preparing for us.

This prayer can be for all of us:

Swift to its close ebbs out life's little day;
Earth's joys grow dim, its glories pass away;
Change and decay in all around I see;
O Thou who changest not, abide with me![13]

[Presented at Ladies' Lectureship, April 12, 1986.]

---

[13]Henry F. Lyte, "Abide with Me," *Great Songs*.

16

Let Your Light Shine

The divine interest in light begins in the first part of the biblical story and runs through the entire Bible until the very last book. In the beginning God said, "'Let there be light'; and there was light. And God saw that the light was good; and God separated the light from the darkness" (Gen. 1:3). Finally, we come to the Revelation to John, the last chapter, to that beautiful description of the holy city—the new Jerusalem. We read, "And night shall be no more; they need no light of lamp or sun, for the Lord God will be their light, and they shall reign for ever and ever" (Rev. 22:5).

The prophets spoke of the Lord as light. In Isaiah 60:19b we read, "The Lord will be your everlasting light." Once I asked Andy T. Ritchie what his favorite psalm was. He had taught devotional literature for many years, and his eyesight was failing. His response was, "Psalm 27." The first verse of that psalm is, "The Lord is my light and my salvation."

More than any other New Testament writer, the apostle John writes of light in his Gospel, in the Epistles, and in the Book of Revelation. We read that "God is light" (1 John 1:5); that "The true light that gives light to every man was coming into the world" (John 1:9; NIV); that Jesus is the light of the world (John 8:12; 9:5); and that "in him was life," and he "was the light of men" (John 1:4). Jesus says of himself, "I have come into the world as a light, so that no one who believes in me should stay in darkness" (John 12:46; NIV).

Then to the followers of this light, Jesus said, "Put your trust in the light while you have it, so that you may become sons of light" (John 12:36; NIV). In 1 John 1:7 we note that the basis of fellowship with one another is walking in the light as Jesus is in the light. In the Sermon on the Mount, Jesus told his disciples, "You are the light of the world" (Matt. 5:14); "Let your light shine before men" (Matt. 5:16). Why? That people who see your good deeds may praise God. Paul in his Ephesian letter repeats what Jesus had earlier said, "You are light in the Lord. Live as children of light" (5:8; NIV). The question now is, if Jesus is the light and we are the children of the light, how then should we live?

William Barclay tells the story of a little girl who was with her mother in a church that had a number of stained-glass windows. "Who are the people in the windows?" she whispered to her mother. "They're saints," her mother whispered back. That very same week the girl was taken by her mother to visit an old lady in the village who was very poor but whose life was very lovely. As they left the house, her mother said, "Well, that's a real saint you've been to see today." The girl did not say anything at the moment, but she was faced with the problem of somehow relating the figures in the stained-glass windows and the little old lady in the cottage in the village. So her mind teased at it, and suddenly she saw it. "I know what a saint is," she said to her mother. "A saint is someone who lets the light shine through."[1] Such is the wisdom of a child.

The *Memphis Commercial Appeal* one year featured a story for many weeks called "A Thousand Points of Light," a theme drawn from an expression President George H. W. Bush used in his nomination speech and again in his inaugural address. He talked about "varied and unique communities in America" and the voluntary work of individuals as "a brilliant diversity spread like stars, like a thousand points of light in a broad and peaceful sky." The paper then cited the volunteer work of about 1,000 people. Jesus, as he always does, sets the example of volunteer work in John 10:18 when he says to the people, "No one takes [my life] from me, but I lay it down of my own accord. I have authority to lay it down and authority to take it up again" (NIV).

---

[1]Barclay, *The All-Sufficient Christ*, 125.

Out of the thousand volunteers, I have chosen two—one we might label as rendering a very great service and another as a very small service. The Lord himself would make no distinction. Dr. Pat Wall, medical director of ambulatory services at Le Bonheur Children's Medical Center and a full-time faculty member of the Department of Pediatrics and associate dean at the University of Tennessee, has established a center for taking care of medical needs of children whose parents cannot afford medical care. Of his work he comments, "I think the center re-establishes the role of the church in taking care of the needy."

The simple service is the category most of us could do. Dean Pearman, 83 years of age, is an extremely early riser. He walks around his neighborhood long before daybreak each morning putting people's newspapers on their porches. For 20 years he has performed this service for more than 35 households. He says, "I just want to do a little something for somebody; it makes the mornings easier not to have to go out in the yard." I suppose this story came home to me since my aunt, who is in her mid-80's and lives in a small town, could not go down the steps on cold and rainy mornings to get her paper. Finally, she told the paperboy she would have to drop her subscription. He didn't seem to care.

In His Steps

I suspect that most of you have read or have heard about *In His Steps* by Charles Sheldon. The book was written in 1896 and has had more circulation than any book except the Bible. In it Henry Maxwell, the preacher at First Church in Raymond, had just finished his sermon when a man came from the rear of the church. He was dusty, worn, and shabby-looking with his faded hat in his hands. He had not shaved, and his hair was rough and tangled. The man began to speak, and nobody interrupted him:

> I've been wondering since I came in here . . . if it would be just the thing to say a word at the close of the service. I'm not drunk and I'm not crazy, and I'm perfectly harm-

> less; but if I die, as there is every likelihood I shall in a few days, I want the satisfaction of thinking that I said my say in a place like this and before this sort of a crowd. . . .
>
> I'm not an ordinary tramp, though I don't know of any teaching of Jesus that makes one kind of a tramp less worth saving than another. . . .
>
> I lost my job ten months ago, I am a printer by trade. . . . I've tramped all over the country trying to find something. . . . I've tramped through this city for three days trying to find a job, and in all of that time I've not had a word of sympathy or comfort except from your minister here, who said he was sorry for me and hoped I would find a job somewhere. . . . I'm not blaming anybody, am I? Just stating facts. . . . My wife died four months ago. . . . My little girl is staying with a printer's family until I find a job. . . . [What do you Christians mean by following the steps of Jesus? What do you mean when you sing, "I'll go with Him all the way" or "All for Jesus"? What do you mean?] It seems to me sometimes as if the people in the city churches had good clothes and nice houses to live in, and money to spend for luxuries, and could go away on summer vacations and all that, while the people outside of the churches, thousands of them, I mean, die in tenements and walk the streets for jobs, and never have a piano or a picture in the house, and grow up in misery and drunkenness and sin.[2]

Then the man, without any warning, fell on his face full length up the aisle. The minister took the man home with him and sent for the man's child. Before the child came, however, her father died.

The next Sunday the minister confessed to his congregation that the "appearance and words of the stranger" had "made a very powerful impression" on him, and he had been compelled

---

[2]Sheldon, *In His Steps*, 14–16.

to ask, "What does following Jesus mean?"[3] At the conclusion of his sermon, he asked for volunteers from the church who would pledge themselves, earnestly and honestly for an entire year, not to do anything without first asking the question, "What would Jesus do?" The volunteers then would follow Jesus no matter what the result might be. About 50 volunteered, including the editor of the local newspaper, a merchant who had at least 100 men employed in his various shops, a superintendent of the great railroad shops, the president of the local college, a medical doctor, an author, an heiress, and a beautiful and gifted choir member. As the story unfolds, we see how this pledge revolutionized their lives.

At the conclusion of the book, the minister asks, "What is the test of Christian discipleship? Is it not the same as in Christ's own time?"[4] I would like to use this story as a backdrop for two areas of life and thought in which the world could see us as the light of this world.

Compassion

The first area in which I believe that Christians can let their lights shine is that of compassion, that ability to enter into the experiences of another, particularly the sufferings of another. Leonard Allen says, "Of all the virtues we might seek, this one brings us closest to the mind of Christ."[5] Compassion is the strongest word for pity in the Greek language. A Christian is to be a man of pity, a man who cannot see suffering or need or distress without a sword of grief piercing his own heart. Shakespeare said long ago, "How far that little candle throws his beams. So shines a good deed in a naughty world."[6] We do not do our good deeds to be seen by men; Jesus warned against such (Matt. 6:1–4). But neither can good deeds be hidden.

The Old Testament pictures throughout the compassion of

---

[3]Ibid., 18–19.

[4]Ibid., 230.

[5]Allen, *The Cruciform Church*, 175.

[6]Shakespeare, *The Merchant of Venice*, 87.

God. Moses assured the people of his day that God loved them even though they had not deserved that love. Ezekiel 16 contains the allegory of the foundling child. In this chapter Israel is compared to a child who had been abandoned at birth, uncared for and unlovely. Yet God loved her anyway. The Book of Hosea is another example of how God loved Israel in all of her unloveliness. Hosea's wife, Gomer, was a harlot and forsook him to go after her lovers. Finally, in utter degradation, she was auctioned off at the slave market. But Hosea bought her back for himself. Although Israel had forsaken God, God still loved her and would take her back if she would return.

Jesus' inaugural sermon in Luke 4:18 has its theme of compassion: "The Spirit of the Lord is upon me, because he has anointed me to preach good news to the poor. He has sent me to proclaim release to the captives and recovering of sight to the blind, to set at liberty those who are oppressed." The cry "have mercy" frequently greeted the ears of Jesus. And he did have mercy. Those who received his compassion were a leper, the widow of Nain, the two blind men of Jericho, the Gerasene demoniac, and the multitudes when he furnished the meal for 5,000 and 4,000 people. He wept at the tomb of Lazarus for the compassion he felt toward the sisters, and he wept over the city of Jerusalem because they had rejected their opportunity.

Lives can speak to us as words cannot. The name of Mother Teresa is a household word for all of us. It would be hard to find any literate person in the world who does not know of her and her work. Robert Fulghum writes of her in his book *All I Really Need to Know I Learned in Kindergarten*:

> . . . in Oslo, Norway, on the tenth of December, in 1980. . . . A small, stooped woman in a faded blue sari and worn sandals received an award. From the hand of a king. . . . Surrounded by the noble and famous in formal black and in elegant gowns. The rich, the powerful, the brilliant, the talented. . . . And there at the center of it all—a little old lady. . . . Servant of the poor and sick and dying. To her, the Nobel Peace Prize.
>
> No shah or president or king or general or scientist

> or pope; no banker or merchant or cartel or oil company or ayatollah holds the key to as much power as she has. None is as rich. For hers is the invincible weapon against the evils of this earth: the caring heart. And hers are the everlasting riches of this life: the wealth of the compassionate spirit.
>
> To cut through the smog of helpless cynicism; to take only the tool of uncompromising love; to make manifest the capacity for healing humanity's wounds; to make the story of the Good Samaritan a living reality; and to live so true a life as to shine out from the back streets of Calcutta takes courage and faith we cannot admit in ourselves and cannot be without.[7]

The second example of compassion was reported by the United Press International in 1986. It is a story of such far-reaching caring that it's almost unbelievable. John Flynn, 64 years old, jokes that he keeps a box of tissues in his living room because he says, "If anyone ever breaks in here, they're going to leave crying." He and his wife do not have a telephone, a television, or a car. They have owned five cars but gave them all away to needy families. His life's work has been giving his money, time, and worldly goods to those needier than himself. For more than 40 years, he has waged a private mission giving away most of his meager salary from a delivery job. He said, "Like Jesus we need to see the old, the lonesome, the blind, the handicapped, the children with no warm clothes, and the people in misery." He tells the children that people can read the gospel story of the Good Samaritan who aided a fallen stranger, or they can act the part. He says it would not take five minutes to throw away all his belongings. All were given to him anyway. His wife says, "I'm contented and peaceful. I'm happy he likes to help people." I must confess I have taught the story of the Good Samaritan all of my adult life, but I have not acted the part as John Flynn and his wife have.

A man asked his two granddaughters what they wanted for

---

[7]Fulghum, *All I Really Need to Know*, 190–91.

Christmas. "Give us a world," they replied. Soon he deduced that what they were asking for was a globe. So happily granddad went out shopping for one and presented it to them on Christmas morning. When his granddaughters opened the present, he could sense their disappointment. "Did you want a different kind of globe?" he asked. "Well, yes," said one of them. "We were kind of hoping for a lighted world." "I can fix that," he said. "I'll take it back and exchange it for a lighted one." Unfortunately, the store where he bought the globe did not sell lighted ones. So he got his money back and set out to find a lighted world rather than a dark one. Finally, he located a globe with a light in it, bought it, and gave it to the granddaughters who were delighted. His wife asked him if he had learned anything from his experience. He said, "Oh, yes, I learned that a lighted world costs more."

A lighted world does cost more. It cost God his Son. It cost Christ his life. And if we are serious about letting our light shine in today's world, it will cost us as well. It cost Mother Teresa, John Flynn and his wife, and scores of others. Tolstoy said long ago, "As a candle shines only when that of which it is made is being spent, so life is only real when it is being spent for others."[8]

In both this area of compassion and the area I am going to mention next, I confess that I do not do what I am advocating. Yet I have the courage to teach because of the words of the seventh-century John of the Ladder who lived 40 years a solitary life at Mt. Sinai: "If some are still dominated by their former bad habits, and yet teach by mere word, let them teach. . . . For, perhaps, being put to shame by their own words they will eventually begin to practice what they teach."[9] Ezra had the correct order.

---

[8]Source unknown. See Davis, *Religion in Action*, 203. See also Tolstoy, *The Light While Ye Have Light*, 94: "As the fire destroys the candle, so the good destroys the personal life"; and "Circle of Readings," v. 42, p. 286; "Notebook for 1879," v. 48, p. 363, http://feb-web.ru/feb/tolstoy/critics/LN1/LN1-561-.htm (accessed March 23, 2009), translated by Professor Steven P. Hill, Professor of Russian, University of Illinois (email from Steven P. Hill, Urbana, IL, to Jean Saunders, Memphis, TN, March 21, 2009): "One candle will light others, while it [the first candle] won't be diminished in its own light."

[9]Climacus, *Ladder of Divine Ascent*, 203.

It is said of him, "For Ezra had set his heart to study the law of the LORD, and to do it, and to teach his statutes and ordinances in Israel" (Ezra 7:10).

Lifestyle

The second area in which I believe the world could see our light shining is that of a more simple lifestyle. William Wordsworth in 1806 wrote these lines in his sonnet "The World Is Too Much with Us":

> The world is too much with us; late and soon,
> Getting and spending, we lay waste our powers;
> Little we see in Nature that is ours;
> We have given our hearts away, a sordid boon![10]

If that were true in 1806, how much more is it true on the verge of the twenty-first century!

The two texts I would like to look at are Colossians 3:1, 2, "If then you have been raised with Christ, seek the things that are above, where Christ is, seated at the right hand of God. Set your minds on things that are above, not on things that are on earth," and Romans 12:2a, "Do not be conformed to this world." We have become so much like the world that non-Christians can't distinguish between the world and us.

As always Jesus is our example in this area of our lives as well as in every other part. Read 2 Corinthians 8:9: "For you know the grace of our Lord Jesus Christ, that though he was rich, yet for your sake he became poor, so that by his poverty you might become rich."

Jesus was born in a stable and raised in poverty. He worked in a carpenter shop and received no money for his preaching. He had nowhere to lay his head. He had to borrow a boat to cross the Sea of Galilee. His support largely came from women. The price that Judas got for him was 30 pieces of silver—the price of a common slave. He ate the Last Supper in a borrowed room and

---

[10]Wordsworth, "The World Is Too Much with Us," 320–21.

went out to give up his life. He commended his mother to John. He gave his garment to soldiers to be gambled for, his peace to his disciples, his forgiveness to the thief on the cross, and his spirit to God.

I think I became more interested in this idea of stewardship of our possessions which would result in a more simple lifestyle after I saw our church budget cut. This limited the money that was available for benevolence, the compassion about which we have just talked. It cut our missions program, making it impossible for us to put another missionary in the field.

The Bible refers to prayer about 500 times, to faith less than 500 times, and to material possessions more than 1,000 times. Sixteen of Jesus' 38 parables are concerned with stewardship of material possessions, things that the citizen of today in America's Middletown is most interested in—food, shelter, clothing (Jesus knew about these needs), comforts, luxuries, education, social position, and enjoyment of things.

John Wright said,

> Our society owns the most sophisticated unused equipment in the world. How often do we purchase shelves of books only to have them occupy wall space collecting dust? Or perhaps we buy the most expensive and proved-efficient exercise equipment that is on the market. But after a week or two of sporadic exertion, we never move again except to lift a fork to our mouth. We buy a beautiful piano that never gets played. We equip an enviable workshop that never gets worked in. We select the most efficient study Bible that is never studied.[11]

Jesus tells us not to lay up for ourselves treasures on earth but to lay them up in heaven (Matt. 6:19, 20). Richard Foster gives us three very good reasons:

1. ". . . this world is a very uncertain place (Matt. 6:19, 20). There simply is 'no hidin' place down here.'" If we do not have moths, rust, and robbers, then we have inflation, which in

[11]Source unknown.

some countries is making money worth half of what we thought it was worth, and/or floods that destroy houses and furnishings.
2. ". . . whatever we fix as our treasure will obsess our whole life." Our heart and treasure will be brought together. It is not just hard to serve two masters; it is impossible.
3. ". . . provision has already been made. The birds of the air and the lilies of the field all witness to an order in the Kingdom of God, in which adequate provision is made for everyone and everything."[12]

In the parable of the rich fool (Luke 12:13-21), there are some things to commend about the man:
1. He acquired his wealth honestly. He farmed.
2. He was wise in his saving of money. In the days before life insurance companies, he took out the best form of insurance; he stored up goods, saved money.
3. He was a good spender. In the building of barns, he would give employment to contractors and laborers.
4. Having secured competence, he was willing to retire and let others have a chance.
5. There is no evidence that he was anything but a good man, a good neighbor.

But the rich man had his defects:
1. He had no spiritual foresight to go with his business sense.
2. He thought he could feed his soul on corn and oats. He thought material things could take the place of spiritual themes.
3. He lost sight of God's ownership of money. His conversation with himself is punctuated with "I" and "my."
4. He neglected his stewardship. He forgot that he owed everything to God.
5. He was a covetous man. He traded the opportunity to help the needy and joy in service for barns and goods.

The following examples of stewardship of possessions should inspire us to try harder to be better stewards. The violinist Fritz Kreisler once said:

---

[12]Foster, *Freedom of Simplicity*, 35–36.

> I was born with music in my system. It was a gift of God. I did not acquire it. So I do not even deserve thanks for the music. Music is too sacred to be sold and the outrageous prices charged by musical celebrities today are truly a crime against society. I never look upon the money I earn as my own. It is a public money. I am constantly endeavoring to reduce my needs to the minimum. I feel morally guilty in ordering a costly meal for it deprives someone else of a slice of bread, some child perhaps of a bottle of milk. My beloved wife feels exactly as I do about these things. In all these years of my so-called success in music we have not built a home for ourselves. Between it and us stand all of the homeless in the world.[13]

Similarly, the Mayo brothers were Christian stewards.

> They believed that money must go back into the service of that humanity which paid it to them. "We try," said Dr. William Mayo, "to take up the medical and surgical education of selected and promising men where the state leaves off. From 1894 onward we have never used more than half of our incomes on ourselves and our families, latterly much less. The very roof of my house goes out of the possession of my family when I die. I wouldn't want my children deprived of the fun and benefit of wanting something and going out to fight for it."[14]

And John Wesley said: "As our income rises, we are all tempted to let our standard of living rise with it. Simply because we can afford it, does that mean we should buy it?"[15] It is hard to find a man who rendered a better account of his stewardship than John Wesley. When he got 30 pounds a year, he lived on 28 and gave away 2; when he got 60 pounds a year, he lived on 28 and gave

---

[13]Source unknown. See White and Kurtz, *The Biblical Review*, 276.

[14]Schroder, "Ownership Versus Stewardship."

[15]Source unknown. John Wesley (1703–1791) was an Anglican cleric and Christian theologian who founded the Arminian Methodist movement. http://en.wikipedia.org/wiki/John_Wesley (accessed March 23, 2009).

away 32; when he later received 90 pounds, he lived on 28 and gave away 62; when he got 120 pounds, he lived on 28 and gave away 92.[16] Wesley said to his sister, "Money never stays with me. It would burn me if it did. I throw it out of my hands as soon as possible, lest it should find its way into my heart."[17]

The U.S. Consultation on Simple Lifestyle began in 1974 at the Lausanne Congress for World Evangelization. This congress summoned Christians to simplify their lifestyles so that the billions who are starving could be fed and the billions who have never heard the Gospel could hear. The congress affirmed that asceticism is not a biblical ideal. This world is a beautiful gift from God, and he intends for us to enjoy and care for it. But "those of us who live in affluent circumstances accept our duty to develop a simple lifestyle in order to contribute generously to both relief and evangelism."[18]

Simple lifestyle is not an end in itself; it is necessary so we can show compassion and so we can evangelize those who are lost. Ron Sider,[19] Richard Foster,[20] and Richard Taylor[21] have all made concrete suggestions for us in this effort to simplify the way we live so that the needy can have care and the lost can hear the Gospel:

1. Seek to be content with what we have. Contentment has always remained elusive but is a quality which can be learned. Paul said that he had learned to be content.
2. Let needs rather than wants govern our choices.
3. Cultivate silence and solitude. Develop close friendships and enjoy long evenings of serious and hilarious conversation. Value music, art, books, and significant travel.
4. Walk, jog, and swim. These are among the best forms of human exercise and require a minimum of equipment.
5. Stop trying to impress people with your clothes and impress them with your life. We should reach the point of maturity

---

[16]Stevens, *History of the Religious Movement*, 207.

[17]Wesley, *Letters*, 5:108–9.

[18]Stott, ed., *Making Christ Known*, 34.

[19]Sider, *Rich Christians*.

[20]Foster, *Freedom of Simplicity*.

[21]Taylor, *The Disciplined Life*.

where we are no longer vulnerable to the opinions of others. George Washington Carver said, "It is not the style of clothes one wears, neither the kind of automobile one drives, nor the amount of money one has in the bank that counts. These mean nothing. It is simply service that measures success."[22] Once when Carver was asked to the White House to meet the president, he was asked if he were not going to buy a new suit of clothes. His response was, "Why? The president wants to see me—not my clothes."

6. Begin a new style of hospitality, simple fare, and a much wider circle of guests. One night we were having company for dinner, and I spent most of the day polishing silver, setting the table, cooking, etc. But at noon that day Jack called to say he was bringing a former student, his wife, and two children for lunch. We had soup, cheese, and fruit—no fuss. And it was as happy a time as the evening meal over which I did fuss.
7. Clothes, shoes, appliances, tools—almost anything can be kept in use with glue, patches, tape, baling wire, and ingenuity. It is now said that the world is no longer held together by baling wire but by duct tape. I married the master of all of these so now I don't throw away a nail, a screw, a tiny piece of anything that might belong on something.
8. Watch your thermostat. Maybe you can take a thermostat set at 60 in the winter, but I can't.
9. Join the resistance movement by claiming, "The price tag is too high."
10. Have a budget book and record expenditures. We would probably be astonished if we knew how much we spend in certain categories in one year. Deficit spending will work no better for us than for the federal government.
11. Listen to G. K. Chesterton: "There are two ways to get enough: one is to continue to accumulate more and more, and the other is to desire less."[23]

---

[22]Carver, *His Own Words*, 17.
[23]Foster, *Freedom of Simplicity*, 110

You yourselves have already put into practice many ideas for a more simple life.

Some Warnings

Simple living is an individual matter; a person chooses before God how best to be a steward of his gifts in today's world of such gross inequalities. We should always be aware of the danger of turning any expressions of simplicity into a new legalism. Christians need not put down people who are wealthy, wasteful, extravagant, or stingy so long as we don't follow their ways. God is their judge and ours. We ought rather to put our energy into being examples of a better way just as Jesus Christ is ours. I love the phrase characteristic of Henry Cadbury, renowned professor at Harvard Divinity School: Frugal but generous. Frugal with himself and generous toward others.[24]

The goal for all of us should be that of Henry Martyn, missionary to India where he worked for seven brief but fruitful years. On arrival to that country he said, "Now let me burn out for God."[25] And he did just that.

Finally, what is our guidebook to living as Jesus would have us live in the areas of compassion and stewardship of what has been entrusted to us, leading to a more simple lifestyle? How will we know that our light is shining in a desperately dark world? Our guidebook is the same as that used by the psalmist: "Thy word is a lamp to my feet and a light to my path" (Ps. 119:105). We can depend on that lamp guiding us to that holy city, the new Jerusalem, where "night shall be no more; [we will] need no light of lamp or sun, for the Lord God will be [our] light" (Rev. 22:5).

[Presented at East Park Church of Christ, Danville, Illinois, May 1990.]

---

[24]Bacon, *Let This Life Speak*, 157.
[25]Smith, *Henry Martyn*, 150.

17

THE CARING HEART

On a recent visit from our four-year-old grandson, he came up to me and said, "Nana, I care about you." I was duly impressed just as you would have been to have that kind of affection expressed. But the words "I care about you" are bandied around so today that everybody cares about us—the automobile dealer, the furniture dealer, the shoe repairman, the waitress, and the salesman of any product from something so innocent as perfume fragrance to something so deadly as alcohol. The phrase is very much like "I love you." We also love the dog, the baby, the ice cream, and the color pink.

To look at the biblical view of caring, we begin just as you would expect us to begin with the One who is the most caring of all—God. The Bible has as its opening words, "In the beginning God created the heavens and the earth" (Gen. 1:1). It closes with the words, "Amen. Come, Lord Jesus! The grace of the Lord Jesus be with all the saints. Amen" (Rev. 22:20, 21). We are the objects of a God who cares about his children.

God planted trees so his child would have food and a shady place to rest. He made rivers to flow so man would have something to drink. Because man needed a sense of purpose, he gave him a garden to care for. God wanted man to be happy, so he provided companionship for man. God brought all the animals, and man saw them and named them. But man needed a deeper companionship, so God provided another human being—bone of his bone and flesh of his flesh.

Man rebelled so that God came very near to ending the whole human experiment. "I will blot out man whom I have created from the face of the ground, man and beast and creeping things and birds of the air, for I am sorry that I have made them" (Gen. 6:7). But then comes, "But Noah found favor in the eyes of the LORD" (Gen. 6:8).

God took care of his people when they were slaves in Egypt for 400 years; he brought judgment on the nation that they served and brought his people out with great possessions. When they came back to Canaan, God gave them great and goodly cities which they did not build, houses full of all good things which they did not fill, cisterns hewn out which they did not hew, and vineyards and olive trees which they did not plant (Deut. 6:10, 11).

God cared so much that "when the time had fully come, God sent forth his Son, born of woman" to redeem us (Gal. 4:4, 5). But then the lowest moment in history came when Jesus was crucified. Divine compassion is most clearly seen in the words of Jesus, "Father, forgive them; for they know not what they do" (Luke 23:34).

And 1,900 years later God is still seeking us through Christ, trying to reconcile the world to himself. "See what love the Father has given us, that we should be called children of God; and so we are" (1 John 3:1a).

Francis Thompson, in his poem "The Hound of Heaven," paints a graphic picture of God's never-ending search for man and an indomitable spirit that will not let him go. We sing of this Love in our hymn:

O Love that wilt not let me go,
I rest my weary soul in Thee;
I give Thee back the life I owe,
That in Thine ocean depths its flow
May richer, fuller be.[1]

Special Groups Who Need Our Care

I would like to focus on five groups of people who need our special care, although you might have chosen other categories since the need for care is as wide as the universe.

---

[1]George Matheson, "O Love that Wilt Not Let Me Go," *Great Songs*.

The first group in need of care is the stranger. We are all too familiar with the mobility of the society in which we live. We look out of our windows and see a moving van across the street telling us that our neighbors are moving either to another part of the city or across country. Drive down any street in the city, and you will count numerous "For Sale" or "Sold" signs in yards. These are constant reminders that, contrary to the lifestyle of a generation ago where people were born in, lived in, and many times died in the same house, we seldom see that phenomenon today. As a result of this transient society in which we live, we find strangers among us.

The law in Exodus 22:21 said, "You shall not wrong a stranger or oppress him, for you were strangers in the land of Egypt." Old and New Testament stories not only show how serious our obligation is to welcome the stranger in our home, but they also tell us that guests are carrying precious gifts with them. When Abraham received three strangers at Mamre and offered them water, bread, and a fine tender calf, they revealed themselves to him as the Lord announcing that Sarah, his wife, would give birth to a son (Gen. 18:1-15). When the widow of Zarephath offered food and shelter to Elijah, he revealed himself as a man of God offering her an abundance of oil and meal and raising her son from the dead (1 Kings 17:9-24). In the judgment scene of Matthew 25, Jesus commends the righteous for giving him a welcome when he came to them as a stranger, and he condemns those on the left because they did not invite him in. The righteous express surprise, and Jesus says, "Truly, I say to you, as you did it to one of the least of these my brethren, you did it to me" (v. 40). When the two travelers to Emmaus invited the stranger who had joined them on the road to stay with them for the night, he made himself known in the breaking of the bread as their Lord and Savior (Luke 24:13-35). Strangers are seen as those who give us a chance to show our love for God by ministering to the needs of others.

When Paul urges the Romans to "Welcome one another, therefore, as Christ has welcomed you" (15:7), he is revealing something close to the heart of the Gospel. Strangers may come to our Sunday morning assemblies, visit for a number of Sundays, and then leave—still strangers. A rose pinned on the lapel, a friendly smile, a "Hello, we are glad to have you today," and even a plea from the preacher that the visitors stay around and visit after the service will not suffice for the stranger in our midst. We can go through that ritual for weeks and never show deep caring for the stranger. The church cannot assume all of the blame for the thousands who move to urban areas and, as we say, "never darken the doors of the church building"; but I think we should recognize that we have not always done what we should have done to welcome at a deeper level the stranger in our midst. We're ingenious in so many ways that I think we should put our minds and, more important, our hearts to determining what we can do to convert the stranger into a friend.

The second group is the suffering. In Luke 4:40 we have a summary of Jesus' ministry to those who were suffering. "Now when the sun was setting, all those who had any that were sick with various diseases brought them to him; and he laid his hands on every one of them and healed them."

Although Capernaum as a town where people live has vanished, the name of Capernaum is immortal, for it was there that much of the ministry of Jesus centered. In the synagogue there was a man who had the spirit of an unclean demon, a familiar affliction in Luke's Gospel. Great numbers of people in Palestine were haunted by the fearsome belief that evil spirits existed and could invade human beings. The man cried, "Have you come to destroy us?" Jesus did not brush aside the man's agony but said, "Come out of him," and the man's distress was lifted (Luke 4:31–37).

The discoveries in modern medicine have made leprosy no longer the hopeless horror it used to be. Many lepers are cured, and those who still have the disease can be in colonies where their treatment is carried on under conditions of kindness and encouragement. But in earlier times, leprosy meant not only physical disintegration but also such exclusion from all decent contacts that it must have seemed to the leper that he was no more than a dead soul. The man full of leprosy in Luke 5 saw Jesus, fell on his face, and besought him, "'Lord, if you will, you can make me clean.' And he stretched out his hand, and touched him, saying, 'I will; be clean'" (Luke 5:12b, 13). Jesus could have healed the leper without touching his vile body, but our Lord communicated a tender love and compassion in his healing touch. This was probably the first time in years that anyone besides another leper had touched this man.

There is hardly a person among us who does not have some sort of back problem, slight or serious, and can all the more appreciate Jesus' miracle in Luke 13. A woman who had had a spirit of infirmity for 18 years and could not straighten herself came to the attention of Jesus. He called her and said, "'Woman, you are freed from your infirmity.' And he laid his hands upon her, and immediately [no therapy, no surgery] she was made straight" (vv. 12, 13).

When Jesus entered the city of Nain, he saw a man who had died being carried out, "the only son of his mother, and she was a widow." And when the Lord saw her, he had compassion on her and said, "Do not weep." He came, touched the bier, and said, "'Young man, I say to you, arise.' And the dead man sat up, and began to speak. And [Jesus] gave him to his mother" (Luke 7:11–15).

In this story we see Jesus' sensitivity to pathos and pain. In the pre-Christian world, women were subordinate; and although they might have their usefulness, they were not treated as being of any consequence. Although the young man is the center of the story, we catch a glimpse of what may be happening in a woman's heart. In the phrase "the only son of his mother, and she was a widow," we see something of the anguish of motherhood and the pathos of the woman left alone. I think in no miracle of Jesus is his compassion more clearly set forth.

All of us can this day pray the prayer we sing:

Once more 'tis eventide, and we,
Oppressed with various ills, draw near;
What if Thy form we cannot see,
We know and feel that Thou art here.

Thy touch has still its ancient pow'r;
No word from Thee can fruitless fall:

Hear, in this solemn evening hour,
And in Thy mercy heal us all.[2]

The third group of people is the poor. In Exodus 22:27 God says, "I am compassionate." In the laws he gave to his people, he demonstrates that compassion. They were not to exact interest from the poor; they were to restore the neighbor's garment before sundown; they were not to reap fields to the border or to strip vineyards bare.

In that Oriental world of the first century, to be poor meant not only to have no money but to have no justice either. The rich and powerful could exploit the little people as they pleased, and the poor were synonymous with the afflicted. One of the psalms pleads with God to "defend the cause of the poor of the people, give deliverance to the needy, and crush the oppressor!" (Ps. 72:4). Jesus had grown up among the poor, and he knew what was often the bitterness of their lot. He understood what it was like for some helpless individual to stand before an unjust judge. In his sermon in the synagogue in Nazareth, Jesus said that one of the features of his messiahship was that he would "preach good news to the poor" (Luke 4:18).

Jesus told the story of the rich man and Lazarus (Luke 16:19–31), not to show that being poor makes a man good and being rich makes a man wicked, but because Jesus knew that out of poverty actually come humility and patience. The poor, having no abundance of material things, may be more sensitive to the value of the things that are unseen. Someday the bitter inequities of this world will be set right.

In Galatians 2:10 Paul, in reporting his meeting with the apostles, said that they asked him to continue to remember the poor, the very thing he was eager to do. A large block of Paul's time was devoted to his collecting money for the poor saints in Jerusalem.

I think one of the commands of Jesus that we have not taken very seriously is, "When you give a feast, invite the poor, the maimed, the lame, the blind, and you will be blessed, because

---

[2]Henry T. Wells, "At Even, When the Sun Was Set," *Great Songs*.

they cannot repay you" (Luke 14:13, 14).

Peter Marshall preached a sermon one Sunday entitled, "By Invitation of Jesus." It told of a wealthy man who sat before the blazing log fire in his handsome house on a wintry night and happened to turn to this passage from Luke 14. He began to think about the dinner that Jesus described, and then he thought about the dinners and parties in his own home and the sort of people he invited. Most of them were listed in *Who's Who in Washington*, and there were those whose names were household words in business, finance, clubs, and government circles—but *they* were not poor or maimed or lame or blind. What, then, if he should try to carry out something like what Jesus pictured? He determined that he would. So he had cards engraved which began this way: "Jesus of Nazareth requests the honor of your presence at a banquet honoring the Sons of Want." Under that was the date for the dinner and the place where the guests were to meet.

A few days later as he went downtown with the invitations in his hands, he gave them to the sort of people he was inviting this time to his dinner—to an old man trying to sell pencils, to the blind man at the corner newsstand, to any forlorn person he met on the winter street. They looked at the cards with puzzlement and some with disbelief. But if you are hungry and cold, you don't pass up a possible chance to be fed. So when evening came, men were waiting in line at the Central Union Mission as was printed on the card. What they found there, though, were cars to take them to the home of the man who had issued the invitation—to be received by him and to sit down with him to the sort of dinner he would have given his most honored guests. When all the shyness and strangeness had melted away, he read them the words of Jesus and said to them, "If I have given you one evening of happiness, I shall be forever glad to remember it, and you are under no obligation to me. This is not my party. It is His! I have merely lent Him this house. He was your Host. He is your Friend. And He has given me the honor of speaking for Him."[3] I know that this sort of activity is seen frequently in homes around the Christmas season, but I hope we can make it more

---

[3]Marshall, comp. and ed., *The Best of Peter Marshall*, 41-52.

than a seasonal occurrence—something that could happen during any week of the year.

The fourth group is the marginal people—the ones who are different from us, the ones we might consider the unlovely ones.

Moses assured the people of his day that God loved them even though they had not deserved that love. "It was not because you were more in number than any other people that the LORD set his love upon you and chose you" (Deut. 7:7). Israel received the love of God because he chose to love her. Even in her unloveliness, God loved her.

Ezekiel 16 contains the allegory of the foundling child. In this chapter Israel is compared to a child who had been abandoned at birth, uncared for and unlovely. Yet God loved her anyway. God cared for her when no one else would care for her.

The Book of Hosea is another example of how God loved Israel in all of her unloveliness. Hosea's wife, Gomer, was a harlot and forsook him to go after her lovers. Finally, in utter degradation, she was auctioned off at the slave market. Hosea loved her in all of her unloveliness and bought her back for himself. The allegory was that of God's relationship to Israel. Even though Israel had forsaken God and played the harlot after other gods, God still loved her, as unlovely as she was, and would take her back if she would return.

The Samaritans were the marginal people of Jesus' day, and no story better illustrates Jesus' compassion toward this group than that of the Good Samaritan in Luke 10. Jesus tells the story in answer to the lawyer's question, "Who is my neighbor?" The priest and a Levite from the temple pass by the man who had been beaten and left for dead. But then comes a man of whom nothing would have been expected—a Samaritan. Between Samaritans and Jews there was the old, inveterate hatred. Although neither considered the other a neighbor, the Samaritan acted as though he were. He went straight up to the beaten man and dressed his wounds. He interrupted his journey long enough to take the wounded man to an inn, pay the innkeeper, and promise to come back and pay whatever more might be owed.

Jesus made the lawyer look at the difference between two

types of people: the men who did not want to find themselves in the neighborhood of anybody who needed help, in contrast with the other man whose spirit made him choose to be a neighbor. Landon Saunders tells the story of the rich lady who was being chauffeured through the poorest section of town. She looked around, obviously distraught, and said, "James, this is so distressing; we must do something about it. I know . . . James, don't drive me through this part of town anymore!"[4]

Neighborliness is not a question of who happens to live next to you but of who needs you and of where you will go and what you will do in answer to those needs. In John 4 the Samaritan woman was surprised that Jesus asked her for a drink: "For Jews have no dealings with Samaritans" (v. 9). Jesus crossed over the boundary of racial prejudice; he reached out and loved the unlovely.

On one occasion Jesus and his disciples found themselves at evening near a Samaritan village. To him Samaritans were also children of his Father. He would seek welcome in their town that night. The Samaritans would not receive him because his face was set toward Jerusalem. James and John were indignant and wanted Jesus to call down fire from heaven and blast these insulting villagers. They had not learned the great compassion of their Master. But Jesus called down no avenging fire; he simply went to another village (Luke 9:51–56).

In Jesus' healing of the centurion's servant recorded in Luke 7, we see a reflection of Paul's statement that in Christ Jesus there is "neither Greek nor Jew, circumcision nor uncircumcision, Barbarian, Scythian, bond nor free" (Col. 3:11; KJV). Even a Roman centurion was the recipient of Jesus' compassion.

The tax collectors were other marginal people in Jesus' day, yet Jesus calls one, Matthew, and makes him an apostle (Luke 5:27, 28). Tax collectors were despised; they served the alien rulers, and their business seemed to the people to be so much a thing of greed and graft that no decent person would be in it.

---

[4]Publication title and date unknown. Used by permission. Email from Landon Saunders, Norwich, VT, to Jean Saunders, Memphis, TN, March 27, 2009.

Levi made a great feast in his house, and the Pharisees and scribes asked, "Why do you eat and drink with tax collectors and sinners?" (Luke 5:30). Jesus did not look at men according to their labels; he could see what the individual person really was. And what he saw in this tax collector was what Dorothy Sayers has imagined as Matthew's description of his own response:

> I shan't forget my first sight of him neither. You don't know me, mister—well, I'll tell you. I was a tax-gatherer. You know what to think about that: I can see it in your face. One of the dirty dogs that works for the government and makes his profit out of selling his countrymen. That's so, and you're dead right . . . Well, see here. When he came down our street the other day, I don't mind telling you I'd had a pretty good morning . . . And I looked up—and there he was. "Hullo!" I thought, "here's the Prophet. I suppose he'll start calling me names like the rest of 'em. Let him. Hard words break no bones." So I stared at him, and he stared at me—seemed as though his eyes was going straight through me and through me ledgers, and reading all the bits as wasn't for publication. And somehow or other he made me feel dirty. That's all. Just dirty. I started shuffling my feet. And he smiled—you know the way he smiles sometimes all of a sudden—and he says, "Follow me." I couldn't believe my ears. I tumbled out of my desk, and away he went up the street, and I went after him. I could hear people laughing—and somebody spat at me—but I didn't seem to care . . . I said to him, "Master, I'm coming with you." And he said, "Come along."[5]

God's love for us removes all reasons we may have for not loving others. If God makes his sun shine on the evil and the good and sends rain on the just and the unjust, what right do we have to refuse our love to anyone, even our enemies (Matt. 5:43-48)? The unlovely around us are the ones who need our love the most.

---

[5]Sayers, *The Man Born to Be King*, 121–22.

In school it is the unlovely child who is most starved for love. The cantankerous brother or sister in the church is the child of God most desperately needing love and acceptance. "For if you love those who love you, what reward have you?" (v. 46).

A certain king was asked why he ate with his attendants and other inferiors. He said, "I dine with some because they are worthy, with others in order that they might become worthy." We love some because they are such lovely people we cannot help it. We love others in order that they may become lovely.

We must welcome marginal people. Jesus ate with outcasts; Paul and Luke took strong stands on behalf of those relegated to the position of second-class citizens in the church. We miss out on this fullness of life when we limit our partnerships to those who most resemble ourselves.

The fifth class of people who most need our care is the lost. The church is not a club or an association of like-minded and congenial people. No people are real representatives of Jesus if they sit still and nurse their own spiritual privilege and have no missionary eagerness.

The three parables that Jesus told in Luke 15 are keyed to one haunting word—lost. What is it like to be lost, to be sought for, and to be ultimately found? Jesus made the divine facts plain, not in any abstract terms but through pictures and parables which every human being could recognize and understand.

The first parable was about a lost sheep. In the Galilean country, there was no one to whom sheep and shepherds were not familiar. But the major emphasis in the parable is not on the sheep but on the shepherd. One sheep might not be much, but the shepherd thinks it is. The one sheep has value and an individuality of its own. In the words of Jesus, the shepherd "calls his own sheep by name and leads them out. . . . for they know his voice" (John 10:3, 4). So the love of God embodied in Christ Jesus knows human souls one by one and cannot rest when any single one has gone astray.

The second comparison is even more familiar than the first. A house was turned upside down for a coin. To the Galilean hearers, one silver coin represented far greater value than it suggests to a modern audience. It was half the annual sum that had to be paid as tax to the temple treasury by every head of a Jewish household. To the poor the loss of one coin would be a major calamity. In comparison to a rejoicing when the coin is found, Jesus said, "Just so, I tell you, there is joy before the angels of God over one sinner who repents" (Luke 15:10).

The third parable, that of the prodigal son (Luke 15:11–32), is the one in which the double theme of human lostness and the love of God becomes most near and poignant.

In Dickens' *David Copperfield,* when "little Emily" had been led astray by the seducer, Steerforth, Mr. Peggotty, who loved her more than his own life, went out to seek for her. And as he left, he said, "Every night, as reg'lar as the night comes, the candle must be stood in its old pane of glass, that if ever she should see it, it may seem to say, 'Come back, my child, come back!'"[6] And so the candle burned in the heart of the father. It was a wonderful day when the son came to himself and turned his heart toward home—to use the phrase of the Dobson film series.

Over all human lostness there is the untiring love of God, and that is the eternal wonder of the Gospel. His saving compassion comes not because we deserve it, but when we know we need it. Unlike the elder brother in the parable, our elder brother sought us, found us, and brought us home.

Jesus has said we are to love one among one hundred sheep. We are to love one from among ten coins. We are to love one from between two sons. Jesus came to save persons one at a time. The lost we love are persons, individuals with first names and addresses. Every life God has created has value in his sight. In the markets of Palestine, nothing could be cheaper than a sparrow. Five of them could be bought for two pennies. Yet not one sparrow could fall and God not know and care (Matt. 10:29). If that were true of a sparrow, how much more of a human soul!

We must never lose sight of the fact that the Great Commission is still in force today, and we must try somehow to recapture the zeal of the early Christians that made them want to compass land and sea to tell others that Jesus came to seek and save the lost.

---

[6]Dickens, *David Copperfield,* 425.

Major Ingredients of Caring

In the last part of this study, I would like to note some of the major ingredients of caring.

1. We must recognize the fact that we are all dependent on others—the yard man, the electrician, the farmer, the automobile mechanic, the policeman, the doctor, the factory worker—and that our ultimate dependence is on God, the giver and sustainer of life. Caring is a kind of debt. How could Paul spend his life crisscrossing the Roman Empire, teaching and enduring the hardships of imprisonments, beatings, stonings, shipwreck, danger from his own people, danger from the Gentiles, danger from robbers, danger from false brethren? He answers in the Roman letter, "We are debtors" (Rom. 8:12). We all owe a debt we can't pay; and in caring for someone we do, I think, show at least some recognition of that debt. We want to say, "Thank you, Lord," with deeds of service.

2. We must know that other person, and that takes time. The mother of Willard Sperry, a homiletics teacher at Harvard, told him when he began his ministry that when tragedy struck in the home of one of the members of his congregation, he should go to that person as a friend and not as a stranger. We have to know what the other person can and can't do—his powers and his limitations.[7]

3. We need to be patient—something akin to what the farmer exercises year in and year out. The person for whom we care may not always meet our timetable. We need something of the lessons we learn from Job—where patience carries the idea of being steadfast, just not giving up on that person. The friends who brought the paralytic to Jesus show something of this quality (Luke 5:17–26). They were not turned aside by any difficulty. More ordinary persons might have started out well enough on what they thought was a proper duty and then given up when the effort looked unreasonable. "Sorry, we wanted to get you there," they could have said, "but you can see for yourself how it is. The street is jammed with people. Jesus is inside that house;

---

[7]Sperry, Class Lecture Notes of Jack P. Lewis, Homiletics.

and there's no way of getting you on this pallet through the crowd even as far as the door. There's nothing left to do, but to turn around and take you home." However, they did not say that. They went up by the outside stairs that led to the flat roof of the Palestinian house; they made an opening in the roof, and they let their friend down directly into the presence of Jesus. This was friendship that amounted to something. How many of us have the spiritual devotion that will go the whole never-to-be-discouraged way to bring someone closer to the living Christ?

4. We must be honest. I must genuinely care for that other person. I must "ring true." I cannot always be thinking of how I might appear to other people. I must not be asking the question, "Is it the expedient thing to do?" but "Is it the right thing to do?"

5. We must trust when we care for another. We can see this characteristic most clearly when we must trust our children when they leave home for school or jobs. When someone knows that we trust him, he very often has a way of wanting to live up to that trust. We want to justify that trust and not to disappoint the person who believes in us. Trust does not mean letting someone go in any direction without guidance. The teacher who cares about his student doesn't leave him free to do whatever he wants to do but provides assistance and encouragement as well as information and helpful experiences. One of the most striking examples of trust in the New Testament is that of Barnabas, who dared to build a bridge of understanding between the recently converted Paul and the suspicious believers of Jerusalem who doubted if their persecutor had really seen the light (Acts 9:26–30).

6. We need to have hope. Someone has said that hope is very much like the coming of spring. I think of all the parables of Jesus, probably there is none more encouraging than the one of the sower or the four soils, as it is sometimes called, found in Mark 4. Surely when the sower sowed his field he hoped for some harvest, and there was that part of the field that brought forth 30-, 60-, and even one 100-fold. Paul's admonition to the Galatians is not to "grow weary in well-doing, for in due season we shall reap, if we do not lose heart" (Gal. 6:9).

7. We need constancy. This takes time, but I believe we have to care without a time limit. We can't say, "I'll care about you for three months, and that's my limit of endurance." It must be an open-ended kind of caring that sets no deadline. Probably all of us have had the experience of giving up too soon, especially when we aren't able to see any results or any fruit. We need something of the philosophy that says, "I'll keep on caring about this person until the Lord comes."

8. We must have the ability to see and to feel as the other person does. Sometimes we need to have had the same experience in order to do this, but sometimes we may have such sensitivity to the feelings of others that we can truly empathize with them. If we have not had the same loss, we have known sorrow; in some ways grief is grief, regardless of the nature of the loss.

The men and women who were in the leper colony of Molokai doubtless had many well-meaning would-be comforters, but certainly no word spoken to them before made their hearts leap as did the two words which one day came from the lips of Father Damien, the priest who had gone to live among them. "We lepers . . . ," he began. Then they knew that nothing they might suffer would be beyond his understanding.[8]

9. This ingredient I think may perhaps be the one that will keep us in the business of caring longer than any other one—think of doing it for Christ. I know of no one in recent times who better exemplified this than Mother Teresa of Calcutta. For more than 34 years she ministered to the old people dying in the streets, to babies that were left in garbage bins, and to leprosy victims driven away by their own families. She was probably the world's most admired woman and was awarded the 1979 Nobel Peace Prize. She also received Britain's prestigious Order of Merit. She rose at 4:30 every morning and turned her hand to anything that needed doing. "This work is done for Jesus," she said.[9] She believed that the most dreaded disease today is not leprosy or cancer but the feeling of being uncared for, of being deserted and alone. The most dreaded disease is indifference toward one's

---

[8]Farrow, *Damien the Leper*, 156–59.

[9]Teresa, *My Life for the Poor*, 52.

neighbor who may be a victim of poverty or disease or exploitation and who is at the end of his life left by the roadside.

A visitor writes of making rounds with Mother Teresa. At one bedside a young nun was cleaning a gaping wound in the neck of a woman being devoured by maggots. The exposed flesh was covered with the squirming creatures, and the nun was removing them, one by one with a pair of tweezers held at arm's length. "No, Sister, you haven't the idea," said Teresa sternly, moving into her place. Using a scalpel, she began to cleanse the wound with expert strokes, her face close to the mass. As she cut into it, the stench increased, but she did not pull back. Finally, she turned to the younger nun, "You must understand that it is Jesus. We're cleaning the wound of our Lord." A parting word to her visitor was, "If we didn't believe it was the body of Christ, we could never do it. No money could make us do it. The whole congregation is built on that: 'Love one another as I have loved you.'"

She wanted no credit for it, however, claiming she was only an instrument in God's hand. She did not want the one writing her story to dwell on her person. She said, "No one thinks of the pen while reading a letter. They only want to know the mind of the person who wrote the letter. That's exactly what I am in God's hand—a little pencil."[10]

10. Finally, care must be within limits. There are ups and downs in caring. Parents, nurses, teachers, friends have good and bad days. We are limited by our own responsibilities to home, children, jobs, physical health, energy, and time. Paul was limited in his care for all of the churches by his imprisonment. Jesus did not heal every blind, deaf, lame, and paralyzed person. He did grow weary and resorted to drawing away from the crowds. As one writer has aptly said, "We are not meant to die on every cross." We can, however, have a kindly interest in all good works, pray for endeavors worldwide, and take an active interest in at least one person.

---

[10]Source unknown. See "Remembering Mother Teresa," *The Passionists' Compassion*.

Conclusion

We have seen God's care from the beginning of time, the different kinds of people who need special care, and some of the major ingredients of caring. We conclude our lesson with a question as old as time, "Am I my brother's keeper?" (Gen. 4:9).

Out of the First World War, there came a recollection of two brothers. They were in the foremost trenches at the worst point of the Flanders battlefront. The young brother ventured out at dusk into no-man's land, was caught in a burst of enemy machine-gun fire, and collapsed into a shell hole, helpless. His older brother, seeing what had happened, determined to go and help him. His comrades in the trench tried to hold him back. He would only be shot himself and do no good. But he did go out and, though he was wounded, he did get to his brother's side. When darkness came, they were both brought in, the older brother with wounds deeper than the younger. And what the younger brother had said to him was this: "I knew you would come."

Perhaps somebody out there is just waiting for us to come.

[Date and occasion of this speech are unknown.]

18

THE GIFT OF ENCOURAGEMENT

The song "Home on the range, where seldom is heard a discouraging word" we think was surely about a land of fantasy when we pick up the morning paper or turn on television for the morning news and there seems to be no encouraging word. There is violence on every hand, and we think the whole world is enveloped in a state of hopelessness. We read Psalm 14:2, 3: "The LORD looks down from heaven upon the children of men, to see if there are any that act wisely, that seek after God. They have all gone astray, they are all alike corrupt; there is none that does good, no, not one." We might think that is speaking of our present age.

But we as Christians can make a difference in the world by a very simple act, which can be done by everyone—the gift of encouragement. Encouragement is universal; everyone needs it, and everybody can give it.

We can't all be an Elizabeth Bernard, who gave her life to mission work in China; or a Sarah Andrews, who gave her life to mission work in Japan; or a Hettie Ewing, who gave 55 years of devoted service on the south coast of Japan; or an Irene Johnson Gatewood, who for over 30 years taught children in postwar Germany and lived to see those children active in the church with many of them now preaching the Gospel in Germany. But we can all be encouragers.

Encouragement is a gift, though you may not have thought of it as one. Paul in Romans 12, in writing about the different gifts, speaks of the gift of encouragement (v. 8; NIV) along with that of prophesying, benevolence, serving, teaching, giving, leadership, and mercy. He does not indicate that teaching is a greater gift than encouragement. A member of my Sunday morning class told me recently that she had discovered what her gift was and that it was one of encouragement.

It seems right to begin with the source of encouragement. Paul, in Romans 15:5, 6, tells us, "May the God who gives endurance and encouragement give you a spirit of unity among yourselves . . . so that with one heart and mouth you may glorify the God and Father of our Lord Jesus Christ" (NIV). A comparison with other Scriptures shows that encouragement is the gift of all three persons of the Trinity. In Philippians 2:1 Paul takes it for granted that believers receive encouragement from being united with Christ. In Acts 9:31 we learn that encouragement comes from the Holy Spirit. "Then the church throughout Judea, Galilee and Samaria enjoyed a time of peace. It was strengthened; and encouraged by the Holy Spirit" (NIV). God the Father is the God of encouragement, God the Son gives encouragement to those who are in union with him, and God the Holy Spirit encourages the believer. How is this done? God encourages us by his Word, "the encouragement of the scriptures" (Rom. 15:4). God encourages us through other believers. Preachers of the Gospel encourage their people "to remain true to the faith" (Acts 14:22; NIV), and fellow believers encourage others by the example of their lives (1 Thess. 3:7; Philm. 7).

The New Testament is filled with admonitions to encourage (sometimes translated "exhort") and gives abundant examples. The early church needed encouragement, and Paul by his life and teaching gave great encouragement to Christians. He sent Tychicus to the Ephesian church and to the Colossian church so they would know about Paul and so that he might encourage their hearts. Tychicus seems to be Paul's emissary for encouragement. He sent Timothy to the Thessalonians to strengthen and encourage them in their faith (1 Thess. 3:2). As much as Paul needed their help, he still considered the encouragement of the brethren so important that he sent them on that mission. Paul told the Thessalonians to strengthen and encourage each other (1 Thess. 4:18; 5:11, 14). Paul in writing to the church at Rome said he longed to see them so that they might "be mutually encouraged by each other's faith" (Rom. 1:12). Paul's final words to Timothy were, "Preach the Word: . . . correct, rebuke and encourage" (2 Tim. 4:2; NIV).

What Encouraged Paul?

In writing to the troubled church at Corinth, Paul could still say he was greatly encouraged by their godly sorrow (2 Cor. 7:8–10), and he was encouraged at the restoration of good relations in the Corinthian church (2 Cor. 7:12, 13). The faith of the Thessalonian church encouraged him (1 Thess. 3:7).

Barnabas

The classic example in the New Testament of an encourager was, as you already know, Barnabas, whose very name means "Son of encouragement" (Acts 4:36). In the early days of the church, he is the one who acted with bold and almost reckless generosity. He is said to have owned a field, to have sold it, and to have donated the proceeds to help those in need. His help was practical. His giving was sacrificial. But Christian love will often challenge the powerful instinct of self-preservation and act in a way that seems almost irresponsibly reckless. A widow casting her only coin into the offering is not acting sensibly. Although the need for funds in the early days of the Jerusalem church may have been short-lived, the principle of the strong helping the weak was never abrogated. When such practical helpfulness (selling a field) ceases to be practiced by Christians, the church loses its true character as a vital brotherhood of believers. If the common faith of Christians does not make them deeply and constantly concerned to supply the need and to minister to the sufferings of their comrades in Christian fellowship, it is indeed a feeble and futile faith.

Barnabas' example challenges us to respond generously when we are confronted by the needs of the deprived whether near or far away. Barnabas encouraged the newcomer. When Saul of Tarsus became a Christian, there were those in the church who found it difficult to trust the man who had previously persecuted them.

How could they be sure of his change of heart? Some of the Christians at Jerusalem were distinctly cool toward him when he visited the city as a new convert. At this point Barnabas, a highly regarded member of the church, came forward and interceded on Paul's behalf. He introduced him to the apostles in Jerusalem, convincing them that Paul's conversion was genuine (Acts 9:26, 27). The Lord used Barnabas to open doors for Paul. Barnabas seemed to have a non-stop sort of love that saw godly potential in problem people. Perhaps we need to rethink our own attitude toward the newcomer. A greeting at the door is not enough. We need to find out the gift of the newcomer and put it to use.

Barnabas exercised a ministry of reconciliation between Jew and Gentile. Some of the exiles who came to Antioch, men originally from Cyprus and Cyrene, began to tell the gospel story to Gentiles and were rewarded by seeing a large number of believers added to the Christian fellowship. The Jewish Christian group at Jerusalem received the news of this innovation with dismay and sent a representative to see whether the step should be approved. Barnabas was the man chosen to execute this difficult mission. When Barnabas reached Antioch, he was convinced that this development was the work of the grace of God. He encouraged it and remained to further and lead the work. Because there was the need for more effective leadership, he sought out Saul of Tarsus and persuaded him to lend his aid in making the most of the open door of Antioch (Acts 11:25ff.).

Another indication of Barnabas' helpfulness is found at a later point in the history of the church. The church at Antioch, upon hearing of the impending famine, determined to send relief to their Christian brothers (Acts 11:27ff.). When the Antioch group chose representatives to take their contribution to Jerusalem, it was Barnabas along with Saul who was selected to head the delegation. Those who sent the gift knew that it was being put into the hands of trustworthy representatives.

Barnabas and Saul envisioned a still greater opportunity for missionary work. They set out on a mission which did not neglect the Jews but which was quick to offer the Gospel to Gentiles. It is to the credit of the church at Antioch that it was willing to give up its most trusted leader and its most promising younger worker for this wider work. Today often when people want to do foreign mission work they hear, "There is still work to do in this city." The church entrusted this mission to Barnabas and Saul. As told in Acts 15, when the missionaries later came to Jerusalem to defend the work which they had done, it was the word of Barnabas and Saul (now called Paul) that carried weight. The church always needs men who can build bridges of sympathy and understanding across the chasm of indifference which divides races and classes. It's a difficult work but a necessary one. Rather than separating because of differences, we need brave souls who can bring about reconciliation. It was Jesus who pronounced a special blessing on the peacemaker—he would be called a son of God (Matt. 5:9).

Barnabas encouraged a man who had failed. John Mark accompanied Paul and Barnabas on their first missionary journey and stayed with them in their preaching through Cyprus and until they reached Perga in Pamphylia. But when they decided to go farther into Asia Minor, his resolve weakened and Mark decided to return to Jerusalem. The Bible does not tell us why Mark gave up his work. Paul felt so strongly about Mark's desertion that he refused to trust him a second time on another missionary venture. Barnabas, however, was equally adamant in his insistence that Mark should be given another chance to redeem himself and declared his intention to take Mark with him in spite of Paul's opposition (Acts 15:36–41). Barnabas clung to the belief that there were greater possibilities in Mark than his past record indicated. He was Mark's relative, and it is no small thing for a man to have relatives who will believe in him when other people despair of him. The family should be the first to offer understanding and sympathy. It is to Barnabas' undying credit that he was prepared to take a risk and put trust in Mark a second time. Mark went on to reward his trust and became a useful servant of Christ. When Paul was a prisoner in Rome, we find that Mark is with him and the apostle is sending him on a mission to Colossae. In Philemon 24 Mark is called a fellow worker of Paul. In 2 Timothy 4:11 Mark is described as useful to Paul for his ministry. Barnabas understood the truth that God's forgiveness not only wipes out our failures but makes possible a new beginning. It was what Jesus did for Peter and what Barnabas did for John Mark.

Paul encouraged Philemon and prayed for him. Philemon's love had given Paul great joy and encouragement. Paul hoped to visit him. Can you imagine greater encouragement than a visit from Paul the aged?

Paul wanted Onesimus to have a second chance, and through Philemon we are sure he had that chance. In asking Philemon to give him that chance, Paul tells him he thanks God for his faith in the Lord Jesus and his love for all the saints.

I think that all of us at some time or another have felt as Louisa Fletcher when she wrote,

> I wish that there were some wonderful place
> Called the Land of Beginning Again,
> Where all our mistakes and all our heartaches
> And all our poor selfish grief
> Could be dropped like a shabby old coat at the door,
> And never be put on again.
>
> I wish we could come on it all unaware,
> Like the hunter who finds a lost trail;
> And I wish that the one whom our blindness had done
> The greatest injustice of all
> Could be at the gates like an old friend that waits
> For the comrade he's gladdest to hail.
>
> We would find all the things we intended to do
> But forgot, and remembered too late,
> Little praises unspoken, little promises broken,
> And all of the thousand and one
> Little duties neglected that might have perfected
> The day for one less fortunate.
>
> It wouldn't be possible not to be kind
> In the Land of Beginning Again;
> And the ones we misjudged and the ones whom we grudged

Their moments of victory here
Would find in the grasp of our loving handclasp
More than penitent lips could explain.

For what had been hardest we'd know had been best,
And what had seemed loss would be gain;
For there isn't a sting that will not take wing
When we've faced it and laughed it away;
And I think that the laughter is most what we're after
In the Land of Beginning Again.

So I wish there were some wonderful place
Called the Land of Beginning Again,
Where all our mistakes and all our heartaches
And all of our poor selfish grief
Could be dropped like a shabby old coat at the door,
And never be put on again.[1]

One of the best examples I know of a second chance is the story of a boy, member of a street gang, who broke out a window in a church building. An elder of the church offered him the alternative of coming to Bible class or of being reported to the police. He chose the Bible class. He became one of the most successful missionaries to the Japanese after World War II and continues to make annual trips back to that part of the world. He is Joe Cannon, once head of Mission 1000 in Memphis. He and his wife in their retirement moved to Okinawa to continue mission work among the Japanese. What a tragedy it would have been had the elder not given Joe a second chance! Hundreds of people from the Far Eastern countries will be in heaven because of Joe Cannon.

Who Needs Encouragement?

Everybody needs encouragement: parents, children, teachers, students, preachers, elders, deacons, Bible school teachers,

---

[1]Fletcher, "The Land of Beginning Again," 101–2.

the maintenance staff, secretaries, the young, the old, the lonely, the bereaved. I have chosen certain groups who especially need encouragement.

People Above Us

Sometimes we may think encouragement is just meant for people on our level—educationally, socially, economically. We may be more inclined to neglect the genuine expression of appreciation to those above us. I remember one time in a faculty meeting at Harding University, Dr. Benson was reporting on the financial needs of the school and his constant work to raise money for the school. He said that he had just received a gift of a million dollars (and this was back in the '40s when a million was more than it is today), and we just sat there as though it was no more than he was supposed to do—that was his job. And I remember—the only time I saw his reaction—he wept. I know how sorry I felt. I could have wept at our ingratitude. He should have received a standing ovation, and we just sat. I think we tried to make up for our ingratitude later, but we had lost that one shining moment when we should have encouraged him.

Children

There are so many negative feelings and expressions toward children these days that I think children of all ages need encouragement. I was interested in a column that recently appeared in our Memphis paper. Each week questions are asked of teenagers. One question recently asked was, "Who has inspired your dreams?" A 14-year-old said, "The person who has inspired my dreams is my mother. She's always encouraged me to strive and do my best at whatever I've attempted to do." A 16-year-old said, "My family has inspired most of my dreams. They've raised me in a warm and loving home and given me a good Christian background. My family has always encouraged me to succeed and has supported me in anything I've tried to do." A 13-year-old said, "My parents are the ones who have inspired most of my dreams. They've given me morals and taught me lessons to get through life. My parents are always encouraging me to do well in school, and they insist that I study hard."

When Luciano Pavarotti was a boy, his grandmother put him on her lap and said, "You're going to be great, you'll see." His mother dreamed he'd be a banker. "Instead," Pavarotti explains, "I ended up teaching elementary school and sang only infrequently. But my father constantly goaded me, said I was singing below my potential." Finally, at age 22, Pavarotti dumped teaching for selling insurance to give him enough time to develop his vocal talent. "Studying voice was the turning point of my life. It's a mistake to take the safe path in life. If I hadn't listened to my father and dropped teaching, I would never be where I am today. And, yes, my teacher groomed me. But no teacher ever told me I would become famous. Just my grandmother."[2]

When I think of helping children, I think of Eddie Grindley, director of Camp Shiloh for many years. Eddie's card read, "Eddie Grindley, Christian." He took the children from the east-side streets of New York to Yankee Stadium where they could see the New York Yankees play ball. The children thought they were in heaven.

When Sharon Draper, a strong Christian, was selected as teacher of the year in 1997, she was asked for her best advice for a first-year teacher. She answered quickly, "Smile at your children." If the children have left home, I think grandparents and uncles and aunts can encourage in many cases as much as or more than parents. Encouragement of children knows no age limit. As someone has said, "You take them on for life."

Senior Citizens

I believe "senior citizen" is the term most often used to describe us older people. I have always loved old people—even before I became old. When I came home from college on vacation, I went to see my mother's friends before my own. Women, as well as men, are often identified by the kind of work they do; so the first question asked is, "What is your work?" When the working years are past, we may wonder about the worth of our lives. But there are so many benefits to be derived in our retirement years. I will admit it took me some time to adjust after 44

---

[2]Source unknown. See Plaskin, "A Perfect Tenor."

years to a life that didn't involve teaching and librarianship. But after that time passed, I find that for the first time in my life I keep a calendar and look at it the first thing every morning. Here are three benefits:

1. We have vast accumulations of friendships. Someone has said, "Age is not measured in years but in friends." I recently had a call from a friend who attended Harding when I did. We had not seen each other for over 50 years (in fact, neither of us could recall the last time), and we closed the gap with a visit at the Freed-Hardeman lectures. You can't accumulate friendships like that unless you have lived a long time. A 20-year-old cannot know the joys of a 50-year class reunion from high school or college. I will admit I do not understand how people I taught could have already retired. I had a recent letter from a student library assistant in the Harding University library thanking me for starting her on a library career that spans 50 years.

2. We have an opportunity to engage in activities not normally possible during the years of child rearing and employment. We have to act out our own agenda; we can't let others do it for us. We have to learn to say "no" to some worthwhile activities because for most of us our energy level goes down as our years go up. I wish we could all be like Caleb who, when he was 85, asked for the hill country of Hebron to conquer.

3. One of the greatest blessings is more time to spend with the written word. Perhaps for the first time in our lives we have time for morning devotionals and intensive Bible study. We have time to read some of the classics. It takes time to read a Dickens novel, but I was delighted when Jack one Christmas gave me the complete works of Dickens. No, I haven't read them all. I know now I never will.

Those with Chronic Diseases

I think about the lame man we read about in John 5 who had been an invalid for 38 years. Crowds passed by him every day near the Sheep Gate where there was a pool, but the lame man was no more to them than a piece of scenery; then Jesus came along and healed him. Jesus had a second encounter with the man when he found him in the temple and admonished him to stop sinning. There are those who are confined to their home and never have a day when they feel really good. Telephone calls, notes, and visits break the monotony of their day. I have a friend who has arthritis all over her body. Her days are long and the nights lonely. She has a hearing problem, so it is difficult to talk with her over the phone or in person. But she is encouraged by notes to let her know she has not been forgotten. I like the story of the woman who went to the bank rather than to the automated teller. When asked why, she responded, "The automated teller doesn't ask me how my arthritis is."

Those in the Hospital

Volumes have been written on how to be helpful to those confined to the hospital. Jack and I belong to that school of thought that believes if someone is sick enough to be in the hospital, she doesn't need visitors. Our doctor friends agree, although we know every generalization has its exception. A few years back when I was in the hospital, I did not feel like visiting. I would not, however, let the nurse put on the door a "No Visitor" sign. One day Betty Copeland came and said, "Would you like for me to read the Bible to you?" That was the one thing I most wanted. She read chapter after chapter.

When the patient goes home, do not bring all the food the first week when one may have to say, "There is no more room in the refrigerator." That food would be most welcome the third or fourth week when the patient is really supposed to be well but doesn't have the energy to cook a meal.

The Bereaved

We can encourage the bereaved by our presence. I read recently of a teenaged son who was killed in a car accident. When a friend came to offer his condolences, the grief-stricken parents were too distraught to welcome their visitor, and they asked him to leave. The man went out to his car and sat there. Hours passed, and that evening a grieving family member looked out the window and noticed that the friend was still in front of the house. One of the parents commented later, "Many kind people visited us and sent us flowers. But in our time of sorrow, nobody encouraged us so much as the man who supported us with his presence."

In a study of 100 senior adult men, all leaders in their congregations, they were asked what was the most helpful ministry when their wives died. They all said, "Just being there." The least helpful, they agreed, were the visitors who talked too much.

Encouragement needs to be continued beyond the first week or even month. By that time the visitors have stopped coming, the long-distance calls have ceased, and the cards and letters have stopped; but the grief doesn't cease. After the crash of an airplane killed 132 people, one widow said, "In a month they will all be gone."

We need to continue our encouragement over long periods of time. Gladys West, the widow of Dr. W. B. West, said recently, "At night the walls just close in on me." If she knew that every night she was going to receive a phone call, it would be helpful. If she knew that every week there would be a friend to say, "This is our day for lunch together," it would be helpful. I suppose this can be overdone. Our neighbor at home, Miss Josephine, said that after her husband died she couldn't get her work done for all her phone calls.

Missionaries

Jack and I spent nine months on a sabbatical in Israel several years back, and we didn't get a lot of mail. We were very thankful for the church bulletin which did come regularly. When I came home, I determined I was going to write a newsletter to send to the missionaries White Station church sponsors and to our students from the Graduate School who were serving as missionaries. The list has now grown to 70. I tell them periodically that I don't expect them to answer but just to send their newsletters which they sent to their sponsoring churches. Many do write letters, though, and I feel as though I'm having a visit with them. I love to hear from them, and it is a reminder to pray for them.

Each Life Group in our congregation has a notebook, and each week every missionary should receive some kind of communication from some Life Group—maybe a card, a letter, or a phone call. We don't want them to think they have been forgotten. I know a couple who has spent over 35 years on the mission field, and their sponsoring congregations simply send the check—no letter. Last week one of our students said all of the time he was on the field, he did not have a letter from his congregation—again the check in the envelope and that was all.

A recent letter from Susan Krumrei, who is serving with her husband in a very difficult field—Holland—said, "Please write to us and let us know how you are doing. We most certainly would enjoy any encouragement that you can send our way. It sometimes becomes hard to be available as a spiritual help to all the people reaching out. I miss my parents very much. Their health is poor, and I ask your prayers for them both."

Elizabeth Bernard gave her life to mission work in China and Hong Kong. In 1951 Jimmy Lovell wrote that there was only "one worker among the 4 million in Hong Kong," and Elizabeth Bernard was that worker. Largely due to her efforts, there are now four congregations of churches of Christ in Hong Kong. When someone asked her about the difficulties she suffered, she said there were so many she hardly knew what to answer; but she spoke of what was on her mind the most—mail. She said, "By the time I write a letter and get an answer, even if they send an answer that day, which they don't, it's been two months, and by then I forgot what I asked." Everyone looks forward to the arrival of the mail boats. Of course, airmail now enables most letters to arrive in two weeks. Someone said a phone call is a utility; a letter is a gift. Email has proved to be a blessing for missionaries to keep in touch with sponsoring congregations, family, and friends.

On a lighter note, I recently saw this encouragement for stay-at-home moms in a Goodman Oaks bulletin:

> Now that I no longer have a small child around the house to care for, I am sometimes the victim of acute bouts with the Almost-Empty-Nest Syndrome. There are times when I begin to question my value as a stay-at-home full-time housewife. Just recently, however, I have begun to

realize that I do have a place in the scheme of things and that there are certain functions that only I am able to do.

The realization first came to me when I noticed that I am the only one in the family who knows how to take down a Christmas tree. In an effort to bolster my ego, I began to make a list of all the other jobs that only I can do. I am the only one who:

Knows how to replace the spare roll of toilet paper.

Can close the basement door.

Can put leftovers into little containers instead of putting the whole serving dish into the refrigerator.

Knows where the scattered shoes of each family member belong.

Knows how to iron.

Is able to take clothes out of the dryer.

Can repair a hem without using Scotch tape or staples.

Is able to roll up the cord on the vacuum cleaner.

Knows to let the dog out. Knows that a dog who has been let out has to be let back in.

Isn't afraid that the heels of the bread are poison.

It's nice to be needed.[3]

The Encourager

Sometimes the encourager (and there is one in every church who stands out) gets tired. Then the rest of us should encourage her and share her load of encouragement. A caring friend confided in me recently, "I am emotionally drained."

It's the Little Things

So often it's the little things that encourage someone else. Mark Twain said he could live for a whole month on one good compliment.

---

[3]Original author, title, and date unknown. *The Oak Leaf* is the bulletin of the Goodman Oaks Church of Christ, Southaven, Mississippi.

Gary Collins tells the story of his plane arriving late in Omaha and his being in a hurry to give a speech on how to help people. He wanted to get off the aircraft and into a taxi as quickly as possible. When he pushed into the aisle and moved toward the front of the plane, he hardly noticed the elderly lady who was struggling to reach the rack where her overnight bag had been placed. He thought, "Somebody should help her." But as he was going into the terminal and toward the baggage claim area, it struck him. In his hand was a briefcase holding notes about how we should help people, and in his pocket was a Bible telling him to encourage others and to give them a hand with their burdens; but he had been too preoccupied to help a fellow passenger with her luggage. He hoped somebody else did. He says that now whenever he goes on an airplane, he looks for opportunities to help a fellow passenger with her luggage.[4] That's one of the little things we can do.

James Turner tells the story of a faculty member who joined the staff of a small college. He was cheerful to his colleagues and warm and enthusiastic in the classroom. Students liked him. The administration found him efficient and innovative. One day several months later he overheard someone compliment him on the good reports he had heard about his teaching. The teacher looked dumbfounded and asked, "Who told you that?" "Why several people!" In four months nobody had said anything to this exemplary teacher about his performance. He said, "This certainly lifts my spirits."[5]

The other day I took a friend (in fact, she was a former student of mine at Harding) to her favorite Chinese restaurant for her birthday. She has had a sad and hard life, and that life has colored her outlook on the world. She surely does love the Lord and the Bible. At this restaurant she read the fortune in her cookie, and it read something about the warm glow she cast. She smiled, saying, "I'm going to put that on my refrigerator." I was so happy for her!

Another of the little things is that of listening. Listening takes

[4]Source unknown.
[5]Source unknown.

time and patience, qualities most of us have in short supply. Jesus took the time and had the patience to have a dialogue with the Samaritan woman in John 4. Jesus talked seven times and the woman six times. Each time Jesus talked, he responded directly to the statement that the Samaritan woman had just made. This is not a series of monologues in which each person resumed talking where he or she had just left off. It was a genuine dialogue with both persons listening carefully and responding concisely. The exciting aspect of this conversation is that Jesus revealed himself as Messiah to the Samaritan woman not through a speech but through a dialogue. The first request was, "Give me a drink" (v. 7). The last response was, "I who speak to you am he [the Messiah]" (v. 26).

Dietrich Bonhoeffer said in his book *Life Together*,

> The first service that one owes to others in the fellowship consists in listening to them. Just as love to God begins with listening to His Word, so the beginning of love for the brethren is learning to listen to them. . . . It is His work that we do for our brother when we learn to listen to him. . . .
>
> Many people are looking for an ear that will listen. They do not find it among Christians, because these Christians are talking when they should be listening. But he who can no longer listen to his brother will soon be no longer listening to God either.[6]

A wonderful biblical passage from Isaiah reminds me,

> The Lord God has given me
> the tongue of those who are taught,
> that I may know how to sustain with a word
> him that is weary.
> Morning by morning he wakens,
> he wakens my ear
> to hear as those who are taught.

[6]Bonhoeffer, *Life Together*, 97–98.

The Lord God has opened my ear,
and I was not rebellious,
I turned not backward (Isa. 50:4, 5).

If it's the little things that give the most encouragement, then why do we hold back?

1. We may not genuinely care about people. But there is no investment that pays such rich dividends as that of investing our lives in people. I think we must have a compassionate heart before we become encouragers. We must put ourselves in the place of the other person. Stephen Vincent Benét wrote, "Life is not lost by dying! Life is lost minute by minute, day by dragging day, in all the thousand, small, uncaring ways."[7]

2. We may be shy. However, I have known people who by nature were shy but who had such compassionate hearts and desire to help people that they overcame their shyness. Rumiko Obata, the wife of a preacher in Tokyo, is a very shy person; but every day she goes next door to the hospital, visits the cancer floor, and brings home the patients' laundry to do.

3. We say we are too busy. Many books have been written on time management, but I think most of us do what we really want to do. We find time for those things. I think the stewardship of time is just as important as the stewardship of money and talent. We are the only ones who can set our own priorities; we must not allow someone else to do it for us. I still like the hymn, "Work, for the night is coming, when man works no more."[8] We have to realize, however, that every need should be met but not by every person. Someone has wisely said, "We are not meant to die on every cross."

4. We may have a feeling of insecurity so that if we praise another, we somehow admit inferiority. That's a lame excuse. God is the one who gives talents, and all that he asks of us is that we be faithful in exercising those talents. It's biblical to rejoice in the good fortune of others.

Stan Paregien writes:

---

[7]Benét, *A Child Is Born*, 23–24.

[8]Annie L. Walker, "Work, for the Night is Coming," *Great Songs*.

> In the tiny village of Henning, Tennessee, there is a little cemetery. In that cemetery is a tombstone with the normal information one would expect to find: a man's name, his date of birth and the date of his death. But chiseled into that granite tombstone, there is also a phrase that summed up the man's life: "Find the Good and Praise It." That tombstone marks the grave of the late Alex Haley, Pulitzer Prize-winning author of *Roots*. He was the man who often said the phrase, "Find the good and praise it," but more importantly lived it out in his life.
>
> "Find the good and praise it" strikes me as sound advice, biblically and psychologically. However, the first part of that phrase, "Find the good," implies that it may be hard to find. Sometimes we have to, like the woman in Luke 15:8 looking for a lost coin, search every nook and cranny to find it.[9]

Paregien tells a story by Arthur Gordon in *A Touch of Wonder*:

> This friend had encountered two different groups of young writers at the University of Wisconsin many years ago. One group of male writers had a club called "The Stranglers." This group of highly intellectual young men would meet and read their essays or stories to the group, and then the group would criticize the writing. They dissected each other's work unmercifully. Meanwhile, across campus, some young female writers formed their own club and called it "The Wranglers." They met and read their manuscripts, just like the men. But their criticisms, if any, were gentle. They actually looked for good things to say.
>
> Well, the group of brilliant young male writers and the group of brilliant young female writers graduated and established careers. Then, some twenty years later, a researcher discovered that not a single man in the highly

[9]Paregien, "Find the Good," 36.

> critical group had made much of a mark in the literary world. The women's group, the praise-oriented club, had produced six very successful writers. One of these writers was Marjorie Kinnan Rawlings, author of the classic novel, *The Yearling*.[10]

Paregien's conclusion: "Praise really does build people up and make them more productive."

Jim Bill McInteer

My choice for a modern-day encourager is Jim Bill McInteer. As you know, his life in recent years has been troubled by the fact that his beloved Betty has suffered some memory loss and that he has suffered from a malignancy. Still, Jim Bill continues to encourage more people than anybody else I know. He has invested his life in people, and what concerns his vast number of friends is of concern to him. He publishes his little newsletter "To Stay in Touch," and every issue is a demonstration of his encouragement to others. He encourages his own family, cooking for them or arranging times for them to be together. He prepares lunch for Betty's garden club. He reports parties at his house and the joy he has in playing host. He tells of the funerals he has preached, and always his comments abound with the faith and noble deeds he has found in those people. By his words he comforts those who sorrow. He will tell about weddings he has performed and the joyful occasions they were. He recounts the invitations he and Betty have had and always says the food is the best. He recommends restaurants to try because he has been there and wants others to know those restaurants are excellent. He reports on the preaching he hears when he travels, and never has he had discouraging words to say about the preacher or his sermons. When I finish reading one of his newsletters, I am most thankful that God has given us a Jim Bill McInteer.

I am sure that you know that the Bible building on the Harding campus was named for him. If ever a building was appro-

---

[10]Ibid., 37.

priately named, it is this one. On a personal note, at the death of my mother, Jim Bill wrote a letter beginning with this statement, "She never knew a day when you did not love her." For 25 years that one statement has brought me comfort.

Four Reminders to Help the Encourager

1. Difficulties are not new. One of the reasons why the Bible is helpful in every generation is that it reflects difficulties on almost every page. It is not about people living in Utopia. Almost every psalm speaks of the hardships of life.

In the New Testament, the reader soon realizes that faith is maintained not in the absence of problems but in the midst of them. Characteristic of the entire New Testament are Paul's powerful words, "We are troubled on every side, yet not distressed; we are perplexed, but not in despair" (2 Cor. 4:8; KJV).

2. God's grace persists. We do not face problems alone. The heart of our faith is expressed in Romans 8:28 with its magnificent statement of how God works in the world: "We know that in everything God works for good with those who love him, who are called according to his purpose."

3. History is a record. Christianity survived the Dark Ages; some of the best Christian literature has been created behind prison walls—Paul's Prison Epistles and Bunyan's *Pilgrim's Progress*. We are part of something which Christ brought into the world with the prediction that it would prevail in spite of all dangers. He said when he first mentioned the church that the gates of Hades would not prevail against it (Matt. 16:18).

4. Finally, the ultimate in encouragement is the blessed hope. "He died for us so that, whether we are awake or asleep, we may live together with him. Therefore encourage one another and build each other up, just as in fact you are doing" (1 Thess. 5:10, 11; NIV). It is then that we will know the reality of the hymn:

When all my labors and trials are o'er,
And I am safe on that beautiful shore,
Just to be near the dear Lord I adore
Will thro' the ages be glory for me.

When, by the gift of His infinite grace,
I am accorded in heaven a place,
Just to be there and to look on His face
Will thro' the ages be glory for me.

Friends will be there I have loved long ago;
Joy like a river around me will flow;
Yet just the smile from my Savior I know
Will thro' the ages be glory for me.[11]

[Presented at Chattanooga, Tennessee, April 26, 1994; White Station Church of Christ retreat, September 23, 1994; Ladies' Day, Hernando, Mississippi, May 1998.]

[11]Charles H. Gabriel, "When All My Labors and Trials Are O'er," *Great Songs.*

19

MOTIVATION

How and why do we keep going in this life we call Christian? How do we motivate ourselves? A paratrooper needs no one to coerce him to listen to instructions. He knows he will soon be pushed out of a plane, and that's motivation enough to get all available help.

Those of us who teach have wondered for as long as we have taught how to motivate capable students to get an education. We say to students, "Get an education so you won't be on the streets, so you can get a good job, so you can be successful as the world counts success." More often than not, these reasons for getting an education are not motivating students to get one. A friend of mine, whose family is on welfare, has a daughter who turned down a $12,000 scholarship to college. We hope the Fogelman proposal will motivate students to pass their work, to stay clear of drugs, and finally to get a college education. But motivation in education continues to baffle administrators and teachers alike. We say if a student is not capable of doing more than "C" work, we can accept that. But the most frustrating student is the one who has God-given ability and doesn't use it. The teacher wishes for the wisdom of Solomon to motivate that student.

Yet we have known some highly motivated students in education. We have a student this semester at the Graduate School who gets up at 3:30 a.m. to drive more than 200 miles for an 8:00 a.m. class. Many students work at Federal Express from midnight till 4:00 a.m. Why do they struggle through Greek and Hebrew when they could take less demanding courses? They want to be able to read the Bible in its original languages. The

University of Tennessee Medical School here gives an award to the graduating student who has earned his degree under the greatest difficulty. I remember when Dr. Henry Farrar won that award. He had a family and worked almost full time to get that M.D. Any doctor's wife who has suffered through an internship and residency knows the struggle. We can see the crucial issue at stake in the world of education, but what about the world of religion in which the stakes are much higher?

Boredom seems to threaten our whole faith. The church has developed a philosophy that places considerable emphasis on excitement and good feelings in regard to serving the Lord. Serving God and doing his will have nothing to do with how it makes you feel in doing it, how excited you get, or how much fun you have. We think we need to get people enthusiastic by positive thinking, making worship services like high school pep rallies, and sending members to workshops, seminars, and lectureships. But then what happens when the adrenalin goes down? Spending long hours at a hospital with those concerned about a loved one is not fun and games. But it does create a sense of peace to know you have served God and have benefited others.

The basis of this lesson on motivation is faith in what God has said in his Word. The Hebrew letter was written to a tired community—written for weary Christians with drooping hands and weak knees (Heb. 12:12). The most devoted Christian will at times experience drooping hands and weak knees. We hope this lesson will give encouragement not to lose heart when these times come.

Even among dedicated servants of the Lord, we may say or we may hear on occasion, "I really do get tired of cooking for fellowship meals, and I get tired of taking casseroles to people." Or "I don't know who will do this particular service when the older generation is gone." Or "I just need to get away." All of these feelings are true and legitimate. Jesus himself grew weary and had to get away. But we must not give up and take a permanent leave from the Lord's work.

Paul in 1 Corinthians 15:58 writes, "Therefore, my beloved brethren, be steadfast, immovable, always abounding in the work of the Lord, knowing that in the Lord your labor is not in vain."

The preceding verse is, "But thanks be to God, who gives us the victory through our Lord Jesus Christ" (1 Cor. 15:57).

In 1 Thessalonians 1:3 Paul commends the Thessalonians for their "steadfastness of hope," and in 2 Thessalonians 1:4 he tells them that he boasts of them for their "steadfastness and faith" in all of their persecutions and in the afflictions they are enduring.

Jesus in Revelation 2:2 commends the church at Ephesus for its "patient endurance," and he also knows the "patient endurance" of the church at Thyatira (Rev. 2:19).

This endurance carries with it the idea of "to the end." Yogi Berra made famous the phrase, "The game is not over till it's over." If you enjoy things like the Super Bowl, you must have had a thrilling day this year when quite a bit of excitement was generated in the fourth quarter. The game was won or lost in the last minute of the fourth quarter. Those of you who follow college basketball games know the outcome of the game may be determined in the last minutes of the game.

In the beginning of the Christian life, there is an excitement as one is baptized into Christ and is warmly greeted by members of God's family. There is the thrill of worship and everything is exciting. But sustaining that interest is often difficult. Charlie Fowler, White Station's minister to the Young Adult Singles, recently in our bulletin asked two questions: "Why is class attendance so inconsistent?" and "What happened to our spirit of service and community?" I thought that if this most active and service-oriented group is asking such questions, what about the rest of us?

Jesus, in his Parable of the Sower, points out that the Christian life is much like that of the farmer sowing seed. Some of the seed falls on the rock, does well for a while, but then dies because it has no root. Eternal life is often won or lost in the fourth quarter. "Be faithful unto death, and I will give you the crown of life" (Rev. 2:10b).

Peter, in his second epistle (2:20, 21), says it is better for one never to begin the Christian life if he is going to foolishly forsake it before the finish. The writer of the Hebrew letter in the context of the warning against falling away from God says in 3:14,

"For we share in Christ, if only we hold our first confidence firm to the end."

Demas was a friend and co-worker of Paul at Rome. But he later deserted Paul (2 Tim. 4:10) because he was in love with this present world. Judas gave up. He should have known after being around Jesus and hearing his teaching on forgiveness that Jesus would have forgiven him too.

But Peter endured to the end. And John Mark, although he disappointed Paul when he left him and Barnabas on their first missionary journey, at the end was very useful in serving Paul (2 Tim. 4:11). Jesus gave the final answer in seeing his faithfulness to his mission through to the very end when he uttered, "It is finished" (John 19:30).

As we have said earlier, the basis of this lesson on motivation is faith in what God has told us. But as children we want to know why. We have an endless listing of whys. Almost everything a child is told to do meets with the inquiring, "Why?" Sometimes we say, "Because I said so." Sometimes we give a reason. So it is in our Christian life when we ask the why of a certain command. God may not always give us a reason, but oftentimes he does. So now we want to look at some of the reasons for some of the instructions the Lord has given to us on how as Christians we ought to live. We will look at four areas—service, family relationships, the marketplace, and times of suffering—and then look at examples to motivate us to hold to God's unchanging hand.

Service

In the area of service ("good deeds," it is often called), we grow tired. But James 1:22–27 tells us to be "doers of the word." God is not interested in people auditing Christianity. The auditor sits through lectures, never takes a test, never turns in an assignment, has no responsibility. He doesn't even have to listen to lectures. However, he never gets a grade or credit for the course.

In Colossians 3:23, 24 we read, "Whatever your task, work heartily, as serving the Lord and not men, knowing that from the Lord you will receive the inheritance as your reward; you are serving the Lord Christ." Whatever your task—making phone calls for prayers and encouragement or working in the clothes closet, you are serving the Lord; preparing meals for your family, you are serving the Lord; taking somebody to the doctor, you are serving the Lord; working in the nursery, you are serving the Lord; cleaning grimy bathrooms, you are serving the Lord. "Whatever your task" covers a multitude of services.

I know of no one today who better exemplifies this than Mother Teresa of Calcutta. For over 35 years, she ministered to the old people dying in the streets, to babies that were left in garbage bins, and to leprosy victims driven away by their own families. She was probably the world's most admired woman, having been awarded the 1979 Nobel Peace Prize. She also received Britain's prestigious Order of Merit. She rose at 4:30 every morning and turned her hand to anything that needed doing. "This work is for Jesus," she said. She believed that the most dreaded disease today is not leprosy or cancer but the feeling of being uncared for, of being deserted and alone, of being left by the roadside at the end of life. The most dreaded disease is an indifference toward one's neighbor who may be a victim of poverty or disease or exploitation.[1]

A visitor wrote of making rounds with her. At one bedside a young nun was cleaning a gaping wound in the neck of a woman being devoured by maggots. The exposed flesh was covered with the squirming creatures and the nun was removing them, one by one with a pair of tweezers held at arm's length. "No, Sister, you haven't the idea," said Teresa sternly, moving into her place. Using a scalpel, she began to cleanse the wound with expert strokes, her face close to the mass. As she cut into it, the stench increased but she did not pull back. Finally, she turned to the younger nun, "You must understand that is Jesus. We're cleaning the wound of our Lord." A parting word to her visitor was, "If we didn't believe it was the body of Christ, we could never do it. No money could make us do it. The whole congregation is built on that: 'Love one another as I have loved you.'"[2]

---

[1]Teresa, *My Life for the Poor*, 52.

[2]Source unknown. See "Remembering Mother Teresa," *The Passionists' Compassion*.

Jesus in depicting the great judgment day expounds this idea. If we give food to the hungry, if we clothe the naked, if we give a drink to the thirsty, if we welcome a stranger, if we visit those in prison, we are in fact doing all of those services for him.

In Titus 3:14 Paul says that people should learn (something that can be learned) to "apply themselves to good deeds." Why? ". . . to help cases of urgent need, and not to be unfruitful." In Philippians 4:17 Paul writes that he seeks not the gift but the fruit which increases to their credit. He wanted Christians to bear fruit, echoing Jesus' teaching on the sound tree and sound fruit.

In his Letter to Timothy, Paul has a word for the rich in this world. "They are to do good, to be rich in good deeds, liberal and generous." Why? By so doing they are "laying up for themselves a good foundation for the future, so that they may take hold of the life which is life indeed" (1 Tim. 6:17–19).

Paul tells the Galatians (6:9, 10) not to "grow weary in well-doing" (he knew the tendency) but to "do good to all men, and especially to those who are of the household of faith." Why? Because there is a harvesting season coming, and we will reap eternal life.

Finally, in this area of good deeds, Jesus shows us by his example and teaching that genuine compassion for hurting people should motivate us to serve them. "And Jesus went about all the cities and villages, teaching in their synagogues and preaching the gospel of the kingdom, and healing every disease and every infirmity. When he saw the crowds, he had compassion on them . . ." (Matt. 9:35, 36).

> As he went ashore he saw a great throng; and he had compassion on them, and healed their sick. When it was evening, the disciples came to him and said, "This is a lonely place, and the day is now over; send the crowds away to go into the villages and buy food for themselves." Jesus said, "They need not go away; . . ." (Matt. 14:14–16).

I stand condemned every time I read this miracle. While working at Camp Shiloh one summer with Eddie Grindley, I learned about compassion. If the parents of the children were coming to visit on Sunday, they were to let the camp know so preparation could be made for the extra people. Sunday came, and so did the crowds—but without any previous notification. I said, "Let them go into town and eat." Eddie, Christ-like as he was, said, "No, we'll feed them here." And we did.

Then again in the very next chapter (Matt. 15:32–37) Jesus tells his disciples, "I have compassion on the crowd, because they have been with me now three days, and have nothing to eat; . . ." (Matt. 15:32). Then he fed the 4,000.

I suppose a favorite miracle for all of us is when Jesus had compassion on the widow of Nain (Luke 7:11–17) and told her not to weep. Then he raised her son, her only son, and gave him to his mother.

Family Relationships

Why do we act as we do in family relationships? Why in Colossians 3:20 are children told to obey their parents? Because it pleases the Lord—and that is reason enough. More than anything, we want to please our parents, at least my generation did. How much more do we want to do that which pleases God!

In the context of husbands and wives, in Ephesians 5:21 Paul writes, "Be subject to one another." Why? "Out of reverence for Christ." You may not be able to respect your husband, but Christ is worthy of all the reverence we can give to him.

In 1 Peter 3:1, we read, "Likewise you wives, be submissive to your husbands." Why? "So that some, though they do not obey the word, may be won without a word by the behavior of their wives." I suppose all of us have known such cases. My friend Helen hoped and prayed for her husband for 20 years. Then her letter came saying that he had become a Christian. He later told me, "I would never have done it except for living with Helen for 20 years."

In 1 Peter 3:7, "Likewise you husbands, live considerately with your wives." Why? "You are joint heirs of the grace of life, in order that your prayers may not be hindered." We read books and we hear sermons on conditions for answered prayer—Is it God's will? Do we pray in faith? Do we have a forgiving spirit?

Do we have an unselfish motive? However, I don't believe I have heard this condition preached—Do I live considerately with my spouse?

Paul, in giving instructions to older women in his letter to Titus (2:3ff.), said, "Train the young women to love their husbands and children, to be sensible, chaste, domestic, kind, and submissive to their husbands." Why? "That the word of God may not be discredited." What a serious charge if by our lives we discredit the Word of God!

In our family relationships, we are motivated to keep on because of future generations. Ever since Alex Haley's *Roots*, we have been more conscious of our heritage. We must know our roots and be able to tell our children so they can pass along their faith to their children.

> When your son asks you in time to come, "What is the meaning of the testimonies and the statues and the ordinances which the LORD our God has commanded you?" then you shall say to your son, "We were Pharaoh's slaves in Egypt; and the LORD brought us out of Egypt with a mighty hand; . . . And the LORD commanded us to do all these statutes, to fear the LORD our God, for our good always, that he might preserve us alive, as at this day" (Deut. 6:20–24).

In later rabbinic thought, when the son asks during the Passover feast, "Wherein is this night different from all other nights?" then the father retells the story of the Exodus. It is a moving experience to be able to participate in a Passover Seder.

So it is today. If we don't remind our children of the great truths of the Gospel—life, death, burial, and resurrection of Jesus—the Lord's Supper will lose its significance. Children will not know its meaning and will finally give it up. It will become a formality with which they can dispense. Timothy, that young man taught by his mother and grandmother, never wavered from the Way and received, I think, the highest compliment any individual received from Paul when he said, "I have no one like him, who will be genuinely anxious for your welfare" (Phil. 2:20).

The Marketplace

Paul, in writing to the Thessalonians about their problem of idleness while they were waiting for the Lord's return, said he did not eat anyone's bread without paying and that he worked night and day so he might not be a burden to anyone (1 Thess. 2:9). Later in that same epistle (4:11, 12), he wrote that the Thessalonians should work with their hands so that they might "command the respect of outsiders, and be dependent on nobody."

Paul's instructions to masters and slaves (Eph. 6:5ff.) might well be transferred to employer and employee in today's world. Employees, be obedient to your employers and render service with goodwill. Employers, do the same. Why? For you both have a Master in heaven, and he doesn't show partiality.

In his Letter to Titus (2:9, 10), Paul writes, "Bid [employees] to be submissive to their [employers] and to give satisfaction in every respect; . . . to show entire and true fidelity." Why? "So that in everything they may adorn the doctrine of God our Savior." In Romans 12:2, we read, "Be transformed by the renewal of your mind, that you may prove what is the will of God"—his good, pleasing, and perfect will. Can you imagine slaves adorning something so perfect as God's will? They can by their fidelity.

Times of Suffering

Jesus said in his Sermon on the Mount, "Love your enemies and pray for those who persecute you." Why? "So that you may be sons of your Father who is in heaven" (Matt. 5:44, 45). If we want to be God's child, to be in God's family, then we must love our enemies and pray for those who may mistreat us. In Romans 5:3 Paul tells us not only to endure the suffering but to rejoice in our sufferings. Why? I think here we have probably the most encouraging passage in all of Scripture for those who suffer, because "suffering produces endurance, and endurance produces character, and character produces hope, and hope does not disappoint us" (5:3–5). I daresay you have seen that passage lived out among some of your Christian friends.

We must remember that every trial is bearable. "God is faithful, and he will not let you be tempted beyond your strength" (1 Cor. 10:13). We have the word of the One who has kept every promise ever made from Genesis on.

Finally, in this matter of suffering, everybody else may desert you, but not Jesus. In 2 Timothy 4:16, 17 Paul writes that at his first defense no one took his part but all deserted him. He adds that the Lord stood by him and gave him strength, and that strength could not have been matched by any of Paul's co-workers.

We have looked at how we might be motivated to finish what we have begun in our Christian life in the areas of service, family relationships, the marketplace, and times of suffering.

Examples of Others

I think the examples of others may motivate us to keep on in all areas of Christian life. Job, with all of his suffering, argued with God, wanted an umpire, but never renounced God. Hebrews 11 is an honor roll of those who did not give up. I love the NIV rendering of Hebrews 11:13: "All these people were still living by faith when they died." Paul, despite afflictions on every hand, never had the slightest intention of giving up. He could three times say, "Imitate me" (1 Cor. 4:16; 11:1; Phil. 3:17). And once (1 Cor. 11:1) he qualifies his statement with "as I follow . . . Christ." Job, Paul, and others assure us that if others held out, so can we.

Harvey Porter read of a woman 107 years old who had been a Christian since she was 11. She had not missed services of the church except when she was sick. "I am sure," he said, "she saw some church fusses in her time, heard some poor preachers, sat through some dull Bible classes, wasn't spoken to by some church members, was neglected by some who knew better; but through it all, she was still there."[3]

We love to hear over and over the story of Polycarp, that early

---

[3]Porter, bulletin article, *The Exhorter* (date unknown). Used by permission. Email from Joel Porter, Dallas, TX, to Jean Saunders, Memphis, TN, April 1, 2009. *The Exhorter* is the bulletin of the Montgomery Boulevard Church of Christ in Albuquerque, New Mexico, where Harvey Porter (d. 1998) peached for 39 years. See some of his sermons at http://www.giftofeternallife.org/about_us/about_sermon.shtml (accessed March 23, 2009).

Christian martyr, who said when urged to renounce God and spare his life, "Eighty and six years have I served him and he has never done me wrong. How can I blaspheme him, my king, who saved me? . . . I am a Christian."[4] And he was burned at the stake.

The ideal example, as always, is Jesus. The writer of Hebrews tells us to "run with perseverance the race that is set before us, looking to Jesus the pioneer and perfecter of our faith, who for the joy that was set before him endured the cross, despising the shame, and is seated at the right hand of the throne of God" (12:1b, 2). We have a certain admiration for the person who is first whether in space travel, mountain climbing, or any other field. Jesus is our pioneer.

Unclassified Motivators

I would like to challenge you to read your Bible looking for sign words—*therefore, if, then, for, inasmuch as, so, because,* and others. To get you started, turn first to the promises given in the beatitudes. IF we are poor in spirit, we will have the kingdom of heaven. IF we mourn, we will be comforted. IF we are meek, we will inherit the earth. IF we hunger and thirst after righteousness, we will be satisfied. IF we are merciful, we will obtain mercy. IF we are pure in heart, we will see God. IF we are peacemakers, we will be called sons of God. And IF we are persecuted for Jesus' sake, we will have a reward in heaven.

Why does John say his Gospel was written? SO that we might believe that Jesus is the Christ, the son of God, and believing might have life in his name (John 20:30, 31). This is the reason that, for those who are seeking to know God's will, we usually say, "Read first the Gospel of John."

Why do we lead a life of purity? BECAUSE we have been bought with a price (1 Cor. 6:20)—and at what cost!

Why do we obey God's commandments such as not forsaking the assembly (Heb. 10:24, 25)? BECAUSE IF we love God, we will keep his commandments (John 14:15). And why do we love

---

[4]Polycarp, *Martyrdom*, 9:3.

God? BECAUSE he first loved us (1 John 4:19).

Why do we pray and work for unity among Christians? SO that the world may believe (John 17:21). The greatest deterrent in evangelism is a divided Christendom.

Why do we forgive anyone whom we think has wronged us, whether family, friend, or enemy? SO we will be forgiven by our Father (Mark 11:25). Even if motivated by self-interest, we cannot afford an unforgiving spirit.

Why must the Lord's servant be kind to everyone, an apt teacher, forbearing, correcting with gentleness? SO that his opponent will repent and come to know the truth and escape the snare of the devil (2 Tim. 2:24–26).

How is it that we can with confidence draw near to God's throne of grace? BECAUSE we have a high priest who in every respect has been tempted as we are and yet without sin (Heb. 4:15).

Why do we refrain from judging? SO that we will not be judged—for whatever judgment we dispense will return to us (Matt. 7:1, 2).

Why do we give? SO that another's wants may be filled and SO proof of our love is given (2 Cor. 8:14, 24).

Why must we work now? BECAUSE night will come—whether it is poor health, death, or something else—when we can no longer work (John 9:4).

Finally, the ultimate motivator for all of us is heaven, where our citizenship is (Phil. 3:20). We look forward to what no earthly father is able to give to us no matter how great his love for us—an inheritance which is imperishable, undefiled, and unfading (1 Pet. 1:4). The Bible doesn't tell us so much about heaven, but everything that we read about it makes us know we want to go there:

We will see God face to face—something that was never given to the greatest of the Bible heroes and heroines.

We will see and have fellowship with all of the saints that have gone before. You will have your list of those you most want to see, and I have mine. When you visit the cave of Machpelah in Hebron where Abraham and Sarah are buried, you think you are standing on holy ground. But think of seeing them face to face. Imagine seeing loved ones who have gone before you. I love the German motto, "Those who live in the Lord never see each other for the last time."

We won't need locks and security doors. There will be no thieves (Matt. 6:20).

We won't have any lack of provisions; we shall hunger and thirst no more (Rev. 7:16).

It will be a place of service and worship (Rev. 22:3).

There will be no more pain, death, or sorrow, and God himself will wipe away every tear (Rev. 7:17b).

There will be no night (Rev. 22:5).

Paul tells us not to lose heart (2 Cor. 4:16) despite disappointments and afflictions of this life because "we have a building from God, a house not made with hands, eternal in the heavens" (2 Cor. 5:1).

I want to close with a thought from Dale Pauls. The world consists of two kinds of people. So does the church. Those who serve and those who insist on being served. Those who give and those who take. Those who meet needs and those whose needs must be met.[5] Inevitably, the heaven-bound church keeps the one group and loses the other. Always and forever.

[Presented at Ladies' class, Highland Street Church of Christ, Memphis, Tennessee, no date; Ladies' class, White Station Church of Christ, Memphis, Tennessee, no date.]

---

[5]Pauls, bulletin article, *The Stamford Messenger* (date unknown). Used by permission. Email from Dale Pauls, Stamford, CT, to Don Meredith, Memphis, TN, August 30, 2007. *The Stamford Messenger* is the bulletin of the Stamford Church of Christ in Stamford, Connecticut.

THE WAY IT IS GOING TO BE

"If my earthly home holds such affection, how much more will my home in heaven!"

Annie May Alston Lewis

Photo by Jeff Montgomery, Harding University Public Relations Office

Annie May and Jack Lewis
March 31, 2005

20

HEAVEN

My first year in college, my parents told me that I could join other students for a Thanksgiving bus trip to Washington, D.C. For a freshman with limited travel experience, a trip to the nation's capital sounded like a dream come true. The week of the trip, my roommate, whose West Tennessee home was a short distance from mine, said, "My daddy is coming for me at Thanksgiving to take me home. Would you like to go with us?" The fascination of the Washington trip very quickly faded with the prospect of going home to spend Thanksgiving with Mama and Daddy.

I cancelled the trip, packed my bag, and was on my way home. To make the event even more exciting, I didn't call home. I knocked at the door. Sixty-eight years later the memory of the initial shock, the open arms, and smiles are as vivid as today's events. What was the nation's capital in comparison with my small hometown? The White House couldn't hold a candle to that white frame house that was home to the two people I loved best in the world.

I have in recent years enjoyed the privilege of travel to distant lands, but I have discovered that whether the distance traveled is ten thousand miles or one hundred miles, whether the absence is nine months or a weekend, I am always eager to return home and inevitably say, "There's no place like home." The oft-repeated phrase may seem trite, but it's true. Scripture uses the literary device, "How much more." So it will be with heaven. If my earthly home holds such affection, how much more will home in heaven!

As Mama and Daddy made such loving preparation for the homecoming of each child, so Jesus is now preparing for my homecoming. There is so little about heaven that I know, but I do know that running up those front steps on that Thanksgiving morning is a foretaste of the joy that awaits me.

On occasion I return to my hometown for visits with cousins and close neighbors, but the people for whom I made those very frequent trips are no longer there. The house still stands and the memories are still there, but those who made the memories have already gone home. I look forward to an association with them that won't include any goodbyes.

Elizabeth Goudge, in her novel *The Dean's Watch*, has the dean say to the watchmaker, Isaac, who is afraid of dying, "We shall see many kindly faces. It is a house, remember, a friendly place."[1] Indeed that and much more. It is home.

[Printed in *Server*, White Station Church of Christ, Memphis, Tennessee, February 2004.]

[1]Goudge, *The Dean's Watch*, 301.

21
Favorite Scriptures

Psalm 27:1—

The Lord is my light and my salvation;
whom shall I fear?
The Lord is the stronghold of my life;
of whom shall I be afraid?

Psalm 27:13, 14—

I believe that I shall see the goodness of the Lord
in the land of the living!
Wait for the Lord;
be strong, and let your heart take courage;
yea, wait for the Lord!

Psalm 37:25—

I have been young, and now am old;
yet I have not seen the righteous forsaken
or his children begging bread.

Psalm 57:2—

I cry to God Most High,
to God who fulfils his purpose for me.

Psalm 103:11–14—

For as the heavens are high above the earth,
    so great is his steadfast love toward those who fear him;
as far as the east is from the west,
    so far does he remove our transgressions from us.
As a father pities his children,
    so the LORD pities those who fear him.
For he knows our frame;
    he remembers that we are dust.

Psalm 118:24—

This is the day which the LORD has made;
    let us rejoice and be glad in it.

Psalm 119:71—

It is good for me that I was afflicted,
    that I might learn thy statutes.

Isaiah 40:28–31—

Have you not known? Have you not heard?
The LORD is the everlasting God,
    the Creator of the ends of the earth.
He does not faint or grow weary,
    his understanding is unsearchable.
He gives power to the faint,
    and to him who has no might he increases strength.
Even youths shall faint and be weary,
    and young men shall fall exhausted;
but they who wait for the LORD shall renew their strength,
    they shall mount up with wings like eagles,
they shall run and not be weary,
    they shall walk and not faint.

Nehemiah 8:10—

> Then he said to them, "Go your way, eat the fat and drink sweet wine and send portions to him for whom nothing is prepared; for this day is holy to our Lord: and do not be grieved, for the joy of the LORD is your strength."

Lamentations 3:22–24—

> The steadfast love of the LORD never ceases,
> his mercies never come to an end;
> they are new every morning;
> great is thy faithfulness.
> "The LORD is my portion," says my soul,
> "therefore I will hope in him."

Habakkuk 3:17, 18—

> Though the fig tree do not blossom,
> nor fruit be on the vines,
> the produce of the olive fail
> and the fields yield no food,
> the flock be cut off from the fold
> and there be no herd in the stalls,
> yet I will rejoice in the LORD,
> I will joy in the God of my salvation.

Romans 8:28—

> We know that in everything God works for good with those who love him, who are called according to his purpose.

James 1:2, 3—

> Count it all joy, my brethren, when you meet various trials, for you know that the testing of your faith produces steadfastness.

Revelation 21:4—

> He will wipe away every tear from their eyes, and death shall be no more, neither shall there be mourning nor crying nor pain any more, for the former things have passed away.

[Scriptures selected by Annie May and read at the memorial service, White Station Church of Christ, Memphis, Tennessee, March 13, 2006.]

BIBLIOGRAPHY

1 Clement. In *The Apostolic Fathers*, vol. 1. Loeb Classical Library. Cambridge: Harvard University Press, 1912.

Allen, C. Leonard. *The Cruciform Church: Becoming the Cross-Shaped People in a Secular World*. Abilene: ACU Press, 1990.

Allen, C. Leonard, Richard T. Hughes, and Michael R. Weed. *The Worldly Church: A Call for Biblical Renewal*. 2nd ed. Abilene: ACU Press, 1991.

Apostolic Constitutions. The Ante-Nicene Fathers, vol. 7. N.p., n.d. Reprint, Grand Rapids: Eerdmans, 1975.

Ashcroft, Mary Ellen. *Temptations Women Face*. Downers Grove: InterVarsity, 1991.

The Babylonian Talmud. 35 vols. Edited by Isidore Epstein. London: Soncino, 1935–48.

Bacon, Margaret Hope. *Let This Life Speak: The Legacy of Henry Joel Cadbury*. Philadelphia: University of Pennsylvania Press, 1987.

Barclay, William. *The All-Sufficient Christ*. Philadelphia: Westminster, 1963.

———. *Discovering Jesus*. Louisville: Westminster/John Knox, 2000.

Barth, Karl. *Fragments Grave and Gay*. Cleveland: Collins, 1971.

Benét, Stephen Vincent. *A Child Is Born: A Modern Drama of the Nativity*. Boston: Walter H. Baker, 1942.

Bernstein, Theodore M. *Miss Thistlebottom's Hobgoblins: The Careful Writer's Guide to the Taboos, Bugbears and Outmoded Rules of English Usage*. New York: Farrar, Straus & Giroux, 1971.

Bonhoeffer, Dietrich. *Life Together*. New York: Harper, 1954.

Bridges, Ronald, and Luther A. Weigle. *The Bible Word Book*. New York: Thomas Nelson, 1960.

Browning, Robert. "Rabbi Ben Ezra." In *Dramatis Personae*, 89–99. Boston: Ticknor & Fields, 1864.

Brueggemann, Walter. "Of the Same Flesh and Bone (Gn 2,23a)." *Catholic Biblical Quarterly* 32 (Oct. 1970): 532–42.

Bunyan, John. *The Pilgrim's Progress*. New York: Dutton, 1954.

Burns, Robert. "To a Louse." In *The Best Loved Poems of the American People*. Selected by Hazel Fellerman, 493–94. Garden City: Doubleday, 1936.

Burroughs, Jeremiah. *The Rare Jewel of Christian Contentment*. London: Banner of Truth Trust, 1964.

Cabot, Richard C., and Russell L. Dicks. *The Art of Ministering to the Sick*. New York: Macmillan, 1936.

Caine, Lynn. *Widow*. New York: Morrow, 1974.

Calvin, John. *Commentary on the Book of Psalms*. Vol. 1. Grand Rapids: Eerdmans, 1948.

Carver, George Washington. *George Washington Carver in His Own Words*. Edited by Gary R. Kremer. Columbia: University of Missouri Press, 1987.

Carver, William Owen. *The Glory of God in the Christian Calling*. Nashville: Broadman, 1949.

Claypool, John. *The Light within You*. Waco: Word Books, 1983.

Climacus, John. *The Ladder of Divine Ascent*. Translated by Lazarus Moore. New York: Harper, 1959.

Dale, Robert. *The Epistle to the Ephesians*. New York: Hodder & Stoughton, n.d.

Davis, Jerome. *Religion in Action*. New York: Philosophical Library, 1956.

Dickens, Charles. *The Personal History and Experience of David Copperfield the Younger*. London: Macmillan, 1904.

Didascalia Apostolorum. Introduction and notes by R. Hugh Connolly. Oxford: Oxford University Press, 1929.

Elliot, Elisabeth. *Through Gates of Splendor*. Wheaton: Tyndale House, 1981.

Emerson, Ralph W. "Gifts." *The Dial* 4 (July 1843): 93.

Farrow, John. *Damien the Leper*. New York: Sheed & Ward, 1937.

Fénelon, François. *Christian Perfection*. New York: Harper & Row, 1947.

Finkelstein, Louis. *Akiba: Scholar, Saint and Martyr*. New York: Atheneum, 1970.

Fletcher, Louisa. "The Land of Beginning Again." In *The Best Loved Poems of the American People*. Selected by Hazel Felleman, 101–102. New York: Doubleday, 1936.

Foster, Richard J. *The Celebration of Discipline: The Path to Spiritual Growth*. San Francisco: Harper & Row, 1978.

________. *Freedom of Simplicity*. New York: Harper & Row, 1981.

________. *Prayer: Finding the Heart's True Home*. San Francisco: Harper, 1992.

Foulkes, Richard. *Lewis Carroll and the Victorian Theatre: Theatricals in a Quiet Life*. Burlington: Ashgate, 2005.

Fulghum, Robert. *All I Really Need to Know I Learned in Kindergarten*. New York: Random House, 1988.

Gish, Arthur. *Beyond the Rat Race*. Scottdale: Herald, 1973.

Gordon, Arthur. *A Touch of Wonder*. Old Tappan: Revel, 1974.

Goudge, Elizabeth. *The Dean's Watch*. New York: Coward-McCann, 1960.

Great Songs of the Church: Number Two. E. L. Jorgenson, comp. Hammond, IN: Great Songs, 1976.

Grubb, Norman P. *C. T. Studd: Cricketer and Pioneer*. Atlantic City: World-Wide Revival Prayer Movement, 1933.

Gupta, Raj. "Valedictory." On the Campus. *Princeton Alumni Weekly* (July 12, 1989): 8, col. 3.

Haley, Alex. *Roots*. New York: Dell, 1977.

Hardin, Joyce. *Three Steps Behind*. Abilene: ACU Press, 1987.

Hawthorne, Nathaniel. "The Great Stone Face." In *Twice-Told Tales*, 21–42. New York: Heritage, 1966.

Henry, Matthew. *Matthew Henry's Commentary on the Whole Bible*. Vol. 1. Old Tappan: Revell, n.d.

Heraclitus. *The Fragments of the Works of Heraclitus on Nature*. Translated by G. T. W. Patrick. Baltimore: N. Murray, 1889.

Hinson, E. Glenn. *A Serious Call to a Contemplative Life-Style*. Philadelphia: Westminster, 1974.

Hodge, Charles. *My Daily Walk with God*. Searcy: Resource Publications, 2000.

The Holy Bible: King James Version. Nashville: Crusade Bible Publishers, 1972.

The Holy Bible: New International Version. Grand Rapids: Zondervan Bible Publishers, 1973, 1978.

The Holy Bible: Revised Standard Version. New York: World, 1962.

Hughes, Richard T. *Reviving the Ancient Faith: The Story of Churches of Christ in America*. Grand Rapids: Eerdmans, 1996.

Hulme, William. *Let the Spirit In: Practicing Christian Devotional Meditation*. Nashville: Abingdon, 1979.

Humphrey, Sandra. "Laura Catherine Keeble: The Woman behind Marshall Keeble." *Christian Woman*, n.s. 1, premier issue (1985): 16–19.

Johnson, James Weldon. *God's Trombones*. New York: Viking, 1927.

Jones, E. Stanley. *Victorious Living*. New York: Abingdon, 1936.

Jones, Jerry. "Service Evangelism." *21st Century Christian* 54 (Jan. 1992): 16–18.

Josephus. *Against Apion*. In *Josephus, with an English Translation*, vol. 1. Loeb Classical Library. Cambridge: Harvard University Press, 1926.

Kelly, Thomas R. *A Testament of Devotion*. New York: Harper & Row, 1941.

Knox, Ronald. *The Holy Bible: A Translation from the Latin Vulgate in the Light of the Hebrew and Greek Originals*. New York: Sheed & Ward, 1956.

Lawrence, Brother. *The Practice of the Presence of God*. Old Tappan: Revell, 1958.

Leclercq, Jean. *The Love of Learning and the Desire for God*. New York: Fordham University Press, 1982.

Lemmons, Reuel. "Community Should Be Aware of the Church." *Christian Chronicle* 44 (Jan. 1987): 19.

Lewis, Annie May. "Translating the Bible." *Christian Woman*, n.s., 3 (Jan./Feb. 1987): 15–19.

Lewis, Jack P. "I Wish She Would Stay Here with Me." *HUGSR Bulletin* 27 (March 1986): 1, 3.

________. *The English Bible from KJV to NIV*. Grand Rapids: Baker Book House, 1981.

Lindbergh, Anne. *Gift from the Sea*. New York: Pantheon Books, 1986.

Lloyd-Jones, Martin. *Truth Unchanged, Unchanging*. Wheaton: Crossway Books, 1993.

Manson, T. W. *The Servant-Messiah: A Study of the Public Ministry of Jesus*. Cambridge: Cambridge University Press, 1953.

Marshall, Catherine, comp. and ed. *The Best of Peter Marshall*. Grand Rapids: Chosen Books, 1983.

Marshall, Peter. *Mr. Jones Meets the Master: Sermons and Prayers of Peter Marshall*. New York: Revell, 1949.

McGinley, Phyllis. *The Love Letters of Phyllis McGinley*. New York: Viking, 1954.

Merton, Thomas. *New Seeds of Contemplation*. Norfolk, CT: New Direction Books, 1961.

Millay, Edna St. Vincent. "Lament." In *Second April*, 64–65. New York: Mitchell Kennerley, 1921.

The Mishnah. Translated by Herbert Danby. London: Oxford University Press, 1933.

Morrison, Phillip. "My Prayer." *21st Century Christian* 54 (Feb. 1992): 12.

Nouwen, Henri J. M. *The Living Reminder: Service and Prayer in Memory of Jesus*. New York: Seabury, 1977.

________. *The Wounded Healer: Ministry in Contemporary Society*. Garden City: Doubleday, 1972.

Oates, Wayne. *Confessions of a Workaholic*. New York: World, 1971.

Origen. *Homily on Genesis and Exodus*. The Fathers of the Church, vol. 71. Translated by Ronald E. Heine. Washington: Catholic University of America Press, 1982.

Ovid. *The Metamorphoses: A Complete New Version*. Translated by Horace Gregory. New York: New American Library, 1960.

Packer, J. I. *Knowing God*. Downers Grove: InterVarsity, 1973.

Paregien, Stan. "Find the Good and Praise It." *Integrity* 25 (March/April 1994): 36–37.

Pascal, Blaise. *Pensées, with English Translation, Brief Notes, and Introduction*, by H. F. Stewart. New York: Pantheon Books, 1950.

Paton, Alan. *Cry the Beloved Country*. New York: Scribner, 1948.

Pauls, Dale. "The More Excellent Way: Reflections on 1 Corinthians 13:4–7." *The Stamford Messenger* (July 31, 1983): 1, 4.

Phillips, J. B. *Letters to Young Churches*. New York: Macmillan, 1947.

Pieper, Francis. *Christian Dogmatics*. Vol. 3. St. Louis: Concordia, 1953.

Plaskin, Glenn. "A Perfect Tenor." *New York Daily News*, December 10, 1990. http://www.glennplaskin.com/Turning_Point_Pavarotte1.pdf (accessed March 20, 2009).

Polycarp. *Martyrdom of Polycarp*. In *The Apostolic Fathers*, vol. 2. Loeb Classical Library. Cambridge: Harvard University Press, 1912.

Powell, Lawrence Clark. *The Alchemy of Books, and Other Essays and Addresses on Books and Writers*. Los Angeles: W. Ritchie, 1954.

Quoist, Michael. *Prayers*. Translated by Agnes M. Forsyth and Anne Marie de Commaille. New York: Sheed & Ward, 1963.

"Remembering Mother Teresa." *The Passionists' Compassion: On-Line Edition* 51 (Winter 1997). http://cptryon.org/compassion/win97/mt.html (accessed March 20, 2009).

Riser, Steven C. "Christian World View." Sermon, Raleigh Presbyterian Church, Memphis, TN, n.d.

Sánchez, Patricia Datchuck. *The Word We Celebrate*. Lanham: Rowman & Littlefield, 1989.

Sangster, W. E. *The Pure in Heart: A Study in Christian Sanctity*. London: Epworth, 1954.

Saroyan, William. *The Human Comedy*. Orlando: Harcourt Brace Jovanovich, 1971.

Sayers, Dorothy L. *The Man Born to Be King*. London: Victor Gollancz, 1943.

________. *Unpopular Opinions*. London: Victor Gollancz, 1946.

Schaeffer, Edith. "Hospitality: Optional or Commanded?" *Christianity Today* 21 (Dec. 17, 1976): 28.

Schaeffer, Francis. *The God Who Is There*. Downers Grove: Inter-Varsity, 1968.

Schroder, Ted. "Ownership Versus Stewardship" (Oct. 24, 2004). VirtueOnline. http://www.virtueonline.org/portal/modules/tinycontent/index.php?id=87 (accessed Sept. 13, 2007).

Shakespeare, William. *The Merchant of Venice*. Boston: D. C. Heath, 1916.

Sheldon, Charles M. *In His Steps*. London: Henry E. Walter, 1948.

Shepherd of Hermas, Mandate. In *The Apostolic Fathers*, vol. 2. Loeb Classical Library. Cambridge: Harvard University Press, 1912.

Shipp, Glover. "No Room in the Bin." *20th Century Christian* 51 (Jan. 1989): 15–19.

Sider, Ronald J. *Rich Christians in an Age of Hunger*. Rev. ed. Downers Grove: InterVarsity, 1984.

Singer, L. E., and Don Wyrtzen. "Finally Home." In *Going Home: 75 Songs for Funerals, Memorial Services, and Life Celebrations*. Franklin: Brentwood-Benson Music, 2005.

Smith, George. *Henry Martyn: Saint and Scholar*. London: Religious Tract Society, 1892.

Songs of Faith and Praise. Alton H. Howard, comp. West Monroe, LA: Howard Publishing, 1994.

Sperry, Willard L. Class Lecture Notes of Jack P. Lewis, Homiletics. Harvard Divinity School, 1944–45.

Stevens, Abel. *The History of the Religious Movement of the 18th Century, Called Methodism*. London: Wesleyan Conference Office, 1878.

Stevenson, Dwight E. *Lexington Theological Seminary, 1865–1965: The College of the Bible Century*. St. Louis: Bethany, 1964.

Stevenson, Robert Louis. *Child's Garden of Verses*. New York: Scribner's, 1905.

Stoddard, Alexandra. *Gift of a Letter*. New York: Avon Books, 1991.

Stott, John, ed. *Making Christ Known: Historic Mission Documents from the Lausanne Movement, 1974–1989*. Grand Rapids: Eerdmans, 1996.

Taylor, Richard. *The Disciplined Life: Studies in the Fine Art of Christian Discipleship*. Minneapolis: Bethany Fellowship, 1962.

Teresa, Mother. *My Life for the Poor*. San Francisco: Harper & Row, 1985.

Tertullian. *To His Wife*. The Ante-Nicene Fathers, vol. 4. N.p., n.d.; reprint, Grand Rapids: Eerdmans, 1968.

Thomas, Joseph. *The Life of the Pilgrim Joseph Thomas*. Winchester: J. Foster, 1817.

Thomas à Kempis. *Imitation of Christ*. San Francisco: Harper San Francisco, 2000.

Thompson, Francis. "The Hound of Heaven." In *The Norton Anthology of English Literature*. Rev. ed., 2:1210–14. New York: Norton, 1968.

Tocqueville, Alexis de. *Democracy in America*. New York: Penguin Putnam, 1984.

Tolstoy, Leo. *The Light While Ye Have Light; Thoughts and Aphorisms; Letters*. Translated from the original Russian and edited by Leo Wiener. London: J. M. Dent, 1905.

Tournier, Paul. *A Place for You*. New York: Harper & Row, 1968.

Tozer, A. W. *The Knowledge of the Holy*. New York: Harper & Row, 1961.

Watson, David. *Fear No Evil: One Man Deals with Terminal Illness*. Wheaton: Harold Shaw, 1984.

Weigle, Luther A. *An Introduction to the Revised Standard Version of the New Testament*. Chicago: International Council of Religious Education, 1946.

________. "Introduction." In *Christian Nurture*, by Horace Bushnell. New Haven: Yale University Press, 1947.

Wesley, John. *Letters of the Rev. John Wesley*. Vol. 5. Edited by John Telford. London: Epworth, 1931.

White, Wilbert Webster, and Robert Merrill Kurtz. *The Biblical Review*. New York: Biblical Seminary, 1929.

Wiesel, Elie. *The Gates of the Forest*. New York: Schocken, 1982.

Williams, John A. *Life of Elder John Smith*. Cincinnati: R. W. Carroll, 1870.

Willis, Wayne. "Listen! Hear!" *Mission Journal* 14 (May 1981): 10–12.

Wordsworth, William. "The World Is Too Much with Us." In *Poems in English 1530–1940*, 320–21. Edited by David Daiches. New York: Ronald, 1950.